Ian Leslie is a journalist and communications consultant who counsels businesses on their internal communications and presentations. He writes on ideas, culture and politics for a variety of titles including the *Guardian* and the *Financial Times*, and he comments on current affairs and culture for the BBC, Sky and NPR. Along with Matthew Taylor, CEO of the RSA, he presented *Polarised*, a podcast about the way we do politics today. He is the author of *Born Liars: Why We Can't Live Without Deceit* and *Curious: The Desire to Know and Why Your Future Depends On It*. He lives in London with his family.

Further praise for *How to Disagree*:

'The world will be a better place if everyone reads this book, and because it's so entertaining they probably will.' Philippa Perry

'What a brilliant idea . . . to help us engage in dialogue by learning how to disagree. Ian Leslie is a master at this sort of book and it shows here.' Daniel Finkelstein

'This is a book full of good insights, stories and practical advice that, taken to heart, will do everyone good.' Margaret Heffernan, author of *Wilful Blindness*

'Leslie is one of our most brilliant science writers, and [*How to Disagree*] is his best yet. It's full of wisdom and surprise and is exactly what we need in a world where disagreement itself feels like it's coming under threat.' Will Storr, author of *Selfie*

'A fascinating deep dive into disagreement: how it goes wrong, and how it can go right. Its powerful insights are wrapped in gripping stories.' Harlan Coben, #1 *New York Times* bestselling author

'Not merely fascinating, [*How to Disagree* is] important. It's the right book at the right time, and Ian Leslie is clearly the right author for the job. And if you encounter ideas that make you squirm – and you probably will – remember, that's part of the point.' David Epstein, bestselling author of *Range*

'As Leslie shows with examples from science, technology and the arts, productive disagreement spurs on creativity and discovery and new thinking: Orville and Wilbur Wright argued almost constantly, so did the Rolling Stones, so did Watson and Crick.' James Marriott, *The Times*

'Essential . . . immediately relevant . . . offers us a toolkit for avoiding the tribalism of social media.' Iain Martin, *The Times*

'A reminder of what we sacrifice by not fighting wisely.' John Gapper, *Financial Times*

How to Disagree

**Lessons on Productive
Conflict at Work and Home**

Ian Leslie

faber

First published in 2021 as
Conflicted: Why Arguments are Tearing Us Apart and How They Can Bring Us Closer Together
by Faber & Faber Limited
The Bindery, 51 Hatton Garden London EC1N 8HN

This paperback edition published in 2022

Typeset by Donald Sommerville
Printed and bound by CPI Group (UK) Ltd, Croydon, CRO 4YY

A CIP record for this book
is available from the British Library

ISBN 978-0-571-37466-3

Printed and bound in the UK on FSC® certified paper in line with our continuing
commitment to ethical business practices, sustainability and the environment.
For further information see faber.co.uk/environmental-policy

Our authorised representative in the EU for product safety is
Easy Access System Europe, Mustamäe tee 50, 10621 Tallinn, Estonia
gpsr.requests@easproject.com

10 9 8 7 6 5

For Douglas, on whom we all agree.

At every opposition, we do not consider whether it be just but, right or wrong, how to disengage ourselves. Instead of extending our arms, we thrust out our claws.
Michel de Montaigne

Without contraries is no progression.
William Blake, *The Marriage of Heaven and Hell*

Everyone nodded, nobody agreed.
Ian McEwan, *Amsterdam*

Contents

Contents

PART THREE
Staying in the Room

PROLOGUE: The Interview

I know very little about the man I'm about to meet except that he is suspected of a horrific crime and that he regards me as the enemy.

I'm sitting in a brightly lit, sparsely furnished room, in an anonymous hotel somewhere in rural England. Thick curtains are drawn across the only window. In front of me is a table; opposite, an empty chair. To my right sits a police officer, who is telling me about the suspect, who, I'm told, is waiting outside. The officer talks me through the excruciating details of the crime. He tells me what we know about it and what we don't, and about the crucial information that I somehow need to extract from the suspect. He tells me that this man is proud, angry and cunning.

I'm trying to concentrate on what the officer is saying, but my brain is whirring away on the encounter to come. This man doesn't want to be here. He doesn't like people like me. How am I going to get someone with whom I am so fundamentally at odds to open up – to tell me anything at all, let alone the truth?

The briefing is finished. I keep my hands flat on the table so that the officer won't see them shaking. 'Are you ready,' says the officer. 'Yes,' I lie. A door opens. The suspect swaggers into the room.

His name is Frank Barnet. He's a delivery driver, a burly man who carries himself with a confidence I certainly don't feel. A minute ago, I was briefed that Barnet had been behaving aggressively while in custody, shouting at the officers. Apparently, he was upset that he had been arrested while dropping off his children at school. Barnet takes the seat opposite and focuses a cold gaze on me. Trying not to betray any evidence of nerves, I start by asking if he can recall what he was doing last Sunday afternoon.

'Why the fuck should I tell you anything?'

Oh man. I am not used to this. Most of my conversations are with people who at least want to talk to me. They usually want it to go well, and so do I. Even if we don't agree on what we're talking about, we agree on how we're going to talk about it. The removal of that unspoken consensus feels alarmingly disorienting. I try again, explaining to Barnet that I just want him to help me understand what he was doing that day.

FB: Why are you talking to me?
IL: We're talking to people who were in the area –
FB: I don't give a fuck about *people*, why are you talking to *me*, Frank Barnet? Why me?

My stomach lurches. A part of me wants to return his hostility, with interest. What right does he have to be so aggressive? He's the one suspected of a crime, not me. Another part of me wants to avoid any confrontation at all and apologise. I feel confused, uncomfortable, stuck.

• • •

For years now, I've been fascinated by the question of why so many of our public disagreements go so badly. People with differing views seem to find it increasingly hard to argue productively, instead becoming mired in acrimony or stuck in a grinding neutral gear. Then I noticed that the same problems apply to our private lives too. Whether it's parents arguing with their children or workplace quarrels, our inability to disagree well seems to act as a roadblock to progress. Shouldn't we be able to express conflicting views without getting into toxic rows or fruitless stalemates? What's getting in our way?

Unable to answer these questions to my satisfaction, I started to do some research. I spent time reading about the principles of good intellectual debate as established and refined by thinkers over thousands of years, from the ancient philosophers onwards. Principles like 'assume good faith', 'get to know your opponent's argument as well as your own', 'don't argue with straw men'. It was wise and enlightening stuff, but something nagged away at me. Like healthy eating or exercise, it seemed much easier to know what you *ought* to do in disagreement than to do it. I grasped the theories, but the moment I got into a row with my boss or my wife or a stranger on social media, theory went out of the window. I came to think of productive disagreement not as a philosophy so much as a discipline, and a skill.

People are not logic machines. We are egotistical, proud, impulsive, insecure and needy. Rather than being a pure exchange of opinions and evidence, an argument is nearly always entangled with how we feel about each other. That's not necessarily a bad thing: emotions can help us fight our corner or make us sympathetic to another's view. But emotions can work against healthy disagreement too. Primordial instincts kick in, clouding our minds and distorting our behaviour. Unspoken tensions simmer under the surface of the politest disagreements, sometimes boiling over into anger, sometimes leading us into sullen withdrawal, but other times pushing us towards truthfulness and intimacy.

When we disagree, we bring the whole of our selves to the conversation: head, heart and gut. The trouble with most treatises on debate or argument is that they only focus on the first. I wanted to address all three. That's why I persuaded an interrogation expert to let me role-play the part of a police interviewer. Most of the disagreements you or I have in our everyday lives do not obviously resemble criminal interviews. Our arguments might be about the best way to run a project at work, or whether it's OK to eat meat, or which of us is drawing too heavily on the joint account. But they do have something fundamental in common with the one I had with Frank Barnet, and it's this: they are, at least in part, related to how we feel about each other. Underneath every disagreement a wordless negotiation over a relationship is taking place. If we don't settle that, the conversation doesn't stand a chance.

The most difficult disagreements can be transformed into productive conversations by paying close attention to this hidden dimension. Some people do this for a living. We can learn a huge amount from those who manage highly charged, high-stakes, adversarial conversations in the course of work: police officers, hostage negotiators, diplomats and others. I've found remarkable similarities between the challenges faced by these experts and those faced by any of us in a marital row, political debate or workplace dispute. By combining this lived expertise with ideas and research from communication science and cognitive psychology, I've been able to identify a universal grammar of productive disagreement, available for any of us to apply to our lives.

In the course of doing so I've not only role-played the part of a criminal interrogator; I've travelled to Memphis to watch cops being trained in how to handle tense encounters on street corners where the prospect of violence is never far away. I've talked to divorce mediators about how they get two people who can barely stand to be in the same room as each other to come to an agreement. I've asked therapists about how they talk to patients who resist every piece of advice they are given, and I've learned how hostage negotiators talk people out of blowing up a building or throwing themselves off a bridge. These professionals do very different things but they are all experienced at retrieving something valuable from the most unpromising of circumstances. They are masters of the conversation beneath the conversation.

I've learnt a lot about humans along the way, including the one writing these words. I'm not one of life's natural warriors; even mild confrontation can make me itch with discomfort. But I've learnt that conflict is not something to be avoided at all costs, and that in the right circumstances, it has immense and gratifying benefits. I've learnt that children are happier when they have open disagreements with their parents – as long as those disagreements don't turn poisonous – and that couples who have vigorous arguments are often more content than those who avoid confrontation. I've learnt that workplace teams function at a higher level when they know how to disagree directly, even passionately, without tearing at the fabric of their relationships. I've learnt that too much agreement is bad for us, and that we can only make the most of our differences when we disagree well.

Knowing how to disagree in a way that leads to progress and understanding instead of stasis and acrimony can help each and every one of us. Productive disagreement is more than just a crucial life skill, however. At a time when humanity is struggling to cope with unprecedented existential challenges, it's a vital necessity for our species. Disagreement is a way of thinking, perhaps the best one we have, critical to the health of any shared enterprise, from marriage to business to democracy. We can use it to turn vague notions into actionable ideas, blind spots into insights, distrust into empathy. We have never been more in need of it.

In case you're under any illusion: disagreeing productively is hard. Evolution has not equipped us for it. Nor is it something for which we get trained. In fact, I think it's fair to say that most us are pretty hopeless at it. That needs to change, or else our increasingly vociferous disagreements are destined to generate heat without light. Either that or they won't generate anything, because we refuse to have them. And the only thing worse than having toxic arguments is not having arguments at all.

PART ONE

Why We Need
New Ways to Argue

1. Beyond Fight or Flight

We live in a society more prone to disagreement than ever before, and we're not remotely prepared for it.

In 2010, *Time* magazine described Facebook's mission as being to 'tame the howling mob and turn the lonely, anti-social world of random chance into a friendly world'. During the first decade of mass internet use, this was a popular theory: the more that people are able to communicate with others, the more friendly and understanding they will become, and the healthier our public discourse will be. As we enter the third decade of this century, that vision seems painfully naive. Howling mobs clash day and night. The internet is connecting people, but it doesn't always create fellow-feeling. At its worst, it can resemble a machine for the production of discord and division.

Silicon Valley entrepreneur Paul Graham has observed that the internet is a medium that engenders disagreement by design. Digital media platforms are inherently interactive and, well, people are disputatious. As Graham puts it, 'Agreeing tends to motivate people less than disagreeing.' Readers are more likely to comment on an article or post when they disagree with it, and in disagreement they have more to say (there are only so many ways you can say, 'I agree'). They also tend to get more animated when they disagree, which usually means getting angry.

A team of data scientists in 2010 studied user activity on BBC discussion forums, measuring the emotional sentiment of nearly 2.5 million posts from 18,000 users. They found that longer discussion threads were sustained by negative comments, and that the most active users overall were more likely to express negative emotions.

We live in a world in which toxic disagreement is ubiquitous, in which people are more frequently offensive and offended, in which we do ever more talking and ever less listening. The technologies we use to communicate with each other have clearly played a part in making us this way but, tempting as it is to blame Facebook and Twitter for our ills, that would be to miss the significance of a wider and more profound shift in human behaviour that has been decades, even centuries, in the making. Socially, as well as electronically, there are fewer one-way channels. Everyone is starting to talk back to everyone else. If we are becoming more disagreeable, it's because modern life demands we speak our mind.

• • •

The American anthropologist Edward T. Hall introduced a distinction between two types of communication culture: high-context and low-context. Like all good theories, it simplifies reality to illuminating effect. In a *low*-context culture, communication is explicit and direct. What people say is taken to be an expression of their thoughts and feelings. You don't need to understand the context – who is speaking, in what situation – to understand the message. A *high*-context culture is one in which little is said explicitly, and most of the message is implied. The meaning of each message resides not so much in the words themselves, as in the context. Communication is oblique, subtle, ambiguous.

Broadly speaking, countries in Europe and North America are low-context cultures, while Asian countries are high-context. To give an example, *bubuzuke* is a simple Japanese dish, popular in Kyoto, made by pouring green tea or broth over rice. If you're at the home of a Kyoto native and they offer you *bubuzuke*, you might decide to answer yes or no, depending on whether you feel hungry. But in Kyoto, offering *bubuzuke* is the traditional way to signal that it's time for a guest to leave. You would need to know the context to get the message.

High-context societies such as Japan's tend to be more traditional and more formal. Good communication means having a deep understanding of shared symbols and unspoken rules of civility, such as deference to seniority of age and rank. The primary purpose of communication is to maintain good relationships, rather than to exchange information or get something off your chest. An emphasis is put on listening, since the listener in a high-context exchange must read between the lines in order to understand what is being said. Speakers in high-context cultures tend to be economical with words, comfortable with pauses, and happy to wait their turn to speak.

Low-context societies, like the USA's, are less traditional and more diverse. They involve more short-term relationships, more flux and less deference. When it comes to speaking or listening, knowledge of tradition, protocol and rank doesn't help quite so much; everybody speaks for themselves. Since you can't trust the context, people rely on language itself. Low-context communication is characterised by what one scholar calls 'the constant and sometimes never-ending use of words'. Intentions are articulated, desires expressed, explanations given. People use first names and engage in small talk. There is more interruption and cross-talking – and more arguing.

This brings us to the most important difference between high-context and low-context cultures: the degree of conflict each generates. In Asian cultures, expressing your opinion directly and forcefully is unusual. It can be interpreted as callow or even offensive. Westerners are more willing to 'speak their mind' and risk confrontation. Differing opinions are expected, even when they generate friction. The difference is relative: even in the West, we have developed cultural strategies to avoid too much argument, like the custom of not discussing politics or religion over dinner. But as such traditions fade, so does their dampening effect on conflict.

HIGH context	**LOW** context
• Implicit	• Explicit
• Indirect, subtle	• Direct, confrontational
• Emotional	• Transactional
• Stronger relationships	• Shallower relationships
• Higher trust	• Lower trust

I'm making broad-brush comparisons between countries by way of illustration, but Hall's high- and low-context culture model is applicable at any scale. People who live in villages where everyone knows each other engage in more high-context communication – nods and winks – than people who live in big cities, who are used to encountering strangers from different backgrounds. In long-established organisations, staff may be able to make their intentions known to each other in a way that leaves newcomers mystified, whereas in a start-up, anything that isn't explicitly articulated will not be heard. Individuals shift between high- and low-context modes: with family or friends, you probably do a lot of high-context communication, but when talking to someone in a call centre, you go low-context. Low-context cultures are better suited to societies undergoing change, with high levels of diversity and innovation. But they can also feel impersonal, brittle and unpredictable, and contain greater potential for strife.

Most of us, wherever we are in the world, are living increasingly low-context lives, as more and more of us flock to cities, do business with strangers and converse over smartphones. Different countries still have different communication cultures, but nearly all of them are subject to the same global vectors of commerce, urbanisation and technology – forces that dissolve tradition, flatten hierarchy and increase the scope for arguments. It's not at all clear that we are prepared for this.

For most of our existence as a species, humans have operated in high-context mode. Our ancestors lived in settlements and tribes with shared traditions and settled chains of command. Now, we frequently encounter others with values and customs different to our own. At the same time, we are more temperamentally egalitarian than ever. Everywhere you look, there are interactions in which all parties have or demand an equal voice. Take the way that marriage has changed. Seventy years ago, there would have been little need for the partners in most marriages to discuss who was going to perform which household chores, or who looked after the children – such things went unsaid. People outsourced those decisions to the culture. With the rise of gender equality, the modern household requires more explicit communication and negotiation. Context no longer tells us who should be doing the laundry. You can believe, as I do, that this change is overwhelmingly a good thing, and still recognise that it increases the potential for thorny disagreements.

For marriage, read society as a whole. Children are less likely to obey parental authority silently; organisations rely less on command-and-control and more on collaboration; journalists no longer expect readers to take their word for it; football managers have discovered that screaming at their players in the dressing room is not necessarily the most effective route to success. Everyone expects their opinion to be heard and, increasingly, it can be. In this raucous, irreverent, gloriously diverse world, previously implicit rules about what can and cannot be said are looser and more fluid, sometimes even disappearing. With less context to guide our decisions, the number of things on which 'we all agree' is shrinking fast.

The low-context shift has been a long time in the making but its speed is being accelerated, at a dizzying rate, by communication technologies. Humans have a highly evolved ability to discern a person's intent from their eyes, posture and movement, the pitch and inflexion of their speech. Online, that context is taken away. Smartphone interfaces and microblogging platforms are low-context by design, restricting the user to a few words or images at a time. We get only a crude read on someone's intent from text, even when the signal is boosted with emojis. Think about what defines low-context culture, at least in its extreme form: endless chatter, frequent argument; everyone telling you what they think, all the time. Remind you of anything? As Ian Macduff, an expert in conflict resolution, puts it, 'The world of the internet looks predominantly like a low-context world.' Meanwhile, we rely on conflict-resolution tactics evolved for the world of 200,000 years ago.

• • •

If humans were purely rational entities, we would listen politely to an opposing view before offering a considered response. In reality, disagreement floods our brain with chemical signals that make it hard to focus on the issue at hand. The signals tell us, this is an attack on *me*. 'I disagree with you' becomes 'I don't like you.' Instead of opening our minds to the other's point of view, we focus on defending ourselves.

This aversion to disagreement is steeped in evolutionary history. Neuroscientists Jonas Kaplan, Sarah Gimbel and Sam Harris used brain imaging to observe what happens when people are presented with evidence that challenges their strongly held political beliefs. They found that it triggers the same areas of the brain that activate in response to physical threat. Even in relatively mild disagreements, our interlocutor becomes a dangerous antagonist out to harm us. That's why our bodies react as they do: the chest tightens, the pulse rate quickens.

Animals respond to threat with two basic tactics, first identified by the Harvard biologist Walter Bradford Cannon in 1915: fight or flight. Humans are no different. A disagreement can tempt us to become aggressive and lash out, or it can induce us to back off and swallow our opinions out of a desire to avoid conflict. These atavistic responses still influence our behaviour in today's low-context environments: we either get into hostile and mostly pointless arguments or do everything we can to avoid arguing at all. In the twenty-first century, both responses are dysfunctional.

You don't have to look far to see the *fight* response to disagreement: just open your social media feeds or read the comments section on your favourite website. This is partly for the reason we've identified – the internet gives everyone the chance to disagree with anyone – but also because social media is custom-designed to turn disagreements into public shouting matches. Social media is reputed to create 'echo chambers', in which people only encounter views they already agree with, but evidence points the other way. Social media users have *more* diverse news diets than non-users – one study shows that they get their news from twice as many places, and while they may still prefer to visit outlets that affirm their worldview, when people use more sources they tend to get wider exposure to different viewpoints, whether they like it or not. Instead of creating bubbles, the internet is bursting them, generating hostility, fear and anger.

Moralising language – *this is utterly disgusting; he's evil* – is a prominent feature of online discourse. Molly Crockett, a neuroscientist at Yale, has pointed out that in our offline lives we rarely encounter behaviours we perceive as immoral – a study conducted in the USA and Canada suggested that witnessing immoral acts accounts for less than 5 per cent of our daily experiences – but on the internet, we come across them all the time. The news can sometimes read like a parade of villains and atrocities. The data suggests that people are more likely to learn online about acts they consider morally outrageous than through traditional media. This is partly because content that outrages is more likely to be shared. A team of scientists led by William Brady, a computational social psychologist at New York University, analysed over half a million tweets made about controversial political issues. They found that using moral and emotional words in a tweet increased its diffusion through the network, via retweets, by 20 per cent for each additional word. Users who post angry messages get the status boost of likes and retweets, and the platforms on which those messages are posted gain the attention and engagement that they sell to advertisers. Online platforms therefore have an incentive to push forward the most extreme and triggering versions of every argument. Nuance, reflection and mutual understanding are not just casualties of the crossfire, but necessary victims.

Social norms developed over centuries to protect relationships from the spread of anger, such as the convention not to discuss contentious subjects with strangers, don't apply online: we blithely post, tweet and forward radioactive messages to people we don't know. When we get angry at strangers, we are less likely to make any effort to see their point of view, or to treat them fairly; psychologists have found that people they prime to feel angry are then more likely to be prejudiced against individuals who are different to them, even though those individuals have nothing to do with the source of their anger.

Of course, social media is not real life and there's little evidence that people are replicating these angry disagreements in person. However, this is not the undiluted good news it seems. The hollow outrage we see online may actually be evidence of the absence of real, reflective disagreements: *fight* as a smokescreen for *flight*. In William Brady's study of the spread of moral outrage on Twitter, the diffusion was happening *within* groups of liberals and conservatives, not between them. People were bonding with each other through shared anger at the out-group, yet nobody was engaging in argument. In a sense, the outrage was only superficially about disagreement. The whole point of engaging in it was to agree with your own side.

In America, Republican and Democrat voters are increasingly divided into different neighbourhoods, churches and shops. Rather than getting into more arguments, voters are doing every- thing they can to avoid them, having been turned off politics by the divisive rhetoric they see in the media. A 2020 study from Columbia University found that politics was the most avoided conversation topic in the USA. Political scientists Samara Klar and Yanna Krupnikov have found that the presence in a neighbour- hood of election placards from either party lowers its attractive- ness to all buyers. In an online survey, just over 20 per cent of respondents said they would be unhappy about the arrival of a new colleague at work with the same political views as theirs, if that person talked about politics in the office. That figure rose to 40 per cent after those same respondents read an article about political polarisation, priming concerns about uncomfortable interactions.

Even in low-context cultures, people are inclined to duck those conversations that have potential for conflict and its associated stress. The truth is that it feels better to be agreed with than disagreed with, and to agree than disagree, particularly with someone we don't want to alienate. But avoidance – *flight* – can lead to alienation too.

• • •

Posterous, a Tumblr-like microblogging platform, was founded by Garry Tan in 2008. It took off like a rocket, becoming one of most popular sites on the internet. Tan and his partner raised millions of dollars and attained celebrity status among their peers in Silicon Valley. But in 2010, traffic to the site flat-lined, and the founders had no idea why. 'We didn't know why we were growing, and we didn't know why we stopped,' Tan told me. He and his partner became locked in disagreement over what to do.

A study from Harvard Business School found that 65 per cent of start-ups fail because of 'co-founder conflict'. To succeed, the leaders of new businesses often have to make a difficult transition from being a group of friends working on a cool idea to being managers of a complex enterprise with multiple stakeholders. People who made choices by instinct and on their own terms acquire new, often onerous responsibilities, with barely any preparation. Staff hired because they were friends or family have their limitations exposed under pressure, and the original gang can have its solidarity tested to breaking point.

Tan, who is scrupulously polite, finds confrontation hard. ('My dad was strong-willed and inconsiderate. I evolved to be the opposite.') The tensions with his friend drove him to the edge of a mental and physical collapse. He couldn't sleep, he could barely eat, and he had the resting pulse of someone taking a brisk run. For the sake of his health, he resigned from the company he had given everything to create. (Posterous was acquired by Twitter, becoming defunct soon after.)

When Posterous went into freefall, Tan and his partner urgently needed to collaborate on solutions. Instead, they avoided each other. The problem, as he came to see it, was that they never had any fights during the years of success: 'I skipped the hard work that it takes to get that relationship and do our best work: embracing conflict and resolving it . . . We rarely spoke directly and honestly with one another.' On the surface, the relationship had seemed strong; underneath, it was brittle.

The modern workplace puts a great emphasis on getting along with colleagues and creating psychological safety. In the worst version of this, everyone feels compelled to nod along, suppress doubts and swallow awkward questions. Different parts of an organisation *should* be in tension with one another and staff should discuss those tensions openly, rather than silently pursuing their own priorities. A culture that tacitly prohibits disagreement makes the organisation more vulnerable to petty office politics, errors of judgement and abuses of power. People around a table should feel not just able but compelled to speak up when they think something, or someone, is wrong.

The costs and benefits of disagreement are not symmetrical. The benefits of avoiding disagreement, or any kind of conflict, are immediate – you can leave the room, literally or psychologically, and instantly feel more relaxed. The benefits of having disagreements are not always apparent in the moment, compared to the discomfort associated with them; they tend to be longer term, cumulative and, ultimately, bigger.

• • •

Psychologists who study personality have identified a handful of consistent traits to measure, like openness (how much a person likes new experiences) and conscientiousness (how efficient and organised they are). Another term they use describes how sympathetic and compassionate a person is, in short, how nice they are. What have the psychologists named this trait? *Agreeableness.* It's not just scientists. In everyday language, we use the word 'disagreeable' to mean something or someone we don't like. We have an ingrained sense that disagreeing is a somehow unwelcome or even shameful behaviour.

Overcoming our difficulty with disagreement cannot entail avoiding it. Instead, we need to change radically the way we think and feel about it. Conflict isn't something that humans fall into now and again by accident. It's a crucial component of life – literally so. Cells and organisms survive by exposing themselves to low doses of toxins. That enables them to learn about the ever-changing environment in which they live, so that when a potentially fatal dose of the same toxin comes along, they're better prepared to cope with it. Human relationships are similar – living things that need conflict in order to survive and flourish.

Psychologists who study conflict in families used to focus on its destructive potential; a high level of parent–child discord is one hallmark of adolescent unhappiness. But increasing attention is now paid to conflict's constructive role. Over the course of a typical day, adolescents report three or four conflicts with parents and one or two with friends. In a study published in 1989, a team of social psychologists led by Abraham Tesser of the University of Georgia asked families with children aged between eleven and fourteen to keep a record of their disagreements, over anything from what to watch on TV to whether it was time to do homework. The researchers found that the kids who had a relatively high number of disagreements with their parents were happier, more socially adapted, and more successful at school.

This applied only to those who had calm disagreements, however; children who had a lot of angry disagreements at home did not do so well. Similarly, a 2007 study, involving teenagers in Miami, found that children with more conflict at home were more likely to do well at school, but only if their underlying family relationships were warm and supportive. This points to something I'll be exploring throughout this book: the extent to which healthy disagreements depend on healthy relationships. It's vital to note, though, that the reverse is also true. Frequent and open disagreement makes a relationship better able to withstand a serious challenge – such as your business imploding.

As an investor, Garry Tan advises start-up founders to have open disagreements. Too many times, he says, he's seen founders make the same error: 'Conflict is bad, therefore we should minimise it.' The most common mistake that managers make is to conclude, from the vivid evidence that fighting is dysfunctional, that conflict is intrinsically undesirable. In fact, the relationship between conflict and successful teamwork is not a simple linear one, in which more conflict leads to less success, or vice versa. It is what statisticians describe as curvilinear. It runs on an inverted U (*see overleaf*):

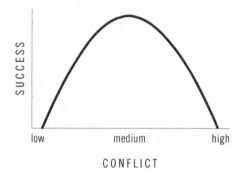

In families, too, the evidence suggests that disagreement is beneficial, because it exposes problems and instigates change. After those benefits are realised, however, additional fighting starts to corrode relationships. For teenagers, some conflict can be productive, but unremitting discord just makes them miserable.

It's telling that we don't have a good word for engaging in a non-hostile disagreement with the shared aim of moving the participants toward a new understanding, better decision, or new idea. 'Debate' implies a competition with winners and losers. 'Argument' comes tinged with animosity. 'Dialogue' is too bland, 'dialectic' too obscure. This linguistic gap is evidence of how unpractised we are at productive disagreement. Fight and flight come naturally to us; disagreeing well does not. Words matter. In their classic work, *Metaphors We Live By*, the linguists George Lakoff and Mark Johnson point out that we talk about argument as if it is war: we say that her claims are *indefensible*, that he *attacked the weakest point* of my thesis, that I *demolished* his argument, that she *shot down* my idea. Those metaphors have real effects; they shape how we argue. We see the person we're arguing with as an enemy who must be defeated. We feel attacked, so we defend our positions. Imagine a culture, say Lakoff and Johnson, where argument is viewed as a dance: a collaborative performance, with the aim being to conduct it in the most satisfying and elegant way. It's possible we would argue, and experience argument, very differently. Instead of finding it stressful and unpleasant, we could find it stimulating and enjoyable. Instead of driving us apart, it could draw us together.

2. How Disagreement Brings Us Closer

Couples and teams are happier when they are in the habit of passionate disagreement. Conflict can draw people together.

Nickola Overall, a psychology professor at the University of Auckland, was raised in a sprawling, rambunctious New Zealand family in which nobody was shy of speaking their mind. 'Whenever friends or colleagues meet members of my family, they say to me, "OK I can see why you study direct conflict!"' Overall is an expert on how and why couples get into rows. She's interested in romantic relationships because couples are interesting in themselves, but also because 'The way people try to manage conflict in a relationship tells you about the strategies people use at work or in politics.'

In 2008, Overall began a study of relationships that was to have a lasting impact on her field. She invited married couples to discuss a problem in their relationship on camera, but without anyone else in the room. Some of the couples discussed their problem reasonably and coolly; others got into a heated argument. 'People often ask me whether couples really get into personal rows in a laboratory but they do, quite easily,' says Overall. 'Each couple has two or three things they frequently fight about, and when they talk about one of those things they very quickly expose their anger and hurt feelings.' Overall and her colleagues then reviewed the tapes of the sessions, analysing each one according to a schema commonly used in the field which categorises four communication styles used by couples having a difficult conversation:

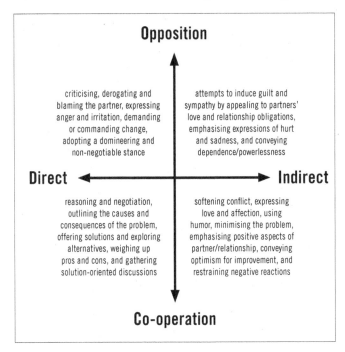

Opposition

criticising, derogating and blaming the partner, expressing anger and irritation, demanding or commanding change, adopting a domineering and non-negotiable stance

attempts to induce guilt and sympathy by appealing to partners' love and relationship obligations, emphasising expressions of hurt and sadness, and conveying dependence/powerlessness

Direct ← → **Indirect**

reasoning and negotiation, outlining the causes and consequences of the problem, offering solutions and exploring alternatives, weighing up pros and cons, and gathering solution-oriented discussions

softening conflict, expressing love and affection, using humor, minimising the problem, emphasising positive aspects of partner/relationship, conveying optimism for improvement, and restraining negative reactions

Co-operation

'Direct co-operation' involves explicit attempts to reason through tough decisions or to solve problems. 'Indirect co-operation' refers to behaviours that soften and reduce conflict, from a hug to an apology or an attempt to lighten the mood. 'Direct opposition' is getting into what we in Britain call a proper barney, involving angry accusations and demands for change. 'Indirect opposition' is popularly known as 'passive aggression' – trying to make the other person feel guilty about something, emphasising how hurt you have been by their actions, ostentatiously declaring that *I* will clean up the kitchen *again*, it's really *no problem*.

In the post-war years, researchers focused on distinguishing couples mired in hostility from those who mostly got along just fine. Hundreds of studies found that unhappy couples have more arguments, whereas happy couples express more agreement and affection. Conflict was framed only as a problem, the solutions to which were found in that bottom-right quadrant. This gave rise to what we'll call the standard model of relationships: a happy couple is one in which the partners frequently share their feelings with each other and avoid hostile arguments. But we all know couples who disagree a great deal and occasionally have shouting matches, yet still seem happy; perhaps you are in one of them.

The couples in Overall's study who engaged in more open conflict stated they did not enjoy it: they experienced tension and felt upset. Afterwards, they told the researchers the conversation had not been successful in solving their problem. But they were not necessarily right about that. When Overall's team invited the couples back to the lab a year later, they asked them whether they had made any progress towards resolving the problem they had talked about. Most relationship experts would have predicted that the couples who engaged in direct opposition – fierce argument – would have made the least progress. Overall found the opposite: the more confrontational couples were the ones more likely to have made headway in solving their issues.

The standard model has a big hole in it. Open conflict is not always harmful to a marriage or long-term relationship. There is now mounting evidence to suggest something like the reverse: that disagreement, criticism and even anger can, over time, increase marital satisfaction. Falling out has benefits.

• • •

As a young research psychologist at the University of Texas in the mid-1970s, William Ickes was dissatisfied by the way human interaction was only studied under artificial conditions, with participants following strict instructions on what to talk about.

He was interested in how well two people were able to read each other's minds during spontaneous conversation – or, in the jargon of the field, 'unstructured dyadic interaction' (a 'dyad' is a pair of individuals – a two-person group). Ickes's resulting body of work offers us a crucial clue to the role of conflict in happy relationships.

Ickes had his respondents, who were university students, arrive at the laboratory in male–female pairs who didn't know each other. Each pair would be ushered into a room that was empty except for a couch and a slide projector. The experimenter would ask them to sit down and explain that he was going to ask them to view and rate some slides. It would then turn out that the projector was broken, and the experimenter had to fetch a new bulb. Left alone, the pair would strike up a conversation, stilted at first but gaining momentum as the minutes passed. Then the experimenter would return and reveal the real purpose of the experiment. A concealed video camera had been recording the pair's interaction.

In the second stage of the study, the respondents would be taken into separate rooms to view a tape of their conversation. They would be asked to pause the tape at any point that they remembered having a specific thought, write down what they were thinking or feeling at that moment, and assess what their conversation partner might have been thinking or feeling too. Later, the tapes would be analysed by the researchers, who assigned scores for the accuracy with which any individual was able to read his or her interlocutor's mind.

In 1957, the influential psychotherapist Carl Rogers defined empathy as the ability to track, from moment to moment, the 'changing felt meanings which flow in this other person'. But until Ickes, nobody had a way of measuring it. Ickes was the first to find a way to assess a person's 'empathic accuracy' – their success at inferring what is going on inside the head of the person they're talking to. His methodology has been adapted to the study of many types of dyad, including friends and married couples.

One of Ickes's major findings about mind-reading is that people are really bad at it. On a scale from 0 to 100, the average empathic accuracy score was twenty-two, and the best scored only fifty-five. (Ickes noted that people on first dates can relax: there's little chance their companion knows what they're thinking.) It's the relationship that makes the biggest difference. Ickes found that friends are better at mind-reading than strangers, because they have a shared store of information about each other, which they can draw on to make quick and accurate inferences. Another way of putting this is that strangers communicate in a low-context environment, in which it pays to be explicit and get all the information out there, whereas friendship is a high-context environment, in which we can deploy heavily coded, highly compressed messages.

Close friends communicate very efficiently and rarely have to make much of an effort to be understood by each other. In contrast, that couple at the next table on a first date have to work really hard at understanding each other, and frequently get it wrong. That said, strangers are quick learners. Ickes found that they got better at reading each other's minds the more information they exchanged, especially when the information established some common ground or shared interest. Friends exchanged more information than strangers, because the talk flowed more freely, but, importantly, that made little or no difference to their empathic accuracy.

That brings us to something important. Friends and strangers process *new* information about each other differently. Strangers pay close attention to it because it helps them form a picture of the other person. Close friends, who rely on what they already know about the other person, tend to discount the importance of new information about them. They don't listen quite as hard because they don't feel they need to.

Generally, men perform worse on tests of empathic accuracy in couples than women. The evidence suggests that it's not that men have any less ability to empathise, it's just that they're less likely to *try*. In the lab, offering cash in exchange for accuracy has been found to wipe out the difference between men and women. So it's not that men can't detect their partner's thoughts and feelings, it's that, for much of the time, they can't be bothered.

This link between our ability to mind-read and our motivation to do so helps to explain a somewhat disturbing finding from the field of relationship science: that while couples get better at reading each other's minds in the first months and years of a relationship, the longer they stay together, the worse they become at understanding each other.

During those initial years, each member of a couple builds a mental model of their partner, through which they interpret whatever their partner says or does. Assuming the relationship is a good one, the model will be pretty accurate – to use the language of a statistician, it will be a good fit for the reality of the person. You learn your partner's predilections and turns of mind. You know that if your partner is grumpy in the morning, it's probably because they had a bad night's sleep or are worrying about work. You can tell, when they ask you what you were doing last night, whether they are genuinely interested or whether they're annoyed at you for staying out. Many of your partner's utterances that would be opaque or meaningless to others make instant sense to you.

A model like this is a wondrous thing, but in its efficiency is its demise. Once you think you've got your partner worked out, you stop noticing new information about them. You might even come to believe that you know them better than they know themselves.

However, no matter how close you and your partner are, you are having different experiences every day, and while people tend not to undergo radical shifts in personality as they age, they do develop and change. Over time, as the gap between model and person grows, your reading of your partner worsens. The model becomes an ill-fitted stereotype, a simplified and inadequate image of the real thing. If that process continues for long, it can end in a shocking rupture – like when your partner turns around and tells you they're leaving.

Talking to each other a lot doesn't mean you will avoid this pitfall. We're led to believe that more talking leads to greater understanding, but while this sounds sensible, several studies have found no correlation between empathic accuracy and how much or how clearly couples communicate. Indeed, more communication can lead to *less* understanding. As the relationship scientist and expert in marital conflict Alan Sillars put it to me, '"Talking it out" doesn't always work. It can make things worse.' If the model of either or both partners has become a distorting lens, then each partner is consistently making mistaken assumptions about what the other is thinking. The more they talk politely, the more the errors pile up, on both sides. Each becomes increasingly frustrated with the other for not understanding them.

Some couples manage to avoid this fate precisely because they never build efficient models of each other. According to Ickes, the couples most likely to retain their empathic accuracy are those who have either a 'continuing ignorance of each other's predilections or an unwillingness to accommodate them'. In other words, ignorance and stubbornness have a role to play in successful relationships. Sometimes it's *good* to be inflexible, even when it creates conflict.

In fact, it may be that creating conflict is the point. 'Listening is one path to understanding,' says Alan Sillars. 'So is negativity.' In a heated argument, you're more likely to hear what your partner genuinely thinks and wants. You find out what they're truly like. 'Conflict provides us with information,' says Nickola Overall. 'The way people respond to us in conflict tells us a lot about how co-operative they are, whether they can be trusted, what they care about.' Conflict in a relationship is not an unfortunate accident. It's a way of learning about others, including and especially those we know most well.

In 2010, American researchers Jim McNulty and Michelle Russell analysed data from two longitudinal studies of relationships. They found that couples who at the beginning of the study engaged in angry rows over relatively trivial problems were less likely to be happy in their relationship four years later. However, couples who were having hostile arguments about deeper problems, such as money or substance abuse, were more likely to feel good about their relationship by the end of the study period.

In a separate paper, McNulty found that for newlywed couples experiencing serious problems, the kinds of 'positive' behaviours encouraged by the standard advice, such as always being affectionate and generous, even hurt some relationships because it stopped the couples facing up to their problems. Indirect co-operation – the softer, subtler approach – can work for minor problems, such as who should be driving the kids to football at weekends, but isn't great for when a couple has something really important to work through, such as whether one partner is drinking too much.

A measure of 'negative directness' seems to be crucial for solving knottier issues. 'In the short term,' Russell told me, 'negative behaviours can make you feel shitty. Nobody likes to be blamed for something or told they're in the wrong. But it can have this motivational effect. It can really get to the root of the problem.' Sometimes, one partner simply hasn't realised that something is a major problem; they need to be enlightened in no uncertain terms. 'A strong emotional response, yelling and anger, can be needed to demonstrate to the person on the receiving end just how much something means to their partner,' Russell told me.

In other words, the occasional row is useful because it updates our mental models. People speak their minds freely, uninhibited by fears about how what they say will affect the relationship, and they do it in a way that demands close attention. That means they often – explicitly or implicitly – disclose new information about how they're feeling and who they are. A good argument blows up the stereotype.

In a study published in 2018, Nickola Overall found evidence for an additional benefit to negative directness: it shows you care about each other. Overall recruited 180 couples and asked each partner, separately, to identify the persistent problems in the relationship, where one partner wanted the other to change. The couples were then asked to discuss one of these problems, in a room together, alone, while being filmed by discreetly positioned cameras. They often got into heated arguments.

Overall and her team coded the interactions for communication style and then checked in with the couples over the following twelve months. She discovered a specific reason that negative-direct arguing can have a beneficial effect on relationship health. When the person arguing for change is previously perceived by their partner to have been less than fully committed to the relationship, their anger, even their hostility, provides evidence that they really do care. Anger is information. 'Expressing negative emotions can convey investment,' said Overall.

The same principles apply to other types of close relationship. Parents do not necessarily gain a greater understanding of their teenage children by talking to them about whatever is troubling the relationship. But pressure and confrontation by the child reliably alerts parents to how their children are feeling. Parents who want a deeper understanding of their children can't simply expect them to 'open up' whenever a problem arises. Greater understanding develops over the course of what Alan Sillars terms 'frequent and unrestrained conversations'. When you keep being candid about the little stuff – including the stuff that annoys you – the big stuff is easier to deal with when it comes up.

'We're still not good at painting a picture of the ways in which dramatic and difficult conflict can be constructive,' says Sillars. 'Relationships can be deeply troubled at points but ultimately better for the people in them as a consequence of confrontation, if that helps them find a new equilibrium.' Michelle Russell agrees: 'Psychology as a whole tends to undervalue the role of negative behaviours and emotions. They can be useful and adaptive. Sometimes you need to feel bad about yourself.'

• • •

Rows may be more useful than we realise, but there is no question that they can be destructive too. What distinguishes the bad rows from the good ones? Answering that question requires us to understand something fundamental about how people communicate.

In an experiment run by Alan Sillars, a wife and husband were filmed discussing their marriage. Afterwards, each of them watched the film separately, and gave their commentary. Here's a sample of the husband's commentary:

– Well, Penny is starting to talk about when she was sick in hospital and she doesn't think I contributed enough at that time or that . . . and I thought I did.

- This is what I get all the time at home, I think . . . I don't go out all that often.
- I was just trying to explain to Penny here that, uh, in my mind, she is always first to me, even though sometimes it seems like I try harder to do other things.

This is a sample of the wife's commentary, on the same part of the conversation:

- Now, I think he was trying to avoid the real issues, so I was getting upset and mad again.
- I wanted him to just understand what I was saying so I was aggravated that he was just kind of smirking and not listening.
- I felt hurt because he wasn't really listening to what I said about my feelings.

You can see there is a mismatch here. The husband is focused on the literal meaning of what's being said – on the events being referred to and the ostensible point of contention, of whether or not he goes out too much. Meanwhile, his wife tracks the conversation at a kind of meta-level. She talks about the feelings she was having during the conversation, and about her husband's desire to avoid the real issues.

In any conversation, we're responding both to its content: to what the discussion or argument is ostensibly about, whether that be money or politics or housework or something else; and also to signals about our relationship: how each sees themselves in relation to the other. The content level is explicit and fully verbalised, and full of concrete references to real-world events, like how much money someone earns or the rights and wrongs of drug policy. The relationship level is implicit and largely unspoken, conveyed as much in our tone of voice and communication style (warm or cold, teasing or sarcastic, animated or taciturn) as in our words. At the content level, there is an exchange of messages; at the relationship level, an exchange of signals.

When the participants are essentially in agreement at this relationship level – when each person is happy with how they think they are being characterised by the other – the content conversation goes smoothly. Problems get solved, tasks performed, ideas hatched. When there is an unspoken disagreement at the relationship level, the crackle and spark of conflict disrupts the content conversation. One or both of the parties find it hard to focus on what they're meant to be talking about because they're engaged in an unspoken, unacknowledged struggle to elicit the other person's respect, or affection, or simply attention. The disagreement either becomes deadlocked or explodes into a damaging row.

According to Sillars, who has observed and coded hundreds of such conversations, when marital disagreements go badly it's often because one of the partners is only tracking the content level of the conversation and not paying any attention to something that's going on at the relationship level. It is also possible to err in the other direction: one partner might have an exaggerated vigilance to the relationship level and so misinterpret what the other person says, seeing insinuations or insults where none were made.

It might not surprise you to discover that, according to the data, men are more likely to be guilty of making the first kind of error, while women are more likely to make the second. In fact, men often become so absorbed in their own words that they fail to notice the relationship signals their partner is sending. Sillars has found that, 'Husbands thought about themselves more than they thought about their partners, whereas wives thought about their partners more than themselves.' Of course, the confusion can occur in both directions. Either way, the person liable to be getting most upset by the dispute is the person most sensitive to the relationship level. A disagreement is more likely to be productive when both partners are paying the same attention to both levels.

How to achieve that? If you have a particularly acute sensitivity to relationship signals, try not to let them dominate your perception of every conversation. When your partner seems upset or preoccupied, do not assume it's about you: listen to what they say and engage in the content of the conversation. If, on the other hand, you suspect yourself to be someone who can get so wrapped up in the content of a conversation that you don't pick up on your partner's feelings, try and pay more attention to non-verbal signals: the pitch of their voice, facial expression and body language. Otherwise you might hear your partner's words but miss what they're saying.

• • •

If conflict can have a surprisingly productive role in romantic relationships, what about the relationships between colleagues? Work is never just about work. The jobs we do are always bound up with our feelings – good and bad – about the people we work with. At the office, even more than at home, we feel pressure to avoid disagreements and the stress and negative feelings that often go with them.

Modern workplaces place a premium on getting along. That's a good thing, but it means that even when our frustration with someone's behaviour is perfectly justified, often the smart thing to do is hide it. The unaired conflict doesn't disappear, however, but manifests itself in office politics, which is essentially the phrase we use for passive aggression at scale. Scholars who study organisations have found that the worst, most unproductive workplace cultures are riddled with passive aggression. That's why the most successful firms make a determined effort to get their internal conflicts out into the open. Carefully managed, conflict can bring co-workers closer together.

Southwest Airlines might just be the most successful airline in history. In 2019, the Texas-based low-cost carrier celebrated its forty-sixth consecutive year of profitability, a unique record in a volatile industry. Southwest's success is often explained with reference to its charismatic former CEO, Herb Kelleher, who co-founded the airline in 1967. Kelleher, who died in 2019, was a man of unquenchable bonhomie and he created a corporate culture in his image: Southwest staff are famous for their conviviality and quirky humour. Jody Hoffer Gittell, a management professor at Brandeis University, argues that the firm's success is not just down to its warm welcome or ukulele-playing baggage handlers, however, but to the way Southwest staff communicate with each other – including how they handle internal conflict.

Gittell spent eight years researching the corporate cultures of airlines during the 1990s. She interviewed staff from the most senior to the most junior, and focused on the major carriers, like American Airlines (AA), United, and Continental. Gittell identified a significant obstacle to profitability: sectarian warfare. The industry, she discovered, has a tradition of status-based competition between the many different functions required to get a plane full of passengers off the ground and back again: pilots, flight attendants, gate agents, ticketing agents, ramp agents, baggage transfer agents, cabin cleaners, caterers, fuellers and mechanics. A ramp agent at AA explained industry politics to her:

Gate and ticket agents think they're better than the ramp. The
ramp think they're better than the cabin cleaners . . . Then the
cabin cleaners look down on the building cleaners. The mechanics
think the ramp agents are a bunch of luggage handlers.

The staff used derisive names for other functions ('agent trash',
'ramp rats') and fiercely guarded their position in a strict hierarchy,
with pilots at the top and cabin cleaners at the bottom. A station
manager at AA confided in Gittell that ramp workers, 'have a
tremendous inferiority complex . . . the pilots don't respect them'.
A cabin cleaner complained that, 'The flight attendants think
they're better than us, when they're sleeping five to an apartment
and they're just waitresses in the sky.'

As Gittell put it, with considerable understatement, the different
functions in an airline 'typically lack shared goals or respect'.
During her research, she kept hearing about an airline called
Southwest, which was said to be different, and so she began to
study it. The contrast was dramatic. Staff across different functions
seemed to respect and even like each other. Pilots appreciated the
work of ramp agents, and cleaners got along with cabin crew. This
culture of respect didn't just make Southwest a more attractive
place to work; it was the reason for its profitability.

The vision of Kelleher and his co-founder Rollin King was
to provide frequent, low-cost flights of under 500 miles in busy
markets. This was brave, since short-haul flights are inherently
costlier than long-haul ones. The more time a plane spends on the
ground, the less money it makes, and planes that fly shorter routes
land more often. What enabled Southwest's counter-intuitive
strategy to work was its relentless focus on reducing turnaround
time, that time spent getting a plane ready for the next flight. Quick
turnarounds are impossible without a high degree of co-ordination

among all the airline's functions. Pilots, flight attendants, baggage handlers and others must constantly communicate any snags in the process and find immediate solutions. To do that well, they need to get along and they need to care about the success of the whole company. Southwest's culture of collaboration means it has the fastest gate turnarounds in the industry. One of its managers told Gittell, 'Sometimes my friends ask me, why do you like to work at Southwest? I feel like a dork but it's because everybody cares.'

It's not that staff from Southwest's different functions don't clash with each other. Argument and annoyance are inevitable in any activity that requires a lot of close and complex co-ordination. But instead of turning their mutual frustrations into seething antipathy, Southwesters air them directly. As one station manager put it to Gittell, 'What's unique about Southwest is that we're real proactive about conflict. We work very hard at destroying any turf battle once one crops up – and they do.'

• • •

Until relatively recently, academics who studied management assumed that workplace conflict was bad for productivity. But, as with marital relationships, there's now an increasing recognition that conflict can have positive effects – and that avoiding it is harmful. In 'conflict-avoidant' workplaces, staff think of conflict only as a dangerous, destructive force that must be shunned. The result is that differences of opinion are channelled into passive-aggression. An employee at an online education service that exemplified this culture told the leadership expert Leslie Perlow, 'I noticed early on that colleagues weren't being frank with one another . . . they smiled when they were seething; they nodded when deep down they couldn't have disagreed more. They pretended to accept differences for the sake of preserving their relationships and their business.'

A crucial challenge for any organisation is to ensure that its employees conceive of conflict as something other than personal rivalry. Management scholars make a distinction between task conflict – arguments over how to solve a problem or make a decision – and relationship conflict, when things get personal. Task conflict, even when it's heated, can be collaborative and productive, if the participants care about solving the same problems. As we'll see later, it flushes out new information and stimulates critical thinking. Relationship conflict is inherently competitive, and usually destructive: personally conflicted groups make inferior decisions, and the people in them feel less happy and less motivated. This holds true in studies of students and professionals, blue-collar workers and executive teams.

The border between task conflict and relationship conflict is a messy one: conflict over a task often slides into personal competition. Evidence suggests that when people interpret disagreements as personal attacks, their cognitive function is impaired, in two principal ways. First, they become rigid in their thinking, clinging to the first position they choose, even when it is shown to be wrong. Second, they engage in 'biased information processing': new information is only absorbed insofar as it fortifies their position. In short, they become exclusively focused on proving themselves right rather than helping the group be right, which makes the group itself a little more stupid.

The organisational psychologist Frank de Wit has examined how a difference in mindset explains why task conflict can tip over into relationship conflict. He draws on a distinction from the science of stress, often used in sports psychology, between *threat states* and *challenge states.* When people evaluate a potentially demanding task, like making a golf putt or giving a public speech, they make an instinctive calculation of whether they have the resources to deal with it. If they feel they do, they go into a heightened state of mental and physiological readiness – the challenge state. If they feel they might be overwhelmed by the task's demands, they focus mind and body on fending it off – the threat state.

Challenge and threat states have different physiological markers. In challenge states, the heart beats faster and also becomes more efficient, maximising the amount of blood it can pump to the brain and muscles. In threat states, the heart beats faster but it doesn't pump more blood. Blood vessels in the heart raise resistance, constricting the flow. Hence the distinctive sensation of anxiety, of being agitated and trapped at the same time. Challenge states involve a measure of anxiety, too, but in a way that converts into physical and cognitive horsepower. In lab experiments, people in challenge states have superior motor control and perform better on mentally demanding tasks, like brain teasers, than people in threat states.

In a series of experiments, de Wit looked at how people responded to direct disagreement in group discussions. He monitored each participant's physiological responses, while assessing their debating tactics. The more that each participant's cardiovascular measures indicated that they had switched into threat state, the less likely they were to shift from the initial opinion and the more likely they were to screen out information that didn't help them win the argument. Participants in a challenge state were more open to divergent viewpoints, and more willing to revise assumptions.

When people feel challenged but not threatened, confident they can handle the disagreement without losing face, they can take a looser grip on their own arguments. That prevents the discussion from degenerating into a personal competition, and keeps the group focused on solving the problem at hand.

Different managers approach team conflicts in different ways. Some try and avoid it altogether; others actively foster a culture of confrontation. Researchers who studied a successful technology firm in the late 1990s observed that, 'Both male and female senior execs were expected to conform to dominant norms: brutal honesty and controlled anger – which often coalesced in the form of screaming arguments that had a scripted, playacting quality.' Theatrical confrontation was also central to the culture of a tech firm known by the pseudonym Playco, studied by the sociologist Calvin Morrill. One employee defined what it means to be a strong executive at Playco: 'A tough son of a bitch, a guy who's not afraid to shoot it out with someone he doesn't agree with, who knows how to play the game, to win and lose with honour and dignity.' Superiors and subordinates were expected to 'joust', and someone was always judged to have 'carried the day' (not necessarily the superior). Skill in jousting was a key component of evaluations. 'We're sharks circling for a kill,' said another Playco executive. 'If someone takes a bite out of you, you take a bite out of him.'

A confrontational culture can facilitate rapid decision-making because weak arguments get quickly weeded out. It works best in organisations that are scrambling to adapt to change. But it encourages fierce personal competition, which distracts from the task at hand. It also – and this is just my personal intuition – selects for assholes. The sweet spot is a culture in which conflicts are played out in the open but everyone is focused on the group being right rather than proving themselves right, a culture in which disagreement is a challenge to be met rather than a threat to be repelled.

If you're a relatively junior employee in a company riven by toxic confrontation or passive-aggressive politics, there may not be much you can do about it except try not to let the culture define you, and look for another job. If you're a leader, however, you can do a lot more. You can model positive disagreements with close senior colleagues, letting everyone know, implicitly and explicitly, that people at this workplace can disagree vigorously and still get along. You can convey to members of your team that if you disagree with them openly, it's not because you don't respect them but because you do. In workplaces where tough decisions have to be taken at speed, communication needs to be direct to the point of abrasiveness; there is little time for subtlety or politeness. The psychologist Nathan Smith, who studies leadership under pressure, told me that he advises senior hospital doctors to prepare junior medics in advance for this style of interaction, so that they don't feel personally persecuted when on the sharp end of it.

Organisations can also introduce simple processes which allow frustrations to be aired and resolved. Relative to other airlines in Jody Gittell's study, Southwest had by far the most proactive approach to conflict resolution. Her analysis suggests that this resulted in faster turnaround times, greater productivity, and fewer customer complaints. A Southwest Airlines employee told Gittell, 'Where there's really a problem [between functions], we have a "Come to Jesus" meeting and work it out. Whereas it's warfare at other airlines, here the goal is to maintain the esteem of everybody.' The meetings were officially termed 'information-gathering' sessions before acquiring their more soulful nickname. They have a regular format: one side gives their version of the problem, then the other gives theirs, before a consensus on the way forward is reached.

Managers at the other airlines studied by Gittell tried to ignore internal disagreements altogether, but when one of them, United, started a new unit, 'United Shuttle', its leaders decided to emulate

Southwest's proactive approach. After Shuttle outperformed the rest of the company, the mainline operation began to hold conflict-resolution sessions too. A ramp manager told Gittell what a difference it made: 'At first we would blame them and they would blame us. So we started having joint meetings, twice monthly. At first they were bitch meetings. Now they've evolved into "I can take that on, I can do that."' One meeting in particular was the turning point: 'The meeting started out with attacks on management and attacks on each other. Terry [a senior manager] came in with flip charts and thought it was chaotic. But Charlie [a middle manager] said it's the best meeting we ever had. Everyone spoke their minds, and people were saying, "Here's what we're going to do."'

• • •

John Gottman, one of the founders of modern relationship science, proposed that the behaviour most deadly to a relationship is contempt, because contempt represents an attack on another person without any focus on the problem, any pretence of a common goal. Nickola Overall agrees that contempt is destructive, but even here, she said, there may be a buried signal waiting to be uncovered. 'I believe that all emotions are important social information. Even with those difficult negative emotions you can sometimes get a glimpse of the other person's perspective. You can get a sense of their dissatisfaction and pain.' That doesn't mean negativity should always be interpreted sympathetically: 'Sometimes, the information you're getting is that this person can't be trusted; that they're not committed to you. The ultimate goal shouldn't always be resolution. Sometimes you need to end the relationship!' But it does mean that there is a role for negative emotions in healthy relationships.

Of course, there is always a risk that a row will get out of hand and damage the relationship we have with our partner, friend or colleague. Awareness of this risk is what leads so many of us to avoid conflict whenever possible. It's what stresses us out about the prospect of even a mild confrontation. What we tend to under-estimate are the risks of *not* airing our differences. When we don't expose our relationship to the relatively minor stress of a candid disagreement, at least two dangers loom.

One of them is that our frustrations, instead of going away, manifest themselves in low-level sniping. Researchers disagree on many issues concerning the complexities of relationships, but one of the clearest findings of the field is that there isn't any useful role for passive aggression. The evidence suggests that 'indirect opposition' is almost always a waste of time, whether that's at home or in the workplace. It neither motivates anyone to change, nor resolves any problems; all it does is corrode trust. If we reach for it often, it's because we want others to know when we are hacked off but are too anxious at the prospect of confrontation to be upfront about it.

The second danger is that we stop learning about each other until, one day, we discover it's too late. What can you learn from a row? You can learn what, or who, that person really cares about. You can learn how they see themselves – which may be different from how you see them, no matter how well you think you know them – and you can learn how they see you.

Under the right conditions, conflict unifies. It can also force people to consider other perspectives, think more deeply about what they're trying to accomplish, and fertilise new ideas. In other words, it can make us smarter and more creative. That's what the next two chapters are about.

3. How Disagreement Makes Us Smarter

Collaborative disagreement is the best way to harvest the intelligence of a group, because it makes a virtue out of our tendency to be unreasonable.

If I asked you to imagine someone doing some really deep thinking, you might conjure up something like Rodin's *The Thinker*. A solitary figure lost in introspection, exploring the recesses of their own mind. This way of thinking about thinking, as something best done alone, is relatively modern. In a much older tradition, thinking and reasoning are essentially interactive, a way of harvesting the intelligence of a group.

Let's take a look at the original thinker. Socrates, the father of Western philosophy, did not write down his ideas so we instead know about him mostly through the accounts of contemporaries. The reason Socrates mistrusted the relatively new technology of writing is because it could not respond to questions. He preferred talking, and he liked to talk with people who disagreed with him – or at least thought they did. His trick was to make them see, through gentle questioning, that they didn't agree with themselves.

Socrates believed that the best way to dispel illusions and identify fallacies was through the exchange of arguments. His took place face to face, in the town square of Athens, often with the town's most respected intellectuals. His favoured technique was to invite someone to put forward an argument (on the nature of justice, say, or happiness) before asking why they believed that – how could they be so sure? Could they account for these exceptions? Eventually, under persistent questioning, the intellectual's initial confidence would be revealed to be based on very little. Socrates was not out to humiliate anyone, but to reveal that we all know a lot less than we think.

Agnes Callard, a professor of philosophy at the University of Chicago and an expert on the ancient Greeks, explained to me that Socrates wasn't just an original thinker, but an innovator too. He was the first to propose, for example, that truth can be reached more reliably and quickly if, instead of one person weighing up both sides of an argument, two or more parties are involved, each assigned a distinct role. Callard calls this method the 'adversarial division of epistemic labour'. One party's job is to throw up hypotheses, the other's is to knock them down. People can co-operatively disagree in order to get to the truth – just as, in a modern courtroom, prosecutor and defender co-operate in a quest for justice by ripping each other's arguments apart.

Theory is one thing, however; practice is another. In order to make this work, Socrates had to innovate in a different way: he had to inculcate a new set of social norms. It's not that Socrates' interlocutors were unaccustomed to debate. This was Athens, after all, a city that prided itself on its vigorous democracy, a city in which every man (although you did have to be a man, with property) was free to express his opinions in public. Athens was a culture of persuasion, however, and so most Athenians conceived of disagreement as a zero-sum game: you either won or lost. Arguments were means to achieve instrumental ends, subordinated to political goals. It was also a culture of one-upmanship. Men competed to be the finest orators, the most skilled debaters. They were not pursuing truth, but prestige.

And so Socrates had to model a new and different kind of conversation. There are moments in the dialogues, says Callard, where Socrates steps aside from the topic under discussion in order to explain to his interlocutors what he, and they, are engaged in.

I don't see myself as superior to the person I'm talking to, he would say. Enquiry isn't a status competition, it's about testing the quality of arguments. Spend time getting clear on your interlocutor's view, and don't worry about finding answers – we're just trying to understand each other a little better. Arguing with someone is a sign of respecting them. From *Hippias Minor* (one of the accounts of Socrates' dialogues made by his pupil Plato): 'Hippias, I don't dispute that you are wiser than I, but it is always my custom to pay attention when someone is saying something, especially when the speaker seems to me to be wise. And because I desire to learn what he means, I question him thoroughly . . . so I can learn.'

Socrates worked hard at communicating to his fellow Athenians that he wasn't trying to beat them at anything. He had no instrumental goal or ulterior motive. He was engaging them in a quest to dispel falsehoods for the sake of it. Nobody had debated like this before, which is why Socrates had to describe what he was doing, as he was doing it, over and again. He was laying the foundation stones of a cathedral: our whole idea of free intellectual enquiry, in philosophy and science, derives from the premise that enquiry is a worthy goal in itself and that people of different views can pursue it together.

To Socrates' listeners, this approach to debate was new, and somewhat strange and unsettling. The intellectuals of Athens would have felt uneasy and sometimes upset as Socrates chiselled away at their arguments. What if I lose face? What if I come out of this looking bad? Socrates had to do a lot of reassuring and soothing; it would hardly be an exaggeration to call it anger management. Callard pointed me to this incident, described in Plato's *Republic*:

While we were speaking, Thrasymachus had tried many times to take over the discussion but was restrained by those sitting near him, who wanted to hear our argument to the end. When we paused after what I'd just said, however, he couldn't keep quiet any longer. He coiled himself up like a wild beast about to spring, and he hurled himself at us as if to tear us to pieces.

Socrates was a troublesome, gadfly-like presence in Athens, always niggling at sacred cows. During his life, the threat of physical violence was never far away, and eventually, the authorities sentenced him to death. We shouldn't regard this as surprising, says Callard – instead, we should be surprised he survived for so long. Athenians were not used to being disagreed with by someone who wasn't clearly trying to best them or persuade them to do something. 'They let him have this flourishing career,' says Callard. 'Why weren't they angrier?' She thinks it was because Socrates worked so hard at assuaging insecurities. In a co-operative disagreement, somebody has to be wrong and Socrates made every effort to let Athenians know that, not only is being proved wrong OK, it is something to be grateful for. In *Gorgias*, for example, Socrates says to Callicles, 'If you refute me, I shan't be upset with you as you were with me; instead you'll go on record as my greatest benefactor.'

The other founding fathers of Western philosophy adopted and developed the Socratic method. We know about Socrates from his pupil Plato, who presented his own ideas in a series of dialogues. Aristotle, Plato's pupil in turn, wrote a textbook on how to be an effective debater, and developed the art of rhetoric: a series of techniques for persuasion. For all these thinkers, however, the clash of views was not just a battle to persuade but a way of generating truth – or at least, dissolving falsehood. Tellingly, the Greeks also founded drama, a form of storytelling that distils truth from conflict.

In medieval Europe, Christian scholars incorporated the rules laid down by the Greeks into the practice of 'disputation': a method of debate, developed first in the monasteries and later in early universities, designed to teach and uncover truths in theology and science. Disputations took place both privately, between master and student, and publicly, in front of the university community. Every disputation followed a similar format. A question is asked. Arguments in favour of one answer to the question are sought and examined. Next, arguments in favour of an opposing answer are considered. The arguments are then weighed against each other, before one or other answer is chosen, or a third one is found. Disputation was competitive; the goal was to convince each other, or an audience. But it was also believed that by examining a problem from different angles, new truths could emerge. The practice was essentially Socratic dialogue, formalised and scaled up. Historians of the period talk of the 'institutionalisation of conflict'.

Institutions have a habit of stagnating. In the sixteenth century, Renaissance thinkers criticised universities for indulging in arid intellectual debates instead of engaging with the real world. But it was the seventeenth-century French philosopher René Descartes who really made the practice seem obsolete. He scorned scholastic disputation as an artificial game that had become entirely about how to win arguments, instead of the discovery of new truths. Sitting alone by the fireplace, Descartes invented a new kind of philosophy, grounded in his certainty of his own existence ('I think, therefore I am'). If you want truth, said Descartes, look within.

The Protestant Reformation, with its emphasis on individual conscience, encouraged this turn towards inner contemplation. The practice of disputation was dealt another blow by the invention of printing; the spread of books meant that individuals could self-educate instead of subjecting themselves to arguments with pettifogging teachers. In the eighteenth century, Enlightenment philosophers presented individual rationality as humanity's supreme gift. Immanuel Kant located the operation of reason in fundamental structures of the mind. Making a 'judgement' had until then been regarded only as an action – as something that officials did in public. Kant was the first to conceive of it as a mental operation, a private act of understanding.

Intellectual exploration had come to be seen as something that happens inside the mind. Only brilliant individuals who freed themselves of the traditions laid down by ancient scholars could make breakthroughs. The idea of the individual genius, exemplified by Newton, became paramount. The irony is that this exaltation of the individual mind took place at a time when thinking was becoming more intensely social and argumentative than ever: scientific societies were formed, philosophers exchanged letters, intellectuals gathered in coffee houses to swap stories and debate ideas.

Even as thinking became more social, thinking about thinking became more abstract. In the nineteenth and early twentieth centuries, the study of reason, now identified with the study of formal logic, became increasingly mathematical. The correctness of an argument was something you could calculate, using algebraic symbols. Ordinary language was not up to the task. Two millennia after Socrates debated all comers in the centre of Athens, the study of reasoning had become truly asocial.

Our ideas about what constitutes good decision-making and judgement still centre around the individual. We are more likely to celebrate individual thinkers, innovators and scientists, than the group or milieu from which they arose. Psychologists study the individual mind, divided into System One and System Two:

conscious and unconscious mental operations. The advent of brain imaging has intensified this focus. Neuroscientists can look at pictures of individual brains, but they can't yet study, with any precision, what happens to brains when we interact with others (you can only fit one person in an MRI scanner). And so, with a few exceptions, they ignore it.

We don't just do our thinking 'in the brain', however. We do it with each other. Our focus on individuals means we underrate disagreement as a route to insight, ideas and good choices.

• • •

Scientists who study group decision-making have observed two major ways in which an absence of disagreement within a group of intelligent people can lead to bad decisions. The better known one is driven by the desire to conform, to follow the lead of a dominant person or people in the room. A popular view instantly prevails and the group herds towards a decision without a full exploration of potential pitfalls or alternatives. The social psychologist Irving Janis, the first to name this phenomenon, in 1972, called it 'group-think'. The problem here, you might say, is that the group acts like an impulsive individual. The second problem is related to this, but subtler. It's called 'shared information bias'. This is what happens when everyone in the room assumes that everyone else knows more than them about the topic at hand. With nobody seriously challenging each other, the participants end up having only a superficial discussion. ('When two men always agree, one of them is unnecessary,' remarked the chewing gum entrepreneur, William Wrigley Jr.)

Disputing a question flushes out new reasons, information and insights that would otherwise remain trapped inside people's heads. These days, we rightly put a lot of emphasis on constructing diverse teams, not just for reasons of social equality but because the more varied the perspectives around a table, the more creative and insightful the discussion will be. But that insight and creativity will only materialise if the people on the team are prepared to challenge each other openly. Disagreement unlocks the benefits of diversity.

As Socrates knew, this may all be good in theory, but in practice, people find it uncomfortable and unpleasant to disagree. Dissenters from a consensus are often disliked, and disagreements can turn into bickering matches. After the notion of groupthink became widely known, some organisations started to look for ways to prevent teams from arriving at a consensus prematurely, without things turning personal, by adopting a solution proposed by Irving Janis: assign a 'devil's advocate'. The practice has its origins in the Roman Catholic Church: when an individual is proposed for beatification or canonisation, the devil's advocate is employed to make the case that the candidate is not worthy. In theory, by explicitly asking someone on the team to argue against whatever decision is being proposed you get the benefits of disagreement – forcing out new information and better solutions – without the costs to team harmony.

There's one problem: it doesn't work. Charlan Nemeth, a professor of social psychology at Berkeley University, ran experiments in which she compared authentic dissent – a group discussion in which the dissenter really believed in her point of view – with a devil's advocate group, in which the dissenter was faking it, and a group in which there was no dissenter. Nemeth found that authentic dissent generated much more productive discussions, with more original thoughts, than either the consensus or devil's advocate conditions. In fact, the devil's advocate condition was counter-productive: it stimulated members of the group to produce more arguments in support of their initial plan, without truly considering the other view (Nemeth calls this behaviour 'cognitive bolstering'). My reading of this is that people became complacent when there was an assigned devil's advocate, believing that they had inoculated themselves against narrow-mindedness. They knew that the devil's advocate didn't really believe what she was saying, so they didn't push themselves to reflect on what she said.

In further studies, Nemeth tested a subtler distinction. In one condition, someone spontaneously dissented from the majority view. In another, that same person was asked to make those same arguments – arguments that the rest of the group knew she truly believed in – after being publicly assigned the role of devil's advocate. Under both conditions, the disagreement created tension in the group, and stimulated some dislike of the dissenter. But the spontaneous condition gave rise to a better discussion, generating more and better (that is, more creative) solutions than the role-play condition, even though the arguments and the person making them were identical.

Nemeth's speculative explanation for the difference in productivity between the discussions is that the group sensed there was less at stake for the dissenter when she was playing the devil's advocate. In the spontaneous discussion, her dissenting position felt more courageous. When she was seen to be carrying out the researcher's instructions, the group perceived someone making smooth, confident arguments, but felt less responsibility to question their own position. In the authentic condition, the other participants responded to the dissenter's vulnerability by opening up a little more themselves, resulting in a much richer discussion in which both sides allowed for the possibility of being persuaded. In other words, people are more likely to confront the possibility that they're wrong when faced with someone who appears truly to believe what they are saying and who is prepared to take a risk by saying it.

Productive disagreement depends on how people feel about each other. We spend a lot of time thinking about how to argue, and not enough on how to shape the relationship that will define how the argument goes. It's often said that in order to disagree well, people need to put emotions aside and think purely rationally, but this is a myth. Disagreeing productively requires a bond of trust: a sense that we're ultimately working with, and not against, each other. That's an inherently emotional question as well as a cognitive one, which is why the previous chapter is crucial to understanding this one. People are not purely rational, and acting as if they are leads to dysfunction. We release the full potential of disagreement when we incorporate our unreasonableness into the process.

• • •

When a company is considering a takeover bid it often hires an investment banking firm, like Goldman Sachs, to advise on the acquisition. The bankers have a strong incentive to persuade the board to do the deal. After all, no deal, no fee. There's an obvious conflict of interest there. The world's most successful investor, Warren Buffett, proposes that companies adopt a counter-balancing measure:

It appears to me that there is only one way to get a rational and balanced discussion. Directors should hire a second advisor to make the case *against* the proposed acquisition, with its fee contingent on the deal *not* going through.

The genius of this approach lies in the fee. Buffett doesn't just advise getting a second opinion; he advises giving the second advisor a financial incentive to win the argument. Why? Because by doing so, the directors can harness the power of biased thinking, while guarding against their own. The second advisor is now strongly motivated to think of as many good reasons as it can that the deal should not go through. The board will then have generated a set of arguments for and a set of arguments against, and so be in a stronger position to make the right call.

When you bring your arguments to the table and I bring mine, and we're both motivated to make the best case we can, the answers that emerge will be stronger for having been forged in the crucible of our disagreement. In 2019, a team of scientists led by James Evans, a sociologist at the University of Chicago, tested this proposition using a vast database of disagreements: the edits made to Wikipedia pages. Evans is interested in the effects of political polarisation, and whether it is possible for polarised individuals to have productive disagreements. Does the clash of strongly opposed political perspectives always lead to hostility or avoidance – fight or flight – or can it be turned into something more fruitful?

Evans realised that Wikipedia is the perfect place to investigate this question (I'm going to use 'Evans' as a shorthand for the team of researchers he led). Wikipedia is a remarkable feat of teamwork. Each page is overseen by an ad hoc community of volunteer editors. Behind every topic there is a 'talk page', which anyone can open up to observe what goes on behind the scenes of the page you see. In the talk page, editors debate proposed additions and deletions, and engage in elaborate arguments, as they try to persuade each other of what should be included on the public-facing page. Some teams produce better-quality pages than others. We know this because Wikipedia assigns a grade for quality to each page, based on how readable, accurate, comprehensive and well-sourced it is.

Evans used machine learning to identify the political leanings of hundreds of thousands of editors – whether they were 'red' or 'blue' – based on their edits of political pages. He was then able to identify the political make-up of thousands of editorial teams, including those working on pages relating to politics and social issues. Some articles were run by highly polarised teams made up of red and blue editors, others by editors who were more in alignment with each other. Here's what Evans discovered: the more polarised the team, the better the quality of the page.

Ideologically polarised teams were more competitive – they had more arguments than more homogeneous or 'moderate' teams. But their arguments improved the quality of the resulting page. The conversations they had on the talk pages were longer, because neither side was willing to give in on a point without a struggle. These longer arguments generated better-quality content, as assumptions were unearthed and arguments honed. Editors working on one page told the researchers, 'We have to admit that the position that was echoed at the end of the argument was much stronger and balanced.' That 'have to' is important: the begrudging way that each side came to an agreement made the answer they arrived at stronger than it otherwise would have been. As Evans puts it, 'If they too easily updated their opinion, then they wouldn't have been motivated to find counter-factual and counter-data arguments that fuel the conversation.'

Egoism – the need to be seen to be right – and tribalism – the desire to see our group win – are usually portrayed only as enemies of good disagreement. Understandably so, because in most cases they are. The productive competition between Wikipedia's editing teams, however, suggests that even tribalism can bear intellectual fruit, providing the participants share a common goal and agree on rules of conduct (of which more later). The best thing to do with our tendency to make self-centred arguments is to harness it.

What connects Socrates, Buffett and the Wikipedians is their understanding of a profound truth about human cognition: our intelligence is interactive.

• • •

Since Socrates' time, the ability to reason has been heralded as humanity's supreme attribute, the thing that sets us apart from other species. This raises a tricky question. If reasoning towards the truth is humanity's superpower, why is everyone so bad at it?

If you were asked to help people arrive at more accurate beliefs and better decisions, you'd probably start by improving their ability to spot their own errors. After all, nobody can be sure they're right about anything until they've fully considered why they might be wrong. But we are all generally very bad at this. We cling to our opinions even in the face of evidence to the contrary. If I believe the world is going to hell in a handcart, I'll only notice bad news and screen out the good. If I've decided that a politician is brilliant, I'll only notice her achievements and ignore her screw-ups. Once I've decided that the Moon landings were a hoax, I'll seek out YouTube videos that agree with me and wave away the counter-evidence.

Psychologists have now established beyond doubt that people are more likely to notice and consider evidence that confirms what they believe, and to discount anything that suggests the opposite. Humans have an instinctive aversion to the possibility they are wrong; they deploy their powers of reason to persuade themselves that they are right even when they're not. Armed with a hypothesis, we bend the world around it. This characteristic, known as 'confirmation bias', appears to be a serious problem for our species. It makes us more likely to deceive ourselves and to believe the lies of others, and less likely to see anyone else's point of view. 'If one were to attempt to identify a single problematic aspect of human reasoning that deserves attention above all others, the confirmation bias would have to be among the candidates for consideration,' says Raymond Nickerson, a psychologist at Tufts University. Cleverness is no cure for this problem; studies have found that intelligent and educated people are just better at persuading themselves they're right, since they are more skilled at generating self-justifying arguments.

This presents a puzzle. Why has evolution endowed us with a tool that is at once both incredibly sophisticated yet faulty enough that if you purchased it from a shop you would send it back? A pair of evolutionary psychologists called Hugo Mercier and Dan Sperber have offered an intriguing answer to this question. If our reasoning capacity is so bad at helping individuals figure out the truth, they say, that's because truth-seeking isn't its function. Instead, reason evolved to help people *argue*.

Homo sapiens is an intensely collaborative species. Smaller and less powerful than other species – weedy, compared to our Neanderthal forebears – humans have nevertheless managed to dominate almost any environment they have set foot in, mainly because they are so good at banding together to get stuff done. To that end, humans have evolved a finely tuned set of abilities for dealing with other humans. In Mercier and Sperber's view, reasoning is one of those social skills. Reason evolved to help people do things with other people – to hunt down prey, make a fire, build a bridge. The giving and asking for reasons enabled individuals to influence others and win them to their side, and it also had the effect of making people accountable for their own actions ('OK, let me explain why I took more than my share of mammoth meat . . .'). The point of being able to come up with reasons is to present them to others in support of your argument, or to knock down someone else's – that is, to argue.

It's not hard to see why those with superior reasoning ability would have been more likely to survive and pass on their genes. The ability to give and examine reasons turns disagreements that might have become violent, even fatally so, into arguments. If I want to start a fire and you want to build a shelter, we can exchange reasons for and against doing so, rather than fighting about it. Those who were particularly skilled at taking part in this back-and-forth would be better at heading off threats, and able to display their competence to the group, winning allies and impressing potential mates.

The giving and asking of reasons is an important way for people to establish the kind of relationship that will enable them to collaborate. For you to trust me as someone with whom you can do business (literally or metaphorically), I can't just say I want something, or that I disagree. I need to explain why and I expect the same from you. The only people we don't expect this from are small children, who, when asked to justify their wants, tend simply to say 'BECAUSE I WANT IT'. Teaching children to say something more persuasive after 'because' is a vital part of their socialisation. Parents can encourage that by modelling it. When you have a disagreement with your child, try and give them reasons for why you want them to do something, even when all you really want to say is 'BECAUSE I SAY SO'.

Mercier and Sperber are 'interactionists', as opposed to 'intellectualist' thinkers. For intellectualists, the purpose of reason is to enable individuals to gain knowledge of the world. But as we've seen, reason often seems to be used to entrench whatever we want to believe, regardless of whether it is true or not. In the inter-actionist view, reason didn't evolve to help individuals reach truths, but to facilitate communication and co-operation. In other words, reasoning is inherently social, and makes us smarter only when we practise it with other people in a process of argument. Socrates was on to something.

The myth of the rational individual who can think his (and it usually has been 'his') way through any problem in magnificent isolation is powerful but misleading. For a start, while humans have accumulated a vast store of collective knowledge, each of us alone knows surprisingly little, certainly less than we imagine. In 2002, the psychologists Frank Keil and Leonid Rozenblit asked people to rate their own understanding of how zips work. The respondents answered confidently – after all, they used zips all the time. But when asked to explain how a zip works, they failed dismally. Similar results were found when people were asked to describe climate change and the economy. We know a lot less than we think we do about the world around us. Cognitive scientists call this 'the illusion of explanatory depth', or just 'the knowledge illusion'.

What enabled humans to conquer the planet is not that we 'think for ourselves'; it is instead our unrivalled ability to think in groups. There is nothing we do, from getting dressed, to using a computer, that does not rely on the knowledge of other people. Each of us is plugged into a vast network of knowledge, passed down from the dead and shared among the living. The more open and fluid your local network, the smarter you can get. Open disagreement is one of the main ways we have of raiding other people's expertise while donating our own to the common pool.

However, as Socrates knew, disagreements only generate truth under certain conditions, one of them being what Mercier and

Sperber call a 'division of cognitive labour'. In the ideal discussion, each individual focuses mainly on the search for reasons for their preferred solution, while the rest of the group critically evaluates those reasons. Everyone throws up their own hypotheses, which are then tested by everyone else. That's a much more efficient process than having each individual trying to come up with and evaluate all the different arguments on both sides of the issue and it's likely to lead to better decisions.

This solves the puzzle of why evolution bequeathed us confirmation bias. In the context of a well-functioning group discussion, confirmation bias is a feature, not a bug, though only if we use it as nature intended. Think about what it's like when someone contradicts you. You feel motivated to think of all the reasons you're right, and to cite them in your support, at least if it's something you care about or when it's important to be seen to be correct (this is why Mercer and Sperber prefer the term 'myside bias' to 'confirmation bias': it only kicks in when your identity or status is threatened). That's an emotional response as much as a cognitive one. Some people might advise you to put your emotions to one side and evaluate arguments purely rationally. But by allowing your emotion to drive your search for good arguments, you're actually doing something productive: contributing new information and new ways of thinking about the problem to the group.

You might be doing it for selfish or narrow reasons – maybe you want to justify yourself and prove how smart you are. Even then, you'll help the group generate a diversity of viewpoints, as people strive to put their reasons forward. Since everyone has an incentive to knock down competing arguments, the weakest arguments get dismissed while the strongest arguments survive, bolstered with more evidence and better reasons. The result is a much deeper and more rigorous thought process than any one of you could have carried out alone. That's exactly how the Wikipedia editing process works, according to James Evans's study. It's how Warren Buffett designs the decision-making process for investment. It's the principle that underlies Socratic dialogue.

Looked at through the interactionist lens, confirmation bias isn't something to eliminate; it's something to harness. Under the right conditions, it raises the collective intelligence of a group. What are those conditions? First, the group must disagree openly, with each individual feeling genuinely compelled, and able, to put their best case forward. Second, and most fundamentally, the members of the group must have a common interest – in the truth, or the right decision. If each member is *only* defending their own position, or trying to get one-up on everyone else, then the weaker arguments don't get eliminated and the group won't make progress. When each person takes a strong position and at the same time allows themself to be swayed by better arguments, the group moves forward.

Confirmation bias, like conflict itself, is curvilinear, operating on an inverted U-curve. A lot of it is bad; so is none of it. I've sat around tables at work where most people don't express a strong point of view and simply accept whatever the most confident person in the room says. The result is a lifeless discussion in which the dominant view isn't tested or developed. Just as in romantic relationships, you can be left wondering how committed those people are to whatever project they are pursuing. You might also, of course, wonder whether the leaders of the company have made it clear that they do not wish to be disagreed with, and that dissenters will be penalised.

I've also sat at tables when different individuals fight their corner, sometimes even slightly beyond the point that seems reasonable to do so. Those discussions can be rumbustious and uncomfortable at times but they are generally higher quality and, when conducted respectfully, they can bring the members of a team closer together. Having said that, individuals who *never* back down from their viewpoint waste everyone's time. There are a lot of annoying people on the far side of the inverted U – and a lot of fruitless debates. You should bring your whole, passionate, biased self to the table, but you also must judge when to separate yourself from the argument you've been pursuing.

The chemistry of disagreement is inherently unstable. It's always threatening to move towards one extreme or the other. Self-assertion becomes aggression, conviction becomes stubbornness, the urge to conform becomes the instinct to herd. Over centuries, we've developed processes and institutions to stabilise this volatility and provide the right conditions for productive disagreement. Foremost among them is the institution of modern science. But even among scientists, bias can get out of hand.

• • •

Four hundred years ago, Francis Bacon warned against what we now call confirmation bias: 'The human understanding when it has once adopted an opinion . . . draws all things else to support and agree with it.' In order to solve this problem Bacon formulated what became known as the scientific method. He instructed scholars to test their theories against real-world observation, so that they could 'analyse nature by proper rejection and exclusion'. Following Bacon, science developed into a discipline, and a community with a division of cognitive labour. Scientists publish research on the topics they care about and try to build a case for their theory. Their work is peer-reviewed and examined by other experts in their field. Scientists try to knock down each other's arguments, at the same time as they learn from each other. Science makes the most of reason's social nature.

Much as we celebrate great individual scientists, it is scientists as a group who make progress. Confirmation bias runs amok when an individual is isolated from people who disagree with them, no matter how brilliant their mind. Isaac Newton spent the last decades of his life immersed in a futile quest to turn base metals into gold. If that work didn't lead anywhere, it was at least partly because he did it alone, without collaborators or reviewers. When he published his groundbreaking work in physics, by contrast, Newton was drawing on the published work of others ('standing on the shoulders of giants', as he put it), and doing so in the knowledge that mathematicians and astronomers across Europe would pounce on any weak arguments.

For the most part, this system has worked very well, leading to the huge advances in medicine and technology that define modernity. It is when science's participants forget how to disagree well that things can get bent out of shape, as the story of John Yudkin illustrates.

In the early 1980s, Western governments, after consulting with the world's top nutrition scientists, told us to change the way we ate. If we wanted to stay healthy, they said, we needed to cut back on foods rich in saturated fats and cholesterol. By and large, we did as we were told. Steak and sausages were replaced with pasta and rice, butter with margarine and vegetable oils, and eggs and toast with muesli and low-fat yoghurt.

Instead of becoming healthier, however, we grew fatter and sicker. In the decades that followed, a public health catastrophe unfolded. Obesity, which until then had been relatively stable, rose dramatically, as did the incidence of related diseases, like diabetes. In recent years, the advice has changed. Although we're still advised to moderate our fat consumption, we are told to beware of another enemy of our health, one that is just as bad, if not worse: sugar.

It would be natural to believe that this sharp change of emphasis came about because nutrition science advanced and new discoveries were made. Not true. The scientific evidence was there all along. It was overlooked because nutrition scientists had forgotten how to disagree with each other and allowed confirmation bias to run riot.

John Yudkin's book *Pure, White and Deadly* was published in 1972. It warned the world that the real threat to people's health was not fat, but sugar. 'If only a small fraction of what we know about the effects of sugar were to be revealed in relation to any other material used as a food additive,' wrote Yudkin, 'that material would promptly be banned.'

Yudkin, a professor of nutrition at Queen Elizabeth College in London, noted that refined sugar has been a major part of Western diets for only 300 years; in evolutionary terms, it is as if we have, just this second, taken our first dose of it. Saturated fats, by contrast, are so intimately bound up with our evolution that they are abundantly present in breast milk. To Yudkin's thinking, it seemed more likely that the recent innovation, rather than the prehistoric staple, was making people sick. He also believed that the evidence that fat is bad for us was relatively weak. He argued that sugar was the more likely cause of obesity, heart disease and diabetes. In the 1960s, the debate over whether sugar or fat was most harmful was a lively one. But by the time Yudkin wrote his book, the commanding heights of his field had been seized by proponents of the fat hypothesis, and most nutrition scientists had signed up to a new consensus: a healthy diet is a low-fat diet. Yudkin led a diminishing band of dissenters.

His book, intended as a warning to the general public, was a last resort. He paid a high price for arguing that sugar was a bigger threat than fat. The world's top nutrition scientists didn't like having their ideas challenged so publicly. Yudkin was disinvited to scientific conferences and shunned by scientific journals. His own college reneged on a promise to let him continue to use its research facilities after his retirement, since it was no longer deemed politic to have an opponent of the fat hypothesis on the premises. Yudkin's research eventually fell out of circulation altogether. He died in 1995, a disappointed and largely forgotten man.

Meanwhile, following advice from the nutrition science elite, American and British governments told their citizens to reduce consumption of fat and cholesterol-rich foods. When people cut back on fat, they usually increase their consumption of carbohydrates. Food manufacturers also responded to the new directives by selling low-fat foods made more palatable by the addition of sugar. It is now becoming increasingly apparent that by turning saturated fats into our number one dietary enemy, we missed the threat of the most versatile, palatable and unhealthy carbohydrate of all.

The story of Yudkin's professional demise scared off any other scientists interested in challenging the consensus that fat was the chief problem with Western diets. Only in the twenty-first century did it become acceptable again, in scientific circles, even to research what sugar does to our bodies. A paediatrician called Robert Lustig led the way. After studying sugar's effects on the metabolic system, in 2013 he published *Fat Chance*, a book exposing the link between sugar and obesity that went on to become a global bestseller. Yudkin's research had been so well buried that Lustig only came across it by accident when a fellow scientist mentioned it to him at a conference. Lustig was astonished to find that it anticipated his own work. When I asked him why he was the first scientist in years to focus on the dangers of sugar, he told me: 'John Yudkin. They took him down so severely – so severely – that nobody wanted to attempt it on their own.'

The obesity epidemic is often blamed on the food industry, and certainly the food companies have a lot to answer for. But if the nutritional advice we have followed for all this time was profoundly flawed, that's also because even scientific enquiry is prone to dysfunctional group behaviour: herding towards majority opinion, intense discomfort with admitting to error, and deference to the dominant.

'Does Science Advance One Funeral at a Time?' was the title of a paper written in 2015 by a team of scholars at the National Bureau of Economic Research in the USA seeking an empirical basis for a remark made by the physicist Max Planck: 'A new scientific truth does not triumph by convincing its opponents and making them see the light, but rather because its opponents eventually die, and a new generation grows up that is familiar with it.' The researchers identified more than 12,000 elite scientists from different fields. Searching obituaries, they found 452 who had died before retirement, and looked to see what happened to the fields from which these celebrated scientists had unexpectedly departed. What they found confirmed the truth of Planck's maxim. Junior researchers who had worked closely with the elite scientists, authoring papers with them, published less. At the same time, there was a marked increase in papers by newcomers to the field, who were less likely to cite the work of the deceased eminence. The articles by these newcomers proved to be substantive and influential, attracting a high number of citations. The newcomers, free of the pressure to agree with dominant elders, moved the whole field along.

Disagreements can make us smarter, as individuals and as groups, by enabling us to learn from others and forcing us to think harder about why we believe what we believe. But, as Socrates knew, for the disagreement to generate insight instead of anger, you have to manage the relationship issues that disagreements inevitably create. Only when there is shared understanding, respect and trust can you really go at it – at which point, anything is possible.

4. How Disagreement Inspires Us

Conflict is the spark that lights the fire of group creativity.

In Dare County, North Carolina, there is a small town called Kill Devil Hills, built on sandy ground near the sea. In September 1902, the town and its airport did not yet exist, but if you had been in the vicinity you might have witnessed a strange scene: two men among the sand dunes, standing face to face next to a piece of heavy machinery, waving their arms in the air, shouting at each other.

For a couple of months, brothers Wilbur and Orville Wright had been going out to Kill Devil Hills with the best glider they had ever built. Using data from wind tunnel experiments, they knew exactly what wing design would provide the best lift and the least drag. But in their test flights, they kept encountering a persistent problem, which culminated in a near-death experience for one of them. On 23 September, as Orville attempted a turn, one wing suddenly went high while the other went low. The glider spun out of control and crashed into the sand. The result, according to Orville's diary, was 'a heap of flying machine, cloth and sticks . . . with me in the centre without a bruise or scratch'.

The problem, which they judged as occurring once every fifty glides, was potentially fatal. The brothers called it 'well-digging'; it later became known as a tailspin. They urgently needed to solve it if they were to realise their ambition of building the first flying machine. On the evening of 2 October, the Wrights discussed the problem, along with their friend George Spratt, and soon got to arguing. Orville, the younger brother, shouted and waved his arms around. Wilbur replied in short, staccato bursts. Spratt felt deeply uncomfortable but he would have known this was far from unusual. The Wright brothers were bare-knuckle debaters.

We're so familiar with the fact that the Wright brothers invented the aeroplane that the miraculous nature of their achievement can go unheralded. Wilbur and Orville were not scientists; they didn't even attend university. They were not attached to any corporation or institution. They ran a bicycle shop in Dayton, Ohio. They had accomplished relatively little right up until they solved one of the greatest engineering puzzles in history.

The Wright brothers, born four years apart, had a close relationship. 'From the time we were little children,' wrote Wilbur, 'my brother Orville and myself lived together, worked together, and in fact, thought together.' The way they thought together was through argument. The sound of their quarrelling was a familiar sound to Dayton locals, who heard it spilling out from the floor above their shop. It was their father, Milton Wright, who taught his sons how to argue productively. After the evening meal, Milton would introduce a topic and instruct the boys to debate it as vigorously as possible without being disrespectful. Then – following the classical rules of debating – he would instruct them to change sides and start again. It proved to be great training.

'In time,' writes Tom Crouch, one of the brothers' biographers, 'they would learn to argue in a more efficient way, tossing ideas back and forth in a kind of verbal shorthand until a kernel of truth began to emerge.' Wilbur noted how discussion 'brings out new ways of looking at things and rounds off the corners'. After George Spratt returned home, he wrote a letter to Wilbur expressing his discomfort at the way the brothers argued. He was particularly perturbed by the way the brothers would switch sides in the middle of an argument, which struck him as dishonest. Wilbur's response is worth reading at length:

It was not my intention to advocate dishonesty in argument nor a bad spirit in a controversy. No truth is without some mixture of error, and no error so false but that it possesses no element of truth. If a man is in too big a hurry to give up an error, he is liable to give up some truth with it, and in accepting the arguments of the other man he is sure to get some errors with it. Honest argument is merely a process of mutually picking the beams and motes out of each other's eyes so both can see clearly . . . After I get hold of a truth I hate to lose it again, and I like to sift all the truth out before I give up on an error.

The brothers didn't argue dutifully; they took delight in it. 'Orv's a good scrapper,' said Wilbur, fondly. In another letter to Spratt, Wilbur chastised him for being too reasonable: 'I see you are back to your old trick of giving up before you are half-beaten in an argument,' he wrote. 'I felt pretty certain of my own ground but was anticipating the pleasure of a good scrap before the matter was settled.'

Charles Taylor, the Wright Cycle Company's only employee and chief mechanic, described the air in the room above him, where the brothers worked, as 'frightened with argument'. He recalled, 'The boys were working out a lot of theory in those days, and occasionally they would get into terrific arguments. They'd shout at each other something terrible. I don't think they really got mad, but they sure got awfully hot.'

How did they get hot without getting mad? Ivonette Wright Miller, a niece of the brothers, identified one crucial ingredient, when she noted that the brothers were adept at 'arguing and *listening*. The tougher they fought, the more intently they listened to each other. Another ingredient was trust, the deep trust that came from their affection for one another and their relentless focus on the same goal.

The night after the brothers argued about how to fix the well-digging problem, Orville did not sleep. Not because he had argued with his brother but because his mind was racing through the possibilities generated by their argument. He reviewed Wilbur's points, then synthesised them with his own. At the breakfast table, he presented the solution: an adjustable rudder. Following a few further suggestions from Wilbur, the brothers made their first fully controllable glider. Now they could move on to a whole new series of arguments.

• • •

In Keith Richards's autobiography, *Life*, he tells a story that captures something about the workplace culture of the Rolling Stones. It's 1984, and the Stones are in Amsterdam for a meeting (yes, even Keith Richards attends meetings). In the evening, Richards and Mick Jagger go out for a drink and return to their hotel in the early hours, by which time Jagger is somewhat the worse for wear. 'Give Mick a couple of glasses, he's gone,' notes Richards scornfully. Jagger decides that he would like to see Charlie Watts, who is in bed. He picks up the phone, calls Watts's room, and says, 'Where's my drummer?' No answer comes. Jagger and Richards have a few more drinks. Twenty minutes later, there is a knock at the door. It is Watts, impeccably attired in one of his Savile Row suits, freshly shaved and cologned. He seizes Jagger by the jacket lapels, shouts, 'Never call me your drummer again,' and delivers a sharp right hook to the singer's chin, which sends Jagger crashing on to a table of champagne and smoked salmon and almost out of a window into the canal below.

It's the kind of incident that would have ended many friendships. But the Stones have kept going for half a century because they're entirely comfortable with the occasional dust-up. Warren Zanes, a rock biographer and former guitarist in the Del Fuegos, told me: 'The bands that stay together aren't necessarily the ones high-fiving each other after every concert and giving each other hugs.'

The Wright brothers were innovators who used conflict to power their mental flights, but conflict seems to be a crucial element of any creative collaboration. You might even say that innovation and creativity themselves arise from arguments with the world. A start-up says: society is doing this all wrong – there is a more convenient way of buying groceries or getting around town. Artists often act in revolt against society or the dominant conventions of their time; the Rolling Stones pitted themselves against post-war Britain's social conservatism. It's hardly surprising, then, that groups of creative people punch as much as they kiss. Some level of internal conflict seems to be advantageous to creativity, but unless the group finds a way to manage that tension productively, the stresses of achieving success can rip the group apart. The history of rock bands is a rich data-set for studying the core problems of any creative enterprise: how to make a group of talented people add up to more than the sum of its parts – and, once you've done that, how to keep the band together.

Successful bands have handled conflict in different ways. Creative disputes don't have to be as fiery as that between Jagger and Watts. The members of R.E.M., one of the longest running and most successful bands of all time, disagreed with each other in a very different style. In 1979, Michael Stipe, then a college student in Athens, Georgia, was browsing in a downtown record store called Wuxtry when he got talking to the clerk, a college dropout called Peter Buck. The two men bonded over a love of underground rock and soon decided to form a band, recruiting two fellow students, Bill Berry and Mike Mills. Thirty-one years after their first gig, R.E.M. broke up amicably, ending one of the happiest collaborations in rock history. Another regular at Wuxtry Records was Bertis Downs, a law student who later became R.E.M.'s manager. He told me that R.E.M. operated – appropriately enough – like an Athenian democracy. 'They all had equal say. There was no pecking order.' Disagreement was still vital, though: 'Everyone had a veto, which meant everyone had to buy into every decision, business or art. They hashed things out until they reached a consensus. And they said "No" a lot.' (Compare this to the culture of Gerry Tan's start-up, Posterous, where conflict was avoided to the point that hashing things out became impossible.)

If democracy worked so well for R.E.M., the obvious question is why is it so rare. The answer is that bands tend to become competitive rather than collaborative. Jeremy Lascelles, formerly CEO of Chrysalis Music, who now runs an artist management company, told me, 'You're dealing with the most toxic element in human relations: ego. A musician needs a big ego to get on stage and bare their soul. But that means you can get these massive egos battling for dominance.' In successful bands, there is plenty of *task* conflict – who should take this solo, whether to do that gig – but relatively little *relationship* conflict – why is the guitarist getting so much attention when I'm the frontman?

Expressing a sentiment that Gerry Tan would recognise, the Silicon Valley venture capitalist Ben Horowitz remarked: 'Most business relationships either become too tense to tolerate or not tense enough to be productive after a while.' Ernest Bormann, a pioneering scholar of small group communication, proposed that every group has a threshold for tolerable tension, which represents its optimal level of conflict. Uncontrolled conflict can destroy the group, he said, but without conflict, boredom and apathy set in. Bormann believed that creative groups did not stay at the tolerance threshold but oscillated around it like a sine wave, alternating frequent episodes of conflict with calmer periods of agreement. Conflict is needed, said Bormann, to clarify goals, illuminate differences, stimulate curiosity, and release pent-up frustration (sometimes you *really* need to tell Mark from accounts how annoying his emails are).

When bands split up they traditionally put it down to 'musical differences'. When the successful British band the Beautiful South split, they explained it was due to 'musical similarities'. Simon Napier-Bell, a manager of multiple successful bands, including the Yardbirds and Wham!, told me that bands who don't fight tend to be creatively moribund. 'Artists don't want to compromise.' When they do, he said, the music becomes safe and boring, as the group merely repeats the formula that made it successful. 'New and interesting art comes from conflict.' He recalled witnessing an argument between the Yardbirds in the recording studio over whether Jeff Beck should be allowed a guitar solo. Beck felt he was not being given enough room to express himself. Eventually, the others grudgingly conceded to him a few bars on a song called 'The Nazz Are Blue'. Napier-Bell sat with the band and watched as Beck recorded his solo. When it came to his bars, Beck simply struck one note and let it bleed into feedback, while glowering with defiance at his bandmates. 'Everything he felt was in that note,' said Napier-Bell. 'It's the highpoint of the album.'

The hard part, of course, is stopping conflict from escalating to the point at which relationships are permanently damaged.

Groups and couples need ways of defusing the stress of vigorous disagreements – of bringing conflict back towards the tolerance threshold. One of the most effective techniques for doing that is humour. In particular, the playful, interpersonal humour we call teasing. For illustration, we need look no further than one of the greatest groups of all time.

In May 1962, Brian Epstein secured an audition for his client with the record company EMI at its studios on Abbey Road in North London. The Beatles had an ardent fan base in Liverpool but this counted for little in the capital, the only gateway to national success. The group knew this could be their last chance to make it big. They had already flunked an audition at Decca. Another failure and they would probably never be heard of outside their home town.

EMI's management had assigned the recording session to an urbane, elegantly dressed producer of novelty records called George Martin. Under Martin's supervision, the band recorded rather jumpy versions of 'Love Me Do', 'P.S. I Love You' and 'Ask Me Why'. When they finished, at around ten in the evening, Martin invited the scruffy, likeable young men up to his control room. He explained, at some length, what they would have to do to become successful, focusing in particular on their inadequate equipment (Paul McCartney's amp had had to be replaced during the session).

Then he paused. 'I've laid into you for quite a long time and you haven't responded. Is there anything you don't like?' After a beat's silence, George Harrison, the youngest member of the group, spoke up. 'Well for a start, I don't like your tie.'

Relationships were very important to the Beatles. Paul McCartney and John Lennon came from families fractured by bereavement, and neither they, nor Harrison, fitted in at school. All of them were hungry for the camaraderie and sense of belonging that came with being in a band.

In their early years especially, the Beatles did everything, on stage and off, as a unit. By the time they met Martin, they had spent years in each other's intimate company, in Liverpool, in Hamburg, in filthy bedsits, tiny dressing rooms and boneshaking vans. As with the Wright brothers, this personal closeness enabled honest professional disagreements. But the Beatles handled conflict in a different way to the Wrights, or the Stones, or R.E.M. There are surprisingly few accounts of them having stand-up rows or fistfights with each other, and as far we know, they generally did not engage in lengthy debating sessions. The Beatles made each other laugh, on stage and off, and they were more likely to rely on humour to see them through difficult issues.

While Lennon was the de facto leader in their early years, each Beatle had a say in how the group was run, and no major decision got taken without agreement from them all. The central relationship tension within the group was over who would dominate, Lennon or McCartney. While Lennon was the charismatic founder and lead singer, McCartney was the more accomplished musician and, over time, an increasingly confident performer, with more than his fair share of adoring fans at the Cavern. Lennon may have accepted McCartney's equal status, but he can't have found it easy all the time, and one way he came to deal with the tension was by teasing his partner.

We get a glimpse of this dynamic on a rough recording of the band's performances at the Star Club in Hamburg, during their final pre-fame visit there in 1962. McCartney is taking the lead on 'Till There Was You', a sentimental ballad from a musical – the kind of song that made the girls swoon for him. Every time he sings a line, Lennon pitches in, one beat behind, with a galumphing great echo: ('*There were birds*'; 'THERE WERE BIRDS' . . . '*No, I never heard them at all*'; 'NO, HE NEVER HEARD THEM'). McCartney carries on regardless, occasionally giggling through a line. He took performing seriously – he wouldn't have allowed anyone else to do that. But this was Lennon. This was funny.

Using humour is an important teamwork skill, somewhat over-looked by management theorists. Humour can be an important safety valve for conflict, a way of acknowledging difficult issues in a way that unites the participants through laughter rather than dividing them in bitterness. Lindred Greer, an associate professor at the University of Michigan and an expert in conflict dynamics, told me that when she teaches MBA courses, it's the former military students who impress her most: 'One of the many leadership skills they have is that they are able to crack a joke at the right moment. They know how to shift the mood of the group in a good way. I've always found that fascinating, and wondered how to quantify it.'

Teasing can go wrong if it isn't practised with sensitivity and affection. But done well, it is one of the most valuable forms of conflict management we have. The teaser gets to say things about the other person's behaviour that if said more bluntly might cause pain or anger, but instead can help them learn something about themselves. Everyone has eccentricities – none of us are 'normal' in every aspect of our behaviour. We shouldn't aspire to be either, but we do benefit from having at least a rough idea of what others consider to be our quirks, good and bad. The teaser lets us know what those are, without insisting that we change them – and they do so while making us laugh.

Teasing can also be a way of gently testing the robustness of a new relationship. The story of George Martin's tie has often been told to illustrate the Beatles' cheekiness, but I think it's also an example of how they used humour to navigate new social terrain. Even as they were being auditioned, I suspect that they were, consciously or otherwise, auditioning Martin. How would this man, clearly their social superior, react when confronted with the opinions of four young working-class men who did not take well to being told what to do? Harrison's joke was a probe. It was also a risk: if Martin responded negatively, that might have been the end of their shot at a deal, and quite possibly the end of the Beatles. Luckily for them, and for us, the signal that came back was positive: Martin laughed.

• • •

In Cambridge in 1951, Francis Crick and James Watson were working on a joint mission to discover the structure of DNA. They knew time was short. A second pair of eminent scientists was working on the same problem, in London. Watson had just attended a conference at which one of their rivals, Maurice Wilkins, presented the first clear images of DNA.

Wilkins was at King's College, the other main centre of DNA research in Britain, after Cambridge. In the X-ray lab there, he met a young researcher called Rosalind Franklin. On their first meeting, he managed to annoy Franklin by assuming she was one of his assistants, rather than a researcher in her own right (she had already made the crucial discovery that there are two forms of DNA). From then on, though a formidable team, Wilkins and Franklin maintained polite but distant relations.

Watson and Crick had a secret weapon, however: rudeness. Crick later recalled that if there was a flaw in his theories, 'Watson would tell me in no uncertain terms this was nonsense, and vice versa. If he would have some idea I didn't like, and I would say so, this would shake his thinking.' Crick believed it was important to be 'perfectly candid, one might almost say rude, to the person you're working with'. The enemy of true collaboration, he said, is 'politeness'.

In 1953, Crick and Watson jointly published their Nobel Prize-winning paper proposing a double-helix structure of DNA, a discovery now regarded as one of the greatest of the twentieth century. 'We had evolved unstated but fruitful methods of collaboration,' wrote Crick later, 'something quite missing in the London group. If either of us suggested a new idea, the other, while taking it seriously, would attempt to demolish it in a candid but non-hostile manner. This turned out to be quite crucial.'

At work, there is often a tendency to deny the role that conflict plays in creative thinking. Hence the much-repeated mantra that, in a brainstorm, 'there are no bad ideas'. Berkeley psychologist Charlan Nemeth (one of the authors of the devil's advocate studies) wanted to see if it was true that barring criticism made groups more creative. She organised ninety-one five-person groups, in America and France, and asked them to come up with ideas to solve a local traffic-congestion problem. Some groups were instructed to brainstorm in the conventional manner, without criticising each other's contributions. Others were told to engage in debate and criticism. Nemeth found that the debaters generated more ideas than the brainstormers. One reason for this, she speculates, is that instituting a norm of open criticism may actually *lower* people's anxiety about being judged. When criticism is framed as a way for the group to reach better answers, people take it less personally.

The sentiment of 'no bad ideas' is well intentioned. If people feel nervous about their ideas being judged or challenged, it is undoubtedly true that they will be less likely to speak up, leaving the conversation less fertile than it should be. But, to me, Nemeth's research suggests that the best way to address this problem is not to try and abolish disagreement, it's to get people feeling more confident about it – and the only way to do *that* is for the organisation's leaders to model and encourage a culture in which it's OK to be wrong, it's OK to show vulnerability, and everyone recognises that open disagreement is a source of creative thinking. We need the bad ideas to get to the good ones.

• • •

Open, passionate disagreement blows away the cobwebs that gather over even the most enduring relationships. Disagreement throws open windows and pulls up carpets, dragging whatever we've chosen to hide under there into the light. It flushes out crucial information and insights that will otherwise lie inaccessible or dormant inside our brains. It fulfils the creative potential of diversity.

As we've seen, though, it can only do all this under certain conditions. There must be mutual trust and some sense of a shared project or common goal. The trust need not be deep; healthy disagreement does not require intimacy. In its minimal form, it means, 'I trust that you are interested in something more from this conversation than "winning" or getting your way.' The shared project could be as shallow as a mutual desire to get through a brief interaction on social media having learnt something from each other. But the stronger the trust and the more important the project to its participants, the more energetic and edifying the disagreement can be. In short, stronger relationships make for higher quality disagreements.

There is no guaranteed route to a good disagreement, because no one person has that in their power. But most of us, most of the time, can do something to make it go better. That's what the next section of this book is about. I'm not going to tell you how to win arguments, because aiming to win an argument isn't very ambitious. Win or lose, it's more important that something new is created between you – insight, learning, ideas. Neither am I going to offer a code of civility (for more on why not, see the last section). What I am going to do is identify the primary conditions for better, more creative arguments.

What follows are nine rules of productive disagreement plus one golden rule on which all the others stand or fall. Since human interactions are infinitely variable, you should treat these rules (except perhaps the meta-rule) as provisional, but I believe they are sturdy guides to better disagreement, whether that be at home or at work or in public life (or on social media, which counts as all three). These rules are born from the practical wisdom of people who manage high-pressure, knotty, often heated disagreements for a living – interrogators, hostage negotiators, cops, mediators and therapists – and from the scientific research into tough conversations. I believe they constitute something close to a universal grammar of good disagreement. They are not intended as techniques or tactics, so much as underlying principles. Having said that, there is obviously a wealth of highly practical tips to be gleaned from our experts, and at the end of the book I've put together a 'toolbox' of techniques available to you when you next embark on a difficult conversation.

PART TWO

Rules of Productive Argument

PART TWO

5. First, Connect

Before getting to the content of the disagreement, establish a relationship of trust.

Over the course of two hot days in August 2017, hundreds of self-proclaimed white supremacists marched through the streets of Charlottesville, Virginia. The marchers, a motley collection of neo-Nazis and Ku Klux Klan members, were there to 'Unite the Right' – to proclaim the unity of the white nationalist cause. They chanted racist slogans and waved Nazi flags. Some carried semi-automatic rifles, others wielded clubs. Despite their attempts to intimidate, they did not go unchallenged: groups of anti-fascists staged counter-protests. They included political activists carrying placards, local clergy in ceremonial robes, and many ordinary residents of Charlottesville, black and white, who turned up to show their disdain for white supremacy.

On 12 August, after a day and a half of tense and sometimes violent confrontations, police finally shut down the rally after Virginia's governor declared a state of emergency. As the crowds dispersed, some of the counter-protestors filed down a narrow street. That was when a young neo-Nazi at the wheel of a Dodge Challenger spotted a murderous opportunity. He drove his car at speed down the street, scattering bodies, killing one of the counter-protesters: a 32-year-old white woman named Heather Heyer.

Heather worked as a paralegal in a Charlottesville law office. Alfred Wilson, her boss, and a friend, vividly remembers the day she died. Alfred, who is African American, had wanted to join the counter-protest, but in the end he and his wife decided against it due to the difficulty of keeping track of their three children in the crowds. They were watching the rally at home on TV when his phone rang. It was Marissa, a co-worker and friend of Heather's, yelling frantically that something had happened, and she couldn't find Heather. Alfred said he'd see what he could do. Less than a minute later, his phone rang again. This time it was Heather's mother, Susan Bro. Susan was calling from the local hospital. 'Heather's gone,' she said, and told him how she had been killed. Alfred got in his car and drove to the hospital.

Over the next few weeks, a storm of grief, anger and controversy raged across the country, with Charlottesville at its epicentre. Heather's death became a flashpoint for national politics, aggravating the racial faultline that runs through America's history. Susan planned and orchestrated Heather's funeral, disposed of Heather's possessions, while dealing with the press from all over the world and taking calls from politicians and celebrities. Meanwhile, at Susan's request, Alfred helped to set up a charitable foundation in Heather's name, so that the funds that were being donated from well-wishers around the world could be put to good use. Nine days after Heather's death, it was registered and accepting donations.

About six weeks after the fatal day there was a benefit concert in Charlottesville for those affected by the violence. It was organised by the Dave Matthews Band; the line-up included Ariana Grande and Justin Timberlake. Alfred's eldest daughter, then in her first year at university, drove home from her college to attend, along with three roommates. When the concert was over, Alfred hugged his daughter goodbye and the four girls set off back to college. About forty minutes later, he got a call from his daughter. Their car had broken down. Alfred drove out to see them. Unable to fix the problem himself, he called a tow-truck.

When the truck driver arrived and met the girls, Alfred was in his car, making a phone call. The truck driver, a white man, was slightly taken aback when Alfred emerged and joined the group. Alfred's daughter has the light brown complexion of his Palestinian wife, and her three friends were white. 'Who are these to you?' the truck driver asked. Alfred told him, before explaining his plan. His daughter and her friends would take his car. He needed the truck to take the broken-down car to a tyre-replacement shop, not far from Alfred's home, about an hour away. Alfred would ride with the truck driver.

Alfred and the driver got into the truck and began the drive down Interstate 64. 'It was quiet,' Alfred recalled. The two men sat in silence for a long time. When Alfred happened to look in the back of the truck, he noticed something: in the window hung a Confederate flag. To some, the flag is associated with pride in the South's cultural heritage. To Alfred and others, it is a symbol of hatred and oppression.

Alfred chose not to say anything. After all, the cab of a truck is a small place. 'I thought, OK, this is going to be a long, awkward hour.'

• • •

We have all been in situations in which there is something difficult we want to say to someone – something we know they will not agree with, at least not at first. The prospect of saying it, and the anger and vituperation that might follow, stops our tongue. I want to tell you not to worry. I want to tell you to put your fears aside and just leap right into the disagreement. But I can't. Beginnings matter.

Scholars from different fields have repeatedly found that subtle differences in how a conversation starts have a disproportionate impact on what follows. Researchers at the Intractable Conflicts Lab at Columbia University discovered that how the participants feel during the first three minutes of a conversation about moral conflict sets the tone for the rest of the discussions. Conversation analysts, who study real-life conversations in minute detail, have established that a pause of as little as 0.7 seconds before someone responds to the initial 'hello' in a phone call is a good predictor that the subsequent conversation will not go well. John Gottman, a relationship scientist, found that the opening exchanges in a married couple's conversations determine how the rest of the encounter will unfold. The same couple can have a productive conversation about something one day and then find themselves stuck in an argument about it the next day, the only difference being how the conversation began.

The reason for this is that humans have a deep-rooted tendency to respond to each other in kind. Without even realising it, we take our cues from the person or people we're talking with, in what we say and how we behave. If someone indicates that they like us, we want to show we like them. If someone discloses to us something they know or feel, we get the urge to do the same for them. And if someone is hostile to us, we have a powerful urge to be hostile to them. This mirroring of behaviour and emotional tenor is not inevitable, but it happens more often than not. Alan Sillars calls it 'the norm of reciprocity'.

Once a feedback loop of positivity or negativity has begun, it's hard to escape. A tense encounter can turn into a raging battle, without either participant willing it. In Gottman's lab, only 4 per cent of couples who began an interaction negatively were able to turn it around in a positive direction. Entering a conversation with noble intentions counts for little. In most marital arguments, says Alan Sillars, both participants want to be seen as playing fair – as trying to achieve their goals without offending the other person. But as the tensions grow, 'people begin to behave more mindlessly and less strategically'. They drop the niceties and make wounding personal comments. They drag in completely unrelated issues in order to get one over on the other. The conflict escalates.

Beginnings matter. So how do you begin?

• • •

In 1943, Major Sherwood Moran, of the US Marines, distributed a memo on the interrogation of enemy prisoners of war to troops throughout the Pacific theatre. Moran was a former missionary who had raised a family in Tokyo before the war. When the Japanese attacked Pearl Harbor in 1941, he was fifty-six, and living in Boston. Realising his fluency in Japanese language and culture might be helpful to the war effort, he enlisted. Moran soon became known as an unusually effective interrogator of Japanese soldiers, who were famously resistant interviewees. And, like Islamist terrorists today, many were fanatically, suicidally committed to their cause, and deeply hostile to Americans.

In his memo, Moran explained why he eschewed the bullying methods used by other interrogators. He believed that if the prisoner was forcibly reminded he was facing his conqueror, he would be placed 'in a psychological position of being on the defensive'. Moran did not believe in making the prisoner feel scared or powerless. Stripping a prisoner of his dignity merely reinforced his determination not to speak. The aim should instead be to achieve 'intellectual and spiritual rapport'.

Moran's premise was that even the most implacable prisoner has a story that he wants to tell. The interrogator's job is to create conditions in which he feels willing and able to tell it. The surest way to do that is to show that you care about him as a human being:

Make him and his troubles the centre of the stage, not you and your questions of war problems. If he is not wounded or tired out, you can ask him if he has been getting enough to eat . . . If he is wounded you have a rare chance. Begin to talk about his wounds. Ask if the doctor has attended to him. Have him show you his wounds or burns.

Today, most experienced interrogators agree. Steven Kleinman, a former army colonel, was one of the US military's most prolific and experienced interrogators and an outspoken opponent of the abusive practices used in the war on terror. He told me about an interrogation he carried out in Baghdad. His colleagues had captured an Iraqi gunrunner who had been selling arms to insurgents. Under aggressive questioning, the prisoner had steadfastly refused to speak, except – Kleinman noticed – to request a call to his daughters. When it was Kleinman's turn to question the prisoner, he began by talking about how bad he felt about leaving his two daughters at home. In exchange, the Iraqi disclosed a worry that his work was making the city less safe for children. 'We began speaking more as two concerned fathers than as an interrogator and detainee,' said Kleinman. Although he didn't it put it this way, Kleinman had used the norm of reciprocity. He opened up a little of himself, which cued the prisoner to do the same. The Iraqi went on to tell Kleinman everything he needed to know.

As distant as this kind of scenario is from the lives most of us live, it offers a model for embarking on a potentially tense disagreement. Before leaping into the dispute itself, focus on creating the right context for it. Figure out what the other person cares about and acknowledge whatever that is in how you talk to them. Behave in the manner with which you would like them to respond; be your ideal interlocutor. Since disagreement makes us nervous, we often put on a mask of invulnerability when we do it, but that's counter-productive. Open up a little to them and they are more likely to open up to you.

Better relationships lead to better disagreements. The sequencing is important. If there's one thing that marks out experts in difficult conversations from the rest of us, it is the way that they devote care and attention to moulding the relationship before they get into the substance of the disagreement. It's the way they begin.

• • •

Divorce mediators meet with couples in the process of splitting up, to try and help them come to agreement in a way that saves on legal fees. Often, the partners can hardly bear to talk to one another. The late Patrick Phear, a pioneer of divorce mediation, explained to an interviewer that he always started with a point of agreement, no matter how trivial: 'I will, if I have to, start with the fact that we can all agree we are human beings and we are in this room.' What you're agreeing about matters less than the act of agreeing. When I spoke to another divorce mediator, Bob Wright, he echoed Phear. 'I tell them, "You both agreed to mediation. That's something."' It's a trick, but it works because the act of agreement on something other than the matter at hand is a small reminder that the disagreement itself need not define the relationship.

Wright, who runs a mediation practice in Grand Rapids, Michigan, regularly sits down with couples in which at least one partner is seething with resentment and anger. In such a situation, you might have thought it best to stay away from the emotions and get straight to the negotiation. But Wright has learnt that the best way to proceed is to get the messy stuff out in the open. He begins by asking each partner to give their side – to talk about what they want, and how they feel about it. Then he asks the other partner to summarise what they heard, and – importantly – to name the underlying emotion. People are generally comfortable with the first task, but find the second one harder. 'Most people – or I should say most American men – don't focus on the emotional component. I tell them, it's OK, you're just guessing.' Wright will help them guess if he needs to, because he knows from experience that just having them say the words out loud transforms the conversation.

What happens, I asked him, when an angry person hears someone say, 'I can see you're furious about that?' 'They often say something like, "DAMN STRAIGHT – and I shouldn't have to tell you!" Then they relax. Once the emotion is on the table it's easier for them to be less angry. It's remarkable to watch.'

Unarticulated emotion is like an unexploded bomb, and naming it somehow defuses it. But you have to be listening. In a commencement speech to UCLA medical graduates, surgeon and writer Atul Gawande told a story from when he was a student. While working the nightshift in a hospital emergency department, he was assigned a prisoner who had swallowed half a razor blade and slashed his wrist. As Gawande investigated his injuries, the man kept up a foul-mouthed stream of invective towards the hospital staff, the policemen who had taken him in, and the incompetent young doctor who was treating him. Gawande had the urge to tell the man to shut up. He thought about abandoning him. But he didn't:

I suddenly remembered a lesson a professor had taught about brain function. When people speak, they aren't just expressing their ideas; they are, even more, expressing their emotions. And it's the emotions that they really want heard. So I stopped listening to the man's words and tried to listen for the emotions.

'You seem really angry and like you feel disrespected,' I said.

'Yes,' he said. 'I am. I am angry and disrespected.'

His voice changed. He told me that I have no idea what it was like inside. He'd been in solitary for two years straight. His eyes began to water. He calmed down. I did, too. For the next hour, I just sewed and listened, trying to hear the feelings behind his words.

• • •

Creating the bond of trust that precedes a productive disagreement is easier said than done, of course, especially when there is little to work with. You might find yourself plunged into a dispute with someone you don't know very well, with barely any time to work on the relationship. But that doesn't mean you should skip the first stage. It just means you need to work fast.

One group of professional communicators who need to strike up a rapport in an instant, a dozen times a day, with people who distrust or even despise them, are the police. We usually hear about police–citizen interactions when things go wrong, but the best cops are highly skilled communicators. For American officers, it's a question of survival, for them and everyone they encounter. In the United States, where cops and many criminals carry firearms, officers are acutely aware of the possibility of potentially lethal violence erupting. Saying the right thing, in the right way, at the right time, can make all the difference.

Over the last several years, a spotlight has been turned on the use of force by American law-enforcement officers, after a series of appalling abuses of power have come to light. In response, the USA's most forward-looking police departments have been rethinking how they interact at close quarters with people from the communities they serve. Police–civilian encounters are often tense and can quickly become confrontational, which is why de-escalation is considered an increasingly important skill. To find out how it is taught I travelled to Tennessee, where the Memphis police department, under its African American director, Michael Rallings, has been leading the way. In 2016, a Black Lives Matter rally blocked a bridge in Memphis for several hours. Rallings persuaded them to clear the way without the threat of force, linking arms with protesters as they left. For three days, I shared a room at the Memphis Police Academy with around twenty cops, most of them experienced officers. They were a mix of white, African American, and Asian American men and women, all of them eager to learn.

The department had hired a training company called Polis Solutions, co-founded by an ex-cop with a philosophy PhD called Jonathan Wender, who we'll hear from later. In Memphis, the Polis team was headed by Don Gulla, a retired cop who had spent over thirty years policing the streets of Seattle. Now, together with his colleagues Mike O'Neill and Rob Bardsley, also retired cops, he trains police officers in de-escalation, although he is not very fond of the term. At dinner with the three of them in their hotel the night before the first day of training, there was a general shrug when I raised it. 'Everyone's talking about de-escalation, but nobody ever really says what it is,' says Gulla, a Filipino American with kind, genial eyes. 'Say there's a guy out there in the lobby going crazy with a meat cleaver. How do I de-escalate that? Probably the best thing to do is shoot him. Is that de-escalation?' His face creased into a smile. For Gulla, de-escalation was a fancy word for good communication.

'What do you do when someone is screaming at you?' asked Gulla of his class, the next morning. 'Do you say, "SHUT UP AND CALM DOWN"? No, you don't say that, because that's going to make him worse.' Just as important as de-escalating, Gulla suggested, was not escalating in the first place. Under pressure, cops can make the mistake of getting caught in a vicious cycle of reciprocity. 'Instead of shouting back at them, you say, "Dude, I get it. We've got work to do, you and I."'

As we've seen, the beginning of a potentially fraught encounter (which, for cops, is most encounters) is crucial. A connection has to be made before the conversation about what to do can begin – and you can't make that connection when you're lecturing the other person on how to feel. In fact, as Gulla's colleague, Mike O'Neill, emphasised, doing so invites the wrong kind of reciprocation: 'As soon as you tell someone to calm down, they're going to say, "NO, YOU CALM DOWN." You've opened the door for an argument or a fight.'

The Polis team advised the Memphis cops to 'start where they're at', a phrase they had picked up from a chance meeting in Louisiana, while running a previous course. The three of them were having lunch in a Chinese restaurant (Gulla and his fellow trainers are dedicated foodies) when a man in a suit walked in and asked what the food was like. They got talking with him, and when they explained why they were in town, the man told them he was an insurance adjuster, responsible for investigating claims. That meant he had to deal with individuals in a variety of emotional states. He shared his approach for fruitful interviews: 'I start where they're at. If they are angry, I go with them. If they are happy, I go with them.' The insurance adjuster didn't mean that he got angry with angry people. He meant that he would always try and respond, in what he said or how he said it, to their feelings. He calibrated his communication style to their emotional temperature. From then on, the phrase became a Polis mantra: *start where they're at.*

Starting where they're at means paying attention to where they're at. In class, Mike O'Neill spoke about the need for an officer arriving at a potentially volatile scene to pause, if only briefly, to assess what is going on, emotionally as well as physically, before intervening. 'I just walk in and *listen* for a couple of seconds. I'm trying to piece it together. Sometimes we turn up to a scene and assume we know what the problem is, but only after we ask some questions do we find out what's really going on.'

A female officer spoke up. 'I try and relate to people. If there's a baby in the house I might ask if I can hold her. Then the focus is on the baby, and everyone calms down. I've walked into someone's living room and seen SIG symbols [SIG Sauer is a popular brand of firearms], I'm like, OK, so there are guns in the house, good to know. But I also see an opportunity to engage. "So what guns do you have?"' Another female officer spoke about disclosing to a person she was arresting, who had a sick parent, that her own mother had recently died from cancer. After the class heard her out in a hush, O'Neill nodded. 'Everything that ever happened to me in my life came back and helped me in my job. Even the fights between my mom and dad. Everything can create empathy.'

Another officer recalled going to the home of a man he needed to arrest for domestic violence. 'I got there, and the mom wanted to leave with the kids but he was standing with the baby in his hands and he wouldn't hand her over. He started asking me questions, like whether I believe in God. At first I was like, none of your business, I'm a cop. But then I thought, why not. We got talking about different religions, about what was going on in the Middle East, what we'd watched on the History Channel. Before

I knew it, he's put the baby down and we're walking to the squad car. Still talking.'

Only some of our disagreements are about achieving compliance, but the principle of making an emotional connection with the person before getting to the hard part applies to all sorts of tough conversations, including political ones. Eli Pariser, the online activist and media entrepreneur, has observed that some of the best American political discussions online take place in forums on the websites of sports teams. Since the participants know they have something in common – a shared love of their team – they find it easier to let their guard down and engage with views different from their own. If the only thing you have in common is the disagreement, it's hard to disagree productively. Too often we talk about finding something in common as if it's an end in itself, instead of what it can be: a springboard to fruitful disagreement.

• • •

After fifteen minutes of sitting silently in the cab of the truck, Alfred Wilson was reprimanded by a voice inside his head. 'I felt this tap on my shoulder,' Alfred told me. 'It was Heather. She said, "Alfred, you need to speak up."' Alfred resolved to take the advice of his dead friend. But he didn't want to get straight to the flag – that would have felt too confrontational. So, he asked himself: what would Heather do now? 'She would have engaged him first.'

Alfred works for a Charlottesville law firm, where he specialises in guiding people through bankruptcy. Five years previously, he had been looking to hire a data-entry clerk – someone to meet new clients on their first visit and enter their information into the system. One of his legal assistants recommended her friend Heather Heyer, but warned him that he would have to be open-minded.

Unlike the other candidates Alfred was interviewing, Heather had no legal experience and no degree. Alfred decided to get her in anyway. He met a nervous but charming young woman. 'This is weird for me,' she told him. 'You're all in suits. All I've ever done is work in a bar.' Alfred asked her how much she earned in tips on a typical weekend. When she told him $200, he concluded that she must be a pretty good communicator and decided to take a chance.

When Heather arrived for her first day on the job, she seemed a little groggy. That morning, she came into Alfred's office and asked if she could change her working hours, which were 8.30 to 5 p.m. Taken aback, Alfred heard her out. 'I've always bartended,' she explained. 'I never got up before noon. I don't know if I can do this.' She proposed working from 12 p.m. until 8 p.m. Alfred was amused by her chutzpah. 'I said, are you kidding? Our clients aren't here at 8 p.m.' But Heather persisted. They negotiated a 10 a.m. start. Alfred laughed as he recalled this to me. 'That was Heather. Getting people to have difficult conversations and compromise.'

Heather was hardworking and a fast learner. She proved to have an exceptional ability to connect with clients. 'People who come to our office are on their worse luck,' said Alfred. 'They might have recently had a heart attack, or they're fighting cancer. Their home is being foreclosed, their car has been repossessed. So when they come in, they are basically embarrassed. Heather would be the first person they met. She had this way of making them feel comfortable, helping them relax.' After a few months, Alfred noticed that Heather was making a difference to his case filings. 'Our clients were telling us much more after they had spoken to Heather, which meant we could help them more. She was opening doors for us.'

Heather got to know Alfred's family. 'She was close to my youngest daughter. Heather would talk to her about the importance of speaking up.' Sometimes, when he walked into her office, she would be crying, usually because she had seen someone vulnerable being abused on social media. One day, when he asked her why she was crying, she said it was about him. 'Alfred, I don't understand why you help some of these people.' She said she had noticed what happened when he met new clients. Alfred, bemused, asked her what she meant. 'You reach your hand out and they don't shake your hand,' said Heather. 'It's like they don't want you to help them.'

Alfred realised she was right. 'I guess it had happened to me so many times in my life that I hadn't been paying attention, or said anything about it,' he told me. 'I had got to the point where I started accepting being treated that way.' Heather also noticed that after leaving his office, an hour later, the same people would be hugging him and thanking him profusely. That only upset her more.

Alfred had been so intent on avoiding the possibility of conflict he had allowed this small injustice to perpetuate itself. He changed his behaviour. 'Now, if I stretch my hand out and they don't respond, I say "Hey, I didn't get to shake your hand." I get them to engage with me, and to deal with the uncomfortable feeling that they're in. Then they open up more. Heather had a gift for those conversations.' He recalled a video clip someone had taken of her from the day of the rally, talking to a white nationalist woman. 'Heather is with three black friends, and she's asking this lady, very calmly, can you explain why you don't like my friends? If you can't explain it, are you sure you're doing the right thing?'

After hearing Heather's voice speak to him in the cab of the truck, Alfred thought for a while about how to start the conversation. Eventually, he said, 'How long you been a tow-truck driver? You're really good at what you do – the way you put that car up.' The driver was responsive, and the two men got talking. 'We found out that we both had three kids, and that we both worked multiple jobs, because we wanted to make sure they had the best future possible.' As the truck drew near the tyre shop, it was about 1 a.m. Alfred asked the difficult question. 'I said, "I just want to ask you something. Why do you have that flag in the back?"'

The truck was still moving, but everything seemed to stop. The driver didn't answer straight away. He had been driving with one hand; now he placed both hands on the wheel and stared straight ahead. Then he said, 'To support my heritage.' 'Did your great-grandfather fight in the Civil War?' Alfred asked, genuinely interested. The driver seemed unsure. 'I think it was a great-uncle or something,' he said. 'OK,' said Alfred. 'You're a public figure. You're towing people's cars. A lot of people are going to feel uncomfortable about that flag. I was, at first. But you and I, we have a lot in common.' The driver agreed.

At the shop, Alfred said thank you and got out. His wife was on her way to pick him up but hadn't arrived yet. The truck stayed parked where it was. 'I went and told him he could leave. He said, "It's dark. You shouldn't be out there by yourself." So I knew he cared.'

About a week later, Alfred got a call from the driver, who said he just wanted to check everything had gone OK. Alfred told him his daughter's car had been fixed and thanked him for following up. 'Oh and I just wanted you to know,' said the driver, 'I took the flag down.'

• • •

A few days after Heather's death, her mother, Susan Bro, delivered a eulogy for her murdered daughter in front of millions watching across America and around the world. Bro had a message for Heather's killer and his allies: 'They tried to kill my child to shut her up. Well guess what, you just magnified her.' Those simple, defiant words instantly went viral, becoming a global headline for Bro's speech. Powerful as they were, they overshadowed something about the speech that was perhaps less tweetable, but just as important. Rather than sanctifying her daughter, Bro described the unvarnished reality of living with a passionate, opinionated young woman:

Oh, my gosh, dinner with her, we knew, was going to be an ordeal of listening. And conversation. And perhaps disagreement, but it was going to happen. And so, my husband would say, 'OK, I'm going to go out in the car and play on my video game for a while.' And she and I would talk, and I would listen. And we would negotiate, and I would listen.

What made Susan Bro's speech so special is that she didn't just tell people to make a difference to the world, or to stay true to their beliefs. She also talked about how *hard* it is to disagree – yet how necessary it is for us to do it:

Let's have the uncomfortable dialogue. It ain't easy sitting down and saying, 'Well, why are you upset?' It ain't easy sitting down and going, 'Yeah, well, I think this way. And I don't agree with you, but I'm going to respectfully listen to what you have to say. We're not going to sit around and shake hands and go 'Kumbaya' . . . The truth is, we are going to have our differences. We are going to be angry with each other. But let's channel that anger, not into hate, not into violence, not into fear, but . . . into righteous action.

Right now, there are people who are here willing to listen to one another and talk to one another. Last night in New England, they had a peaceful rally in Heather's name to have some difficult dialogues. If you ever want to see what one of those dialogues looks like, look at her Facebook posts. I'm telling you, they were rough sometimes. But they were dialogues. And the conversations have to happen.

Susan is a former teacher who lives with her second husband in a trailer park in Virginia, about a half-hour drive from Charlottesville. Since Heather's death she has been on a personal mission to promote difficult political conversations. On Facebook and Twitter she tries to marshal tough, sometimes vitriolic arguments over race and politics. She is impressively polite to antagonists, even those who spout conspiracy theories about her daughter's death.

Bro does not, she told me, think everyone can be engaged in good faith. She doesn't see much point in having dialogues with people who organise white nationalist rallies. But she is interested in reaching those who might have some passing sympathy with their cause.

Twitter is a place where people stand on the corner and yell at each other. Children do that sometimes when they're afraid and they don't know what else to say. I think we can say more, but we've gotten into the habit of doing what's easiest, which is just to yell and then block somebody. We're not trying to learn from each other.

Susan talked about finding the right context for connection.

If I tell them I live in a trailer park, they instantly assume a certain set of political views and level of education. If I tell them I was a teacher, that changes perception again. Or I might tell them I love rock 'n' roll. If you're willing to be little transparent, you can open up the conversation.

6. Let Go of the Rope

To disagree well, you have to give up on trying to control what the other person thinks and feels.

In 2013, a British man was arrested for planning to kidnap and murder a soldier. The suspect, who had a criminal history, had posted messages on social media in support of violent jihad. In a raid on his home, the police found a bag containing a hammer, a kitchen knife and a map with the location of a nearby army barracks.

Shortly after his arrest, the suspect was interviewed by a counter-terrorism police officer. The interviewer wanted him to provide an account of his plan and to reveal with whom, if anyone, he had been conspiring. But the detainee – we will call him Nick – refused to divulge any information. Instead, he expounded grandiloquently on the evils of the British state for over half an hour with little interruption. When the interviewer attempted questions, Nick responded with scornful, finger-jabbing accusations of ignorance, naivety and moral weakness: 'You don't know how corrupt your own government is – and if you don't care, then a curse upon you.'

Watching a video of this encounter, it is just possible to discern Nick's desire, beneath his ranting, to tell what he knows. In front of him, a copy of the Qur'an lies open. He says that he was acting for the good of the British people, and that he is willing to talk to the police because, as a man of God, he wants to prevent future atrocities. But he will not answer questions until he is sure that his questioner cares about Britain as much as he does: 'The purpose of the interview is not to go through your little checklist so you can get a pat on the head. If I find you are a jobsworth, we are done talking, so be sincere.'

It is impossible to watch the encounter without feeling tense. Periodically, Nick turns away from the interviewer and goes silent, or leaves the room, having taken offence at something said or not said. Each time he returns, Nick's solicitor advises him not to speak. Nick ignores him, though in a sense he takes the advice: despite the verbiage, he tells his interviewer nothing.

Nick: Tell me why I should tell you. What is the reason behind you asking me this question?

Interviewer: I am asking you these questions because I need to investigate what has happened and know what your role was in these events.

Nick: No, that's your job – not your reason. I'm asking you why it matters to you.

The interviewer, who has remained heroically calm in the face of Nick's verbal barrage, is not able to move the encounter out of stalemate, and eventually his bosses recall him. When the new interviewer takes a seat, Nick resumes his inquisitorial stance. 'Why are you asking me these questions?' he says. 'Think carefully about your reasons.'

What would you say?

The interviewer could simply repeat what the last interviewer had said; after all, it was the truth. But that would probably trigger the same response. I was struck, watching this video, by how it resembled arguments I have been in: ones where you get stuck in a battle of wills in which nobody wants to give an inch. Only when somebody shifts position or simply changes their tone is the conversation unblocked. You realise, the argument wasn't really about what you thought you were arguing about. It was about who is in charge.

The new interviewer begins speaking. 'On the day we arrested you,' he says,

I believe that you had the intention of killing a British soldier or police officer. I don't know the details of what happened, why you may have felt it needed to happen, or what you wanted to achieve by doing this. Only you know these things, Nick. If you are willing, you'll tell me, and if you're not, you won't. I can't force you to tell me – I don't want to force you. I'd like you to help me understand. Would you tell me about what happened?

The interviewer opens up his notebook, showing Nick its empty pages. 'You see? I don't even have a list of questions.'

'That is beautiful,' Nick says. 'Because you have treated me with consideration and respect, yes I will tell you now.' Nick went on to give a full account of the planned crime.

• • •

What was it about the second interviewer's approach that meant Nick opened up? Laurence Alison thinks it was the way the interviewer spelt out, so clearly, that Nick did not have to talk. The worst way to get someone to share a secret is to tell them to do it.

Laurence is a professor of forensic psychology at Liverpool University, and one of the world's leading authorities on effective interrogation. I watched the video with him and with Emily Alison, a professional counsellor. Husband and wife, the Alisons are responsible for having constructed, in close co-operation with the British police, the world's first empirically grounded model of effective interrogation.

Pausing the video, Emily Alison grimaced. 'When I watched this tape the first time I had to switch it off and walk away. I was so outraged, my heart was pounding in my chest. Of course, in the room, it's one thousand times worse.' Laurence nodded. 'As the interviewer, what you *want* to say is, "You're the one in the fucking seat, not me." He's trying to control you, so you try and control him. But then it escalates.' The moment an interrogation turns into a struggle for dominance, it fails. As we watched the Nick video, an officer in Britain's counter-terrorist police force was in the room. 'Cops are used to being in control,' he remarked. 'A big thing we talk about is leaving your ego at the door.'

Emily met Laurence after arriving in the UK from her home in Wisconsin to study forensic psychology at Liverpool University. Laurence, then a PhD student, was already a rising star of the field. As Laurence built an academic career, Emily, who had worked as a counsellor in Wisconsin prisons, started a consultancy helping social workers counsel families afflicted by domestic abuse. Laurence sometimes got calls for advice from the police on the conduct of tricky interrogations and he would partner with Emily, whose counselling experience had taught her a lot about interviewing difficult people. The Alisons soon gained a reputation for unlocking the most challenging suspects.

In 2010, Laurence was offered funding by a US government agency that was commissioning research into non-coercive methods of interrogation. He set his sights on an audacious goal: persuading Britain's counter-terrorism unit to give him access to video of interviews with terrorist suspects. Two years and over a hundred phone calls later, they agreed. The videos included interviews with Irish paramilitaries, al-Qaida operatives, and far-right extremists.

Some were incompetent bunglers caught up in something they didn't understand, others were highly dangerous operatives.

The Alisons analysed the interviews in minute detail, using an intricate taxonomy of interrogation behaviours. They studied the tactics employed by suspects (total silence? humming?), the manner in which the interviewer asked questions (confrontational? authoritative? passive?), and, crucially, the amount and quality of information yielded by the suspect. They gathered data on 150 different variables in all. When the process was complete, a statistical analysis of the data was performed. The results showed that interviewers who struck up better relationships with suspects elicited more and better information from them. The Alisons had made the first empirical proof of what had, until then, been something between a hypothesis and an insider secret: rapport is the closest thing interrogators have to a truth serum.

That wasn't the full extent of the Alisons' discovery. They also got further than anyone else towards defining what, exactly, rapport *is*. Despite its reputation among elite practitioners, the concept was vaguely defined and poorly understood, and often conflated with simply being nice. In fact, Laurence observed, interviewers could fail because they were *too* nice, acquiescing too quickly to the demands of a suspect. The best interviewers knew when to be sympathetic, and when to be direct and forthright. What they never did was make the interviewee feel like he was being pressured to speak. Interrogators who emphasised the suspect's ability to make their own choices were more likely to be successful. For instance, ineffective interrogators tended to mumble through the legal declaration of rights at the start of the interview ('You have the right to remain silent . . .'). The successful ones are more likely to make a big deal out of it, explicitly emphasising the suspect's right not to talk. In Laurence's paraphrase, they might say something like, 'I can't tell you what to do. This guy [the solicitor] can't tell you what to do. It's up to you. You can leave the room now if you like. I'm just really interested in how you got here.' Then they listen.

During the years when she worked on police cases with Laurence, Emily Alison had come to see interrogation as a close relation of addiction counselling. Both involve getting someone who does not want to be in the same room as you to talk about something they do not want to talk about. As she pointed out to me, around two decades ago the practice of addiction counselling was transformed by the incorporation of a simple truth: nobody likes being told what to do.

• • •

In 1980, a 23-year-old South African called Stephen Rollnick started work as a nurse's aide in a rehabilitation centre for alcoholics. The centre's clinicians took a confrontational approach to the job. They believed their clients were lying to themselves, and others, about the severity of their problem. Before setting the patient on the road to recovery, the clinician needed to challenge the patient on their dishonesty and strip away their illusions – to break their resistance.

This clinic was not atypical. The post-war medical consensus on addiction treatment regarded patients as wayward children who needed to be taught how to behave. The counsellor's job was to tell the addict the truth about their condition, and, if they denied it, to do so again more forcefully until they accepted it. To Rollnick, this seemed bound to poison the relationship. In the coffee room, he observed that the off-duty conversations of the counsellors were tinged with contempt for their patients.

One of the clients under Rollnick's care was an alcoholic called Anthony, who would leave group sessions having barely said a word. One day, he walked out for the last time. Rollnick discovered the next morning that Anthony had shot his wife and then himself in front of their young children. Shattered by this tragedy, Rollnick resigned from the centre and left South Africa, settling in the UK. He embarked on a course in clinical psychology at Cardiff University and began to search for a different way of helping addicts.

A couple of years in, Rollnick came across a new paper written by a young American psychologist called William Miller and was startled by the extent to which he agreed with what it said. Miller, who specialised in the treatment of alcoholism, argued that counsellors were having the wrong kind of conversations with the addicts. Miller understood them to be caught between a desire to change and a desire to maintain their habit, and being told what to do had a perverse effect: as soon as they felt themselves being judged or instructed, they thought of all the reasons why they did not want to change. By positioning himself as an authority figure, the counsellor might make himself feel better, but he reinforced the addict's determination to carry on.

Miller proposed an alternative approach. Rather than insisting on change and instigating confrontation, counsellors should focus on building a relationship of trust and mutual understanding. The patient should be allowed to talk through her experiences without ever feeling the need to defend her choices. Eventually, she will begin making the arguments for change herself. Then, because she has reached her own decision, rather than acting on someone else's instruction, she will be much more motivated to change. Miller called this approach 'Motivational Interviewing', or, MI. Rollnick began using MI in his clinical practice, with transformative results. One day, he met Miller at a conference, and told him about his enthusiasm for MI. The two men ended up writing a book together, developing Miller's ideas.

In the book, Miller and Rollnick note that most addicts sincerely want to change. They understand the impact that their habit is having on their lives and on those around them. They want it to stop, but at the same time, they want to carry on. They are ambivalent. Ambivalence is often misunderstood. It doesn't mean not caring about what happens. It means the opposite: an ambivalent person has an excess of motivation: she wants two incompatible things, which battle against each other in her psyche. This isn't just true of addicts: we all experience ambivalence. Miller and Rollnick showed how it can manifest itself over the course of a sentence:

I need to do something about my weight (*desires change*) but I've tried everything and it never lasts (*desires to sustain*).

An ambivalent person has a committee meeting going on inside their brain. Some on the committee are arguing for change; others are arguing against it. When the counsellor argues for change, he adds a voice to one side of the committee. But the ambivalent person's instinctive response is to add a voice to the other side – to come up with the reasons why she shouldn't change. This might sound like a stalemate, but actually it's a win for 'no change', since people tend to trust themselves more than others. Hence Miller and Rollnick's unsettling conclusion: by making arguments to someone about why they should change, you make it *less* likely they will do so.

In the context of addiction treatment, ambivalence is good: an addict who is ambivalent is one step closer towards recovery than one still fully committed to their habit. But ambivalence can be where addicts get stranded unless the therapist is able to help them win their own internal battle – not by lecturing, but by listening. Miller and Rollnick's book pioneered a method of drawing out the patient's thoughts, called 'reflection': responding to or summarising what the speaker says in a way that forms a guess about what they mean ('So if I understand you correctly, you're saying . . .'). The speaker can either accept the interpretation, or correct it; either way, they feel listened to, and empowered, while the therapist gains insight into how they think and feel.

Miller and Rollnick's book became a bestseller in its field and proved hugely influential among therapists of all stripes, not least because its methods work. Over 200 randomised control trials have found MI to be more effective than traditional methods across a range of areas, including gambling addiction and mental health; William Miller is now one of the world's most frequently cited scientists. The principles behind MI proved to be applicable to many types of tough conversation.

Emily Alison had been trained in Motivational Interviewing when she worked as a counsellor for Wisconsin's probation service. Later, while working with Laurence and the British police, she noticed that interrogations failed or succeeded for similar reasons as therapeutic sessions. Interrogators who made an adversary out of their subject left the room empty-handed; those who made them a partner yielded information. This observation became the basis of the Alisons' model of rapport, for which they went on to find such powerful empirical support. Rapport is a sense of trust or liking, yes, but also a sense that the partners in the conversation see each other as equals, capable of making their own choices and having their own thoughts, with neither trying to control or dominate the other.

It's important to bear this in mind during any kinds of disagreement, including those we have at home. 'I tell the police, if you can deal with teenagers you can deal with terrorists,' said Laurence. He gave me the example of a father who opens the door to his daughter when she comes home late. The father tells her off for breaking their agreement. His daughter, who feels pushed around, pushes back. A power struggle ensues, until one or both stomp off to their room. Of course, teenagers can be impossible, but what's certain is that a conversation fails when it becomes a struggle for dominance. If the father had emphasised his concern for his daughter's safety, said Laurence, a more productive conversation might have unfolded. 'In a tug of war, the harder you pull, the harder they pull. My suggestion is, let go of the rope.'

• • •

Implicit in Miller and Rollnick's critique of traditional addiction therapy was the uncomfortable suggestion that counsellors should question their own motivation. Their instinct to 'fix' the other person – to correct them or *put them right* – represented a desire to dominate the conversation, and the relationship. Miller and Rollnick coined a name for this instinct: the 'righting reflex'. As soon as I read about it, I started seeing it everywhere. The righting reflex lies behind so many of our dysfunctional disagreements.

In their classic book on child-rearing, *How to Talk so Kids Will Listen & Listen so Kids Will Talk*, Adele Faber and Elaine Mazlish outline a typical mother–child exchange:

Child: Mommy, I'm tired.
Me: You couldn't be tired. You just napped.

Child: [louder] But I'm tired.
Me: You're not tired. You're just a little sleepy. Let's get dressed.
Child: [wailing] No, I'm tired!

Faber and Mazlish observe that when conversations turn into arguments like this it's often because the parent flat out tells the child that their perceptions are wrong. There is only one right way to perceive the world: the way of the parent. The child's response, quite naturally, is to insist even more strongly on their own view.

Many adult disagreements are like this too. Confronted with someone we think is in the wrong, we desperately want to correct them. If only we can articulate the right arguments, we tell ourselves, or provide the critical facts, we can break their resistance to the truth, just as counsellors believed they could break the resistance of addicts. We fantasise about (someone else's) Damascene conversion, fondly imagining our interlocutor will turn to us after we've made some clinching argument and say, 'My God, you're right. I've been completely wrong about this.' It comes true, now and again, but more often than not the other person simply becomes more entrenched in their position.

We usually engage in righting behaviour with sincere intent. But try and recall a time when you were being told off, or someone was explaining to you, at length, why you are wrong about something. How did you feel? You probably felt annoyed or even humiliated, as if the other person was trying to order you around or squash you. Think about the language we use for this kind of feeling: *I was put in my place; I felt small.* That's why we often push back even when we know the other person is right. In fact, the more right they are, the more we push – and the other person in turn reciprocates. The result is a conversation that either escalates into a full-blown row or shuts down.

The righting reflex exists for emotions, not just beliefs. The Polis team's advice to the Memphis cops, about never telling a distraught person to calm down, reminded me of arguments I have had with my young children. I've found myself telling them to *stop being upset* about something that to me seems trivial – like not getting the correct mug for their morning milk. I have to tell you, it rarely goes well. But then, I don't respond positively to being told by people on Twitter that I should or shouldn't be *outraged* about whatever is in the news. Come to think of it, my wife doesn't seem to like it when I tell her to *calm down* (as Mike O'Neill could have told me, it has precisely the opposite effect). Apart from anything else, we're making a category error when we do this: emotions are not subject to rational intervention; that's what makes them emotions. So why do we insist on telling people what to feel? For the same reason that we are over-confident in our powers of rational persuasion. We find it hard to accept that other human beings have minds as real and as complex as our own.

Being wary of the righting reflex is not the same as avoiding disagreement; it means not getting to the disagreement too soon, before the two of you have had a chance to understand each other's position. Neither does it mean giving up on right and wrong. Crucially, it requires you to put aside the belief that you can control the other person's mind with your words. Not just the belief, but the wish; you have to approach the disagreement, not as a threat to be fended off, but as a collaboration from which both might gain. After all, there is usually something to learn from a person with whom we're disagreeing, and some truth to what they are saying. It's also true that the other person is probably less certain than they appear – that there is an element of ambivalence to their beliefs; some tension or contradiction that can be teased out, as long as they are not too busy defending themselves. It's probably true of you, too.

If your interlocutor does not wish to co-operate in any way at all there may not be much you can do about it, but at least you won't get pulled into a draining battle of wills. By resisting the righting reflex, and actively listening, you send the signal that you're interested in learning, not dominating. That relaxes them, which relaxes you. The two of you may still vigorously disagree, but you'll be treating each other as equals, which changes everything, even minds – even your own.

• • •

Maybe I'm avoiding the really hard question here. It's easier to resist the righting reflex when you at least respect the other's opinion. If I think your view is wrong but reasonable, and that I might even be persuaded to believe it, I'll be better at listening and less inclined to go into lecture mode. But let's test the value of this approach under more extreme circumstances. What if the person I'm talking to is staunchly attached to a belief that is obviously, unequivocally, wildly wrong. Isn't it important I tell them so directly at the first opportunity?

The question has acquired an urgency in recent years. The internet has enabled those who dispute basic tenets of established scientific knowledge to congregate into groups in which false beliefs are shared and disseminated. In some cases, there are serious ramifications. The so-called anti-vax movement, made up of those who oppose vaccinating children against infectious diseases, is making it more likely that diseases, like measles, which have previously been eradicated in developed nations, will re-emerge.

Since we often call such people 'delusional', I wondered if there was anything to learn about how to deal with them from experts in the treatment of clinical delusions, which is why I went to see Dr Emmanuelle Peters at her office in King's College, London. Peters is a clinical psychologist who specialises in therapy for patients with psychotic delusions: false beliefs that make it difficult for them to conduct their lives. To be clear: disbelieving a widely accepted scientific fact or believing in a conspiracy theory about the Moon landings is not the same as being psychotically deluded. But as it turns out, it's not completely different either.

More often than not, clinically delusional beliefs are paranoiac: the patient might believe that everyone she passes in the street is part of a secret plan to destroy her, or that she is receiving coded messages from outer space about a forthcoming attack. Other patients have more positive, or 'grandiose' delusions, which can nevertheless be debilitating, like the man who believes he is a king who will one day inherit a fortune, and has therefore never bothered to make any income and now finds himself on the edge of destitution. Delusional people come to see therapists not to have their delusion cured – they don't believe it is a delusion – but because their beliefs are making the world a stressful, difficult place. Somebody who is convinced that the government has put a contract out on their life may find it too scary to leave the house to go to work or visit the shops. The therapist's first job, says Peters, is to understand what that feels like. 'The right attitude isn't, "I must get this person out of their misery by showing them that they're wrong." It's "I must understand where this person is coming from."' That is, they need to start where they're at.

Dr Peters listened intently to my questions before answering in fast, fluent sentences. Her demeanour was confident although her turns of phrase were tentative – she uses *might*, *perhaps*, and *could* a lot – and she habitually checks that her interlocutor is coming along with her. She told me that some mental health professionals feel the need to tell delusional patients how things really are: 'That person in the park who spat on the ground? Of course he wasn't sending a signal to you – he was just spitting. There is no vast conspiracy. This is all in your head.' They soon find out that doing that puts them on a hiding to nothing. The patient has endured months or years of people telling them they're wrong. They've been told they're crazy. They've heard it all. They're not going to change their mind suddenly just because a doctor is telling them the same thing.

'The moment you try to change the belief they push back,' Dr Peters told me. 'If you go in head-on you won't be able to help them, because they will spend all their time trying to convince you otherwise.' Instead, the therapist should offer to help the patient deal with the difficulty they find themselves in. She is not colluding in the false belief – the patient is not going to believe it any more than they already do. By putting herself on the patient's side, however, the therapist makes it more likely they will listen to her suggestions.

Gently, over time, Dr Peters tries to reduce the patient's certainty in their belief. Wherever there is a glimmer of doubt, she works with it, inviting the patient to consider evidence for and against. 'I wouldn't say to the patient, "devil worshippers don't exist", but I might say, "In this *particular* instance, when someone pushed you on the bus, I wonder whether it might have been an accident?"'

Sometimes, the mere act of listening to someone talk about their delusion can weaken their conviction in it. In a 2015 paper, Kyle Arnold and Julia Vakhrusheva, psychiatrists from Coney Island Hospital in New York, relate the case study of a young woman who had been in therapy for several months before it became apparent that she suffered from delusion. In one session, she was complaining about not being able to make friends. When the therapist asked why that might be, she replied, 'Well, there is something I hadn't told you about. You're going to think I'm crazy if I tell you.' Her therapist invited her to continue. The patient said, 'It's all about the Big Kahuna.'

'The Big Kahuna?' the therapist inquired. 'Yes,' the patient said, 'It's a video game I'm trapped in. I am the Big Kahuna, and the title of the game is also "The Big Kahuna".' The patient explained she believed the entire world population participated in a video game in which the objective was to transfer credit from her bank account into theirs. 'How can you tell when people are taking your credit?' the therapist inquired. 'Phones!' the patient exclaimed. 'Whenever I walk through a group of people, they pull out their phones and use them to transfer my credit to them.' The therapist asked her to rate how certain she was about these 'beliefs' and she said she was 99.9 per cent sure they were true.

Arnold and Vakhrusheva agree with Dr Peters that while it's not a good idea to challenge a delusion head-on, that doesn't mean you can't probe and prod it. A therapist can ask about the evidence for it and prompt the patient to consider that maybe, at some level, it doesn't add up. The crucial point, they say, echoing Miller and Rollnick, is that it should be the *patient* who articulates the arguments against their delusion. The therapist's role is to help the patient think about their own thinking. In some cases, that can mean saying very little at all. When the young woman explained that she was living in a video game, her therapist didn't raise his eyebrows in disbelief or shake his head. He listened. At the next session, the patient rated her level of conviction at just 80 per cent.

When the therapist asked why it had dropped so steeply, the woman said, 'I hadn't really thought about the Big Kahuna as a "belief" before. When you think of something as a "belief" that means it might not be true, so then you have to think about that.' 'And what did you think about it?' asked the therapist. 'Well,' said the patient, 'it just seemed so . . . *weird*. I mean if somebody told me about the Big Kahuna, I'd think they were totally crazy.'

What applies to delusional patients also applies to people who deny that vaccines work. Call them deluded or crazy and you only make them more determined to assert themselves. Carli Leon, a mother of two, used to be a vociferous anti-vaccination supporter, before changing her mind on the issue. She told *Voice of America*, 'When people would ridicule me and call me a bad mother, it only made me dig my heels in more.' Insults strengthen resistance.

Like other people in positions of authority, doctors are these days exposed to more disagreement than ever. Patients come armed with information they have read online and expect to have a say in any decisions. The spread of anti-vax beliefs presents the medical profession with a particularly tough challenge. In the USA, where the anti-vaccination movement is widespread, public health officials have learnt to distinguish between hard-core refuseniks and the many parents who are merely uncertain – in other words, the ambivalent. With the latter, the best strategy has proved to be taking their concerns seriously, listening properly and winning trust, rather than taking on the belief directly.

Emma Wagner gave birth in a hospital in Savannah, Georgia, in 2011. When the paediatrician on the ward asked if she was interested in the hepatitis B vaccine, Wagner, who was anti-vaccines, expressed doubts. The paediatrician did not tell her she was wrong or attempt to persuade her there and then. Instead, he told her he would support her decision, 'and in a few years we'll talk about immunisations for school'. Wagner, impressed by the respect and care he showed for her, began to reflect on whether she had been listening to the wrong people. She has since become a staunch supporter of vaccination.

Resisting the righting reflex requires humility and self-discipline. Even when you know, intellectually, that telling someone they're wrong can make things worse, the urge to do so can be overwhelming. Therapists who have been trained not to do this still struggle with it. The reason for that, suggest Arnold and Vakhrusheva, is that it's upsetting to hear someone flagrantly contradict your own model of reality. Just like everyone else, therapists feel the need to push back, even when it gets in the way of helping the patient.

That chimes with an intriguing finding from research into the effectiveness of individual therapists: the ones who experience more self-doubt are better at their job. A 2011 study in the *British Journal of Clinical Psychology* found that therapists who rated themselves more negatively were typically judged as more competent by independent experts. Inspired by that paper, a German study compared how much therapists thought their patients were progressing with how the patients themselves felt about it. The researchers found that the less success therapists thought they were having, the better the patients felt. Helene Nissen-Lie, an associate professor of clinical psychology at the University of Oslo, who has also studied this question, finds that therapists with greater self-doubt achieve better outcomes because they are better at listening.

When we meet someone who is deluded, or even just someone with whom we strongly disagree, we want to cure them of the belief. By attempting to do so, we only make their condition worse. Better to create conditions in which the patient heals herself. In fact, perhaps it's best not to think of yourselves as patient and physician at all, but as two equally benighted and confused people relying on each other to reach better answers. That way, they're more likely to see things your way and you're more likely to learn something. Often there is a kernel of truth to a false belief, and you are more likely to spot it once you put aside your desire to be right. Give up on trying to control what the other person is thinking and you free your own mind too.

7. Give Face

Disagreements become toxic when they become status battles. The skilful disagreer makes every effort to make their adversary feel good about themselves.

On 6 May 1993, 15,000 white men marched through the town of Potchefstroom, not far from Johannesburg, South Africa. They were heavily armed and wore brown shirts with swastikas. The men were members of competing factions within the South African far right, who shared a belief in the genetic superiority of white Afrikaners. The Afrikaners, many of whom were ex-military and had fought in the war against Angola, were uniting forces against what they saw as a hostile black takeover of their country.

Just over three years previously, the South African government had released Nelson Mandela from prison after twenty-seven years, following intense domestic and international pressure. They had also legalised his party, the African National Congress (ANC). Apartheid, the system that enabled the country's white minority to rule South Africa and exclude its black majority, was on its way out. Mandela, now in a power-sharing arrangement with the white government, was planning democratic elections, in which everyone, black and white, could vote. That would inevitably mean the ANC taking power, with Mandela as president. The white 'Afrikaner nation' would be lost forever – unless it was won through force of arms.

The Potchefstroom march culminated in a fiery speech by Eugene Terreblanche, leader of the Afrikaner Resistance Movement, and an admirer of Adolf Hitler. At the climax of the ceremony, Terreblanche singled out a figure from the crowd.

Constand Viljoen, a silver-haired man with a martial bearing, was rapturously applauded as he stepped on to the podium.

General Viljoen was a decorated military veteran, and the commander of the South African Defence Force during the most violent years of confrontation with black activists. He had been a ruthless enforcer of white supremacy, organising assassinations of black leaders and imposing brutal punishments on black communities which threatened disruption. Now, he was called upon to vanquish Mandela, whom white nationalists believed should have been hanged a long time ago. Viljoen was apartheid's last best hope. To thunderous cheers, he promised the crowd he would lead them to the promised land of a separatist white state: 'A bloody conflict which will require sacrifices is inevitable, but we will gladly sacrifice because our cause is just.'

Mandela was understandably alarmed by what unfolded at Potchefstroom. He had received word that Viljoen was organising a force of as many as 100,000 men, many of them trained fighters. Mandela could have had Viljoen arrested for treason or inciting violence. But he calculated that this would make a martyr out of Viljoen, just as his own arrest had done for him, decades before. Mandela was also uncertain whether the South African military would back him in a fight against a man many of them revered.

More than this, Mandela's objective wasn't merely to win power. His overriding goal was to see South Africa become a full democracy, in which all races, and all political factions, felt included. So he decided on a different course, less obvious and in some ways harder. He invited Viljoen to tea.

In September 1993, Mandela met Viljoen, after contacting him via secret channels. Viljoen showed up to Mandela's home, in a Johannesburg suburb, accompanied by three other former generals. He knocked on the door and waited for a servant to open it. To his surprise, it was Mandela who greeted them. With a wide smile, the ANC leader shook hands with his visitors, declaring himself delighted to meet them. Ushering them in, Mandela suggested that he and Viljoen talk privately first, before the formal meeting began.

The two men went into Mandela's living room. Mandela asked Viljoen if he took tea. Viljoen said yes. Mandela poured him a cup. Mandela asked Viljoen if he took milk. Viljoen said yes. Mandela served him milk. Mandela asked if Viljoen took sugar, and Viljoen said yes, and Mandela added some sugar.

Thirteen years later, Viljoen recounted every detail of this encounter to the British journalist John Carlin. The elderly Viljoen was stiff and cautious. In telling the story of the tea, he allowed himself a rare expression of amazement. 'All I had to do was stir it!'

• • •

Suppose you are meeting someone for the first time – an employer who is interviewing you for a job, or your new tutor at university. As you start talking, what impression of yourself do you want to convey? The sociologist Erving Goffman called this desired impression your *face*: the public image a person wants to establish in a social interaction.

We put effort into establishing the appropriate face for each encounter. The face you want to show a potential boss will be different to the face you want to show someone on a date. Goffman called this effort *facework*. With people we trust and know well, we don't worry so much about face. With those we don't know – especially if those people have some power over us – we put in the facework. When we put in the facework and we still don't achieve the face we want, it feels bad. If you want to be seen as authoritative and someone treats you with minimal respect, you feel embarrassed and even humiliated.

Skilful disagreers don't just think about their own face; they're highly attuned to the *other's* face. One of the most powerful social skills is the ability to *give face*: to confirm the public image that the other person wishes to project. You don't need to be selfless to think this is important. In any conversation, when the other person feels their desired face is being accepted and confirmed, they're going to be a lot easier to deal with, and more likely to listen to what you have to say.

Nelson Mandela was a genius of facework, particularly when it came to the art of giving face. His elaborate show of courtesy towards Viljoen was strategic. He knew that difficult conversations lay ahead between him and the former general, and a less sophisticated operator would have got straight into them. Mandela knew he had some work to do first.

• • •

At the 1972 Olympic Games in West Germany, a group of Palestinian terrorists seized eleven Israeli athletes. The terrorists made their demands, the authorities refused them. The Munich police resorted to firepower. Twenty-two people were killed, including all the hostages. In the wake of what became known as the Munich Massacre, law-enforcement agencies around the world realised they had an urgent problem. Officers communicating with hostage-takers in order to avoid or minimise violence had no protocol to follow. Police departments realised that they needed to learn negotiation skills. Hostage negotiators, who may be specialists or trained officers with other responsibilities, are now deployed in a wide range of situations. The best ones are not just expert in tactics, but in the subtle art of giving face.

In 'instrumental' crises, the interaction tends to be relatively rational in character. The hostage-taker sets out clear demands, and a bargaining process ensues. In 'expressive' crises, the hostage-takers want to *say* something – to people at home, to the world. They are usually people who have acted impulsively: a father who has kidnapped his daughter after losing custody, a man who has tied up his girlfriend and is threatening to kill her. Most often, negotiators are dealing with individuals who have taken themselves hostage: people who have climbed to the top of a tall building and are threatening to jump. The hostage-taker in an 'expressive' scenario is usually on an emotional edge – angry, desperate, deeply insecure, and liable to act in unpredictable ways.

Negotiators are taught to soothe and reassure the hostage-taker before getting to the negotiation. William Donohue, a professor of communication at the University of Michigan, has spent decades studying conflict-ridden conversations – some successful, some failed – involving terrorists, Somalian pirates, and people on the brink of suicide. He talked to me about a key component of face: how powerful a person feels. Hostage-takers in expressive situations want their importance to be recognised in some way – to have their status acknowledged.

Donohue and his collaborator Paul Taylor, of Lancaster University in the UK, coined the term 'one-down' to describe the party, in any kind of negotiation, who feels most insecure about their relative status. One-down parties are more likely to act aggressively and competitively, at the expense of finding common ground or coming up with solutions. In 1974, Spain and the United States opened negotiations over the status of certain US military bases on Spanish soil. The political scientist Daniel

Druckman looked at when American and Spanish negotiators adopted 'hard tactics' or 'soft tactics'. He found that the Spanish team used threats and accusations three times as often as the American team. The Spanish, one-down, were aggressively asserting their autonomy.

When a hostage-taker feels dominated, he is more likely to resort to violence. 'That's when words fail,' Donohue told me. 'In effect, the hostage-taker says, "You haven't acknowledged respect for me, so I have to gain it by controlling you physically."' People will go to great, even self-destructive lengths to avoid the perception that they are being walked over. One-down parties often play dirty, attacking their adversary from unexpected, hard-to-defend angles. Instead of looking for solutions that might work for everyone, they treat every negotiation as a zero-sum game in which someone must win and the other must lose. Instead of engaging with the content, they attack the person as a way of asserting their status.

By contrast, there are those who enter a negotiation expecting to succeed because they are, or perceive themselves to be, in the stronger position. They may well therefore adopt a more relaxed and expansive approach, focusing on the substance of the disagreement and looking for win–win solutions. They may also take more risks with their face, making moves that might otherwise be seen as weak, offering a more friendly and conciliatory dialogue. Since they don't fear losing face, they can reach out a hand.

This is why giving face is so important. It is in a negotiator's interest for their counterpart to feel as secure as possible. Skilled negotiators are always trying to create the adversary they want. They know that when they're one-up, the smart thing to do is to narrow the gap. Mandela's tea service was a way of charming Viljoen but it wasn't just that; it was a way of lowering himself in order to make Viljoen feel he was not one-down.

Donohue analysed the transcripts of twenty mediated disputes between husbands and wives in California, over custody and visitation rights. Donohue found that husbands used much more aggressive tactics, while wives focused on the facts. Husbands were more likely to bring up issues relating to the relationship, to complain about the lack of consideration for their rights, to question the trustworthiness of their spouse. These tactics tended to raise the emotional temperature of the conversation, harden the positions of both parties and turn the dispute into a pure power struggle, making progress towards an agreement difficult or impossible. Why did the husbands behave like this? Because they felt one-down: the courts tend to award custody rights to wives.

If this is a reversal of the stereotypical marital dispute, in which the woman is more emotionally driven than the man, the difference is instructive. As Alan Sillars found, there is some truth to the stereotype: women tend to be more tuned in to the relationship level of marital conversations, while men focus more on content. But as you'll recall, this is a function of motivation – when men want to tune in to emotions, they can. The question of who is acting emotionally, then, isn't so much to do with gender as it is to which partner is on the wrong side of a power relationship.

In any conversation where there is an unequal power balance, the more powerful party is more likely to be focused on the top line – on the content or matter at hand – while the one-down party focuses on the relationship. Here are a few examples:

- An interrogator says, 'Tell us what you know, or you're in big trouble.' The suspect thinks, 'You're trying to control me.'
- A parent says, 'Why did you come home so late?' The teenage daughter thinks, 'You're treating me like a little kid.'

- A doctor says, 'We can't find anything wrong with you.' The patient thinks, 'You don't care about me.'
- A customer service representative says, 'The reason we didn't get the package to you is . . .' The customer thinks, 'Can't you just say sorry like you mean it?'
- A politician says, 'The economy is growing more strongly than ever.' A voter thinks, 'Stop talking to me like I'm an idiot.' (Indeed, one way that politicians misjudge their electorates is when they under-estimate the extent to which the voters feel one-down from them. Politicians can become so absorbed in the content of their debates that they pay insufficient attention to the relationships underlying them.)

When a debate becomes volatile and dysfunctional it's often because someone in the conversation feels they are not getting the face they deserve. This helps to explain the pervasiveness of bad temper on social media, which can sometimes feel like a status competition in which the currency is attention. On Twitter, Facebook or Instagram, anyone can get likes, retweets or new followers – in theory. But although there are exceptions, it is actually very hard for people who are not already celebrities to build a following. Gulled by the promise of high status, users then get angry when status is denied. In 2016, researchers from the University of Southern California set out to quantify this phenomenon. Focusing on Twitter, they identified a random sample of about 6,000 users and monitored their activity over the course of a month. They found that the top 20 per cent of Twitter users 'own' 96 per cent of all followers, 93 per cent of retweets, and 93 per cent of mentions. They discovered a 'rich get richer and poor get poorer' effect. Users who already have a lot of followers are more likely to gain new ones; users who are 'poor' in attention are more likely to lose them.

Social media *appears* to give everyone an equal chance of being heard. In reality, it is geared to reward a tiny minority with massive amounts of attention, while the majority has very little. The system is rigged.

So far, we've been talking about one aspect of facework: status. However, there is another, closely related yet distinct component of a person's face, which is not so much about how high or low they feel, as who they feel they are.

• • •

Having served Constand Viljoen a carefully prepared cup of tea, Mandela switched gears. He pointed out to Viljoen that if their respective sides went to battle, there was no way Viljoen's forces could defeat the government's forces, but they could do great damage. Many lives would be lost on both sides with no clear winner. It was in the interests of both sides to come to an agreement. Viljoen did not dissent.

Mandela then surprised Viljoen for a second time. He started speaking about his respect for the Afrikaner people – the very people who had branded him a terrorist and a traitor, imprisoned him for decades, destroyed his family life, and oppressed his fellow blacks. The Afrikaners, said Mandela, had done him and his people a huge amount of harm, but he still believed in their humanity. Mandela said that 'if the child of an Afrikaner's [black] farm labourer got sick, the Afrikaner farmer would take him in his [truck] to the hospital, phone to check up on him, and take his parents to see him.'

We can't know for sure that Mandela believed what he said about Afrikaners, but certainly Viljoen didn't doubt his sincerity. Mandela's directness about the damage that Afrikaners had done to him made Viljoen more convinced that he was speaking honestly. Something else convinced him too – Mandela spoke to him, then and throughout their subsequent meetings not in English, but in Afrikaans.

When people are used to being on the wrong end of a power relationship, they often become very good readers of people. They gauge the relationship level of conversations, in order to convert their psychological insight into influence. If Mandela was an exceptionally skilful reader of other people, it was at least partly because he had spent so long figuring out how to get what he wanted from a position of powerlessness. In prison, he turned the white guards into his allies and in some cases close friends, in order to eke out some freedoms in captivity. One of the ways he went about this was by making them see that he respected them *as Afrikaners*.

One of the first tasks Mandela set himself in prison was to learn the language of his captors. Some of his fellow political prisoners were upset with Mandela for this. To them, it felt like giving in to the enemy, but to Mandela, who was thinking far into the future, it was a way to co-opt his oppressors. He studied Afrikaner history, too, including the exploits of their war heroes. He read Afrikaans novels and poetry. None of this was a trick. Mandela genuinely believed that Afrikaners were South African; that he and they belonged to the same land. He also believed that one day they could be persuaded to agree with him.

At least from his early days in captivity, Mandela had decided that black South Africans could not fight their way to freedom: they would only achieve democracy by talking. That meant talking to South Africa's white rulers, and in order to have a successful conversation with them, Mandela realised he would have to teach them not be afraid of him, and not to hate him. He would have to create the adversary he wanted. That meant reassuring them that their identity was not under threat.

In the months after their first meeting, Mandela tried to convince Viljoen and his allies to give up their guns and participate in the democratic process. He made one particular gesture that went a long way towards convincing Viljoen to surrender his cause. South Africa's national anthem was an Afrikaans song of conquest. Now that apartheid was being dismantled, most ANC leaders wanted it replaced with their own liberation anthem. Mandela disagreed. To stamp on such a symbol of Afrikaner pride, he said, would be a grave mistake.

Mandela proposed an awkward but workable solution: both anthems would be sung at official occasions, one after the other. Was this a substantial political concession? No, it was a gesture – but a powerful one. It was another way for Mandela to reassure Viljoen that he would never have to give up who he was.

• • •

Elisa Sobo, a professor of anthropology at San Diego State University, has interviewed parents who refuse vaccines. Why were these people, many of them smart and highly educated, ignoring mainstream medical advice that was based on sound science? Sobo concluded that for these individuals opposition to vaccines is not just a belief, but an 'act of identification' – that is, it's more about opting in to a group than opting out of a treatment, like 'getting a gang tattoo, slipping on a wedding ring, or binge-watching a popular streamed TV show'. The refusal is 'more about who one is and with whom one identifies than who one isn't or whom one opposes'. Sobo points out that this is also true of those who opt *in* to vaccines: our desire to be associated with mainstream views on medicine is also a way of signalling who we are. That's why arguments between the two sides quickly become clashes of identity.

William Donohue, who has studied the topic for several decades, told me that what drags participants into destructive conflict is usually a struggle over who they are. 'I've seen it in hostage situations, in politics, in marital arguments. *You* don't know anything, *you* have problems, *you're* insensitive. One person feels like the other is attacking who they are, so they defend themselves, or hit back. It escalates.'

That our opinions come tangled up with our sense of ourselves is not necessarily a bad thing, as we saw earlier, but it is something we need to be aware of when trying to get someone to do something they do not want to do, whether that's stop smoking, adapt to a new working practice, or vote for our candidate. Our goal should be to prise the disputed opinion or action away from the person's sense of self – to lower the identity stakes. The skilful disagreer finds a way of helping their adversary conclude that they can say or do something different, and still be themselves.

One way to do that is to have the disagreement away from an audience. In Boston in 1994, in the wake of a shooting at an abortion clinic, the philanthropist Laura Chasin reached out to six abortion activists, three of them pro-life, three pro-choice, and asked them to meet in secret to see if they could build some kind of understanding. Hard and even painful as it was, the six women met, clandestinely, over a period of years. At first, they found their positions hardening, and none of them ever changed their minds on the fundamental points. But over time, as they got to know each other, they felt able to think, communicate and negotiate in more unconstrained, less simplistic ways. Note, too, that at their first meeting, Mandela took Viljoen aside. The less that people feel compelled to maintain their face in front of allies, the more flexible they feel able to be.

The same principle applies to workplace conflicts. In front of an audience of colleagues, people are more likely to focus on how they want to be seen, rather than on the right way to solve the problem. If it is important to me to be seen as competent, I might react angrily to any challenge to my work. If I want to be seen as nice and co-operative, I might refrain from expressing my strongly felt opposition to a proposal in terms strong enough for anyone to notice. That's why, when a difficult work conversation arises, the participants often propose to 'take it offline'. The phrase used to mean simply an in-person discussion, but it has gained the additional nuance of, 'Let's take this potentially tough conversation to a place where there is less at stake for our faces.'

Taking a disagreement offline can work but it should only ever be seen as a second-best option. It means the problem at hand is exposed to the scrutiny of fewer minds, losing the benefits of open disagreements. The best way to lower the identity stakes is to create a workplace culture in which people *do not feel much need to protect their face*; a culture in which different opinions are explicitly encouraged, mistakes are expected, rules of conduct are understood, and everyone trusts that everyone else cares about the collective goal. Then you can really have it out.

Still, in most disagreements, face is at stake in some way, and while getting out of sight of an audience is one way of lowering the identity stakes, another way is to give face – to affirm your adversary's ideal sense of themselves, as Mandela did with Viljoen. When you show me that you believe in who I am and want to be seen as, you make it easier for me to reconsider my position. By being personally gracious, you can depersonalise the disagreement.

Sometimes that can be as simple as offering a compliment at

the very moment your adversary feels most vulnerable. Jonathan Wender, the ex-cop who co-founded Polis Solutions, has written a book about policing in which he notes that the act of arrest is a moment of potential humiliation for the suspect. Wender argues that when police officers are making an arrest they should do what they can to make the person being arrested feel better about themselves. He gives the example of arresting a man he calls Calvin, suspected of violent assault:

The officer and I each took hold of one of Calvin's arms and told him he was under arrest. He began to struggle and was clearly ready to fight. Given his large stature and history of violence, we wanted to avoid fighting with Calvin, which would inevitably leave him and officers injured. I . . . told Calvin, 'Look, you're just too big for us to fight with.'

Wender writes, 'Officers can de-escalate a potential fight by . . . affirming his dignity, especially in public.' As we've seen, it is in a cop's interest to make the person they have arrested feel good, or at least less bad, about themselves, just as it was in Mandela's interest to affirm Viljoen's dignity. This is common sense – or at least it ought to be. It is amazing how often people commit what you might call the overdog's mistake: when, having achieved a dominant position, they brutally ram their advantage home, wounding the other party's sense of self. By doing so, they might gain some fleeting satisfaction, but they also create the adversary they do not want.

Wounded people are dangerous. In Memphis, I watched as the Polis trainer Mike O'Neill told the class that when he was a cop, he had seen officers hit suspects after they had been cuffed, sometimes in front of the suspect's friends or family. Not only was that wrong, he said, it was dumb: the act of humiliating someone in an arrest 'can kill your colleagues'. There was a grave murmur of assent in the room. Suspects who have been humiliated do not forget it, and often look for ways to get their own back on a cop – any cop – years down the line. It is a pattern familiar to students of history. Humiliation hurts the humiliators and those associated with them. In a study of ten international diplomatic crises, political scientists William Zartman and Johannes Aurik described how, when stronger countries exert power over weaker countries, the weaker ones accede in the short term but look for ways to retaliate later on.

Imagine if Mandela had entered that conversation with Viljoen the way that people argue with each other in public today. First of all, he would have attacked his identity: he would, in front of as many people as possible, have called Viljoen a white supremacist with blood on his hands. Then he would have explained to the former general, in an aggressive tone, why he needed to disarm and accept Mandela's terms, since it was the only morally correct and practically viable course for him to take. Mandela would have been perfectly justified in doing all this; he would have been in the right on every count. But how do you think Viljoen would have reacted?

The American politician Alexandria Ocasio-Cortez has described how to have a conversation with someone with whom you strongly disagree. You don't have to share her politics to see that it is good advice:

I have this mentor. And one of the best pieces of advice that he gave me is 'always give someone the golden gate of retreat', which is: give someone enough rope, give someone enough compassion, enough opportunity in a conversation for them to look good changing their mind. And it's a really important thing to be able to do, because if you're just like, 'Oh you said this thing!

You're racist!' And now you're forcing that person to say, 'No I'm not.' Et cetera. There's no golden gate of retreat there. The only retreat there is to just barrel right through the opposing opinion.

When we're in an argument with someone, we should be thinking about how they can change their mind and look good – maintain or even enhance their face – at the same time. Often this is very hard to do in the moment of the dispute itself, when opinion and face are bound even more tightly together than they are before or after (writer Rachel Cusk defines an argument as 'an emergency of self-definition'). However, by showing that we have listened to and respected our interlocutor's point of view, we make it more likely that, like the vaccination convert we heard from earlier, they will come around at some later point. If and when they do, we should avoid scolding them for not agreeing with us all along. It's amazing quite how often people in polarised debates do this; it hardly makes it more tempting to switch sides. Instead, we should remember that they have achieved something we have not: a change of mind.

. . .

Within six months of that first cup of tea with Mandela, Viljoen took what he described as the toughest decision of his life: he ordered his followers to lay down their arms. Shortly after that, he announced that not only would he not disrupt the upcoming democratic elections, he would take part in them. In return for no political concessions whatsoever, Viljoen had given his blessing to a political process that, ten months earlier, he vowed to fight to the death. Mandela had transformed his most formidable enemy into an opponent with whom he could peacefully disagree.

It's impossible not to admire Mandela's shrewdness and skill in dealing with a dangerous enemy he needed to win round (part of his shrewdness was seeing that he needed to win him round). But his adversary deserves credit here as well. Viljoen made a deep, painful change to his mindset. He abandoned his original position in order to accept that black South Africans could be fellow citizens and Mandela his leader. He then had to sell that vision to his own side, taking enormous risks with his 'face'. What Mandela did was help Viljoen realise that he did not have to surrender his identity. He could be part of the nation and still be proudly himself: an Afrikaner, a military veteran, a South African citizen.

Nelson Mandela was inaugurated as president in May 1994, and a new parliament opened, one that reflected the racial diversity of South Africa: two-thirds of the new representatives were black. Viljoen himself had won a seat, after his party picked up nine seats in the election. John Carlin, who was there for the opening, watched Mandela walk into a chamber that had previously been all-white and overwhelmingly male and which now embodied the diversity of South Africa. Carlin noticed something in particular: Viljoen was staring at Mandela, entranced.

Twelve years later, Carlin put it to Viljoen that what he had seen on his face that day was profound respect, and even affection. Viljoen, who was uncomfortable with sentiment, replied tersely: 'Yes, that would be correct.' Then he remembered something else. 'Mandela came in and he saw me and he came across the floor to me, which he was not really supposed to do according to parliamentary protocol. He shook my hand and he had a big smile on his face and said how happy he was to see me there.' A voice had called out from the gallery: 'Give him a hug, General!' 'And did you?' asked Carlin. 'I am a military man and he was my president,' said Viljoen. 'I shook his hand and I stood to attention.'

8. Check Your Weirdness

Behind many disagreements is a clash of cultures that seem strange to each other. Don't assume that yours is the normal one.

Schneider: Ever since I was a very small child – I've always like yourself looked up at the stars and wondered why is this – where are we going, how did we get there, what's this vast expanse about?

FBI: Yeah.

Schneider: Why is this earth a cemetery, everything dies here, plants, people, animals, six thousand years of woe and human history. We get a little bit of pleasure but we're never satisfied and fulfilled and relatives can be taken out of your life, friends, accidents. God, what's going on?

FBI: Yeah.

Schneider: Who are you, God? But I've never really claimed to know God. I tried it, the Christian routine for the majority of my life and in honesty, I mean, I've never really known God but I've always wanted to know God.

FBI: Um-hum.

Schneider: I do see something about a book that's very logical and clear and this man also has opened up very deep sciences, physics, astronomy, and these are the things that not many have gotten to hear recently . . .

FBI: You know, I've just been handed a note that David did a radio interview and that's been completed. How is he feeling with his injuries?

On the morning of Sunday 28 February 1993, around eighty armed law-enforcement agents descended on a sprawling property near the town of Waco, Texas, known as the Mount Carmel complex. The agents were from the ATF (Bureau of Alcohol, Tobacco and Firearms), which investigates crimes involving unlawful firearms. They had a warrant for the arrest of Vernon Wayne Howell, also known as David Koresh, leader of the religious community that lived at Mount Carmel, known as the Branch Davidians. The agents had reason to believe that the group had amassed a large stockpile of illegal weapons.

The ATF had been told that Koresh never left the compound and so resolved that the only way to arrest him was to spring a surprise. But the Branch Davidians were tipped off, and had prepared defensive positions. An intense gun battle ensued, in which six Mount Carmel residents were killed, along with four ATF agents. Koresh was wounded but survived. A local deputy sheriff, Larry Lynch, negotiated a ceasefire.

The next day, the FBI took over, surrounding Mount Carmel, and demanded that the Davidians surrender peacefully and face justice. The Davidians refused. So began a barricaded siege. The FBI assembled what may have been the largest military force ever gathered against civilians on US soil. It parked ten Bradleys – armoured fighting vehicles – inside the compound. In addition to personnel from the US Army and local law-enforcement agencies, a total of 899 government officials were gathered at Mount Carmel. Meanwhile, the FBI's tactical team made conditions as uncomfortable as possible for the Davidians. They cut the phone lines and electricity to the building. At night they flooded the compound with bright lights and blasted music through powerful speakers.

A team of crack FBI negotiators, trained in precisely this kind of situation – a barricaded siege – were flown in from around the country. They set up shop in a nearby aircraft hangar, with access to the one remaining phone line into Mount Carmel. Their conversation with Davidian leaders was to last fifty-one days. The transcripts, later published in full, are a unique record of a painfully difficult negotiation. To read them is to witness two parties talking at great length while barely communicating at all. The exchange above features Steve Schneider, David Koresh's closest friend and aide, talking to an unnamed FBI negotiator. While Schneider ruminates on the meaning of life, the negotiator seems uninterested, joining in only when he finds a reason to return to what he thinks of as the purpose of the conversation.

The FBI negotiators were, for the most part, professional and thorough, following standard procedures: they tried to show respect for the Davidians, to give them reasonable options, to cultivate rapport. They even took advice from psychologists on how to handle different personality types. In short, they did everything by the book. But the book turned out to be missing a crucial chapter.

• • •

The linguist Richard Lewis was one of the first academics to grasp the importance to negotiation of cultural difference. When people from different countries meet to thrash out a business deal or a political agreement, using a common language is no guarantee that each side will understand the other. Cross-cultural negotiations that degenerate into confusion and personal acrimony can do so not because the parties are disagreeing on substance, but because each is engaged in different kind of conversation to the other. Lewis pointed out that before you negotiate with an Italian, you should make it your business to understand what an Italian thinks a negotiation *is*. He made diagrammatic representations of how different nationalities negotiate. Here's a few of them:

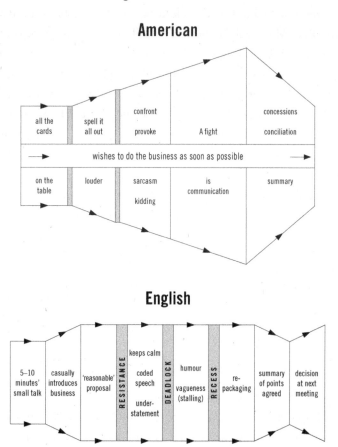

American

all the cards / on the table

spell it all out / louder

confront / provoke / sarcasm / kidding

A fight / is communication

wishes to do the business as soon as possible

concessions / conciliation / summary

English

5–10 minutes' small talk

casually introduces business

'reasonable' proposal

RESISTANCE

keeps calm / coded speech / under-statement

DEADLOCK

humour / vagueness (stalling)

RECESS

re-packaging

summary of points agreed

decision at next meeting

Lewis's models are not based on quantitative empirical research; they are a mixture of his own observations and his expertise in the use of language. But his essential insight is an important one: unless you take time to understand the other party's cultural worldview, you are liable to misunderstand what they are saying and misread their motivations. If the American doesn't understand

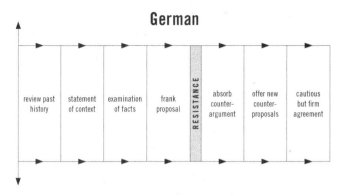

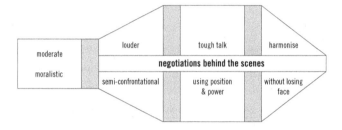

why the German she is talking to is not engaging in small talk, the American thinks he is haughty and rude – nearly as bad as that insufferably vague and flippant English person. The Chinese misinterpret the American's impatience to get things done as aggression. The English under-estimate the German desire for due process and think they're just being difficult. Everyone under-estimates how much the French love to argue.

Culture shapes how people behave and what they say, which is why trying to have a tough conversation with someone without knowing where they're coming from – culturally, as well as personally – is self-defeating. The FBI agents deployed to Waco were practiced in negotiating with Americans, not Chinese or

Germans; the idea that they needed to take time to understand the cultural outlook of fellow countrymen would hardly have occurred to them. But culture is not just a matter of country.

• • •

The Waco siege instantly became a national crisis and an international event. The world's news media feasted on an irresistible story: a brainwashed religious cult with a charismatic leader defying the might of the US government. Lurid rumours abounded. It was said that David Koresh had over a hundred wives who did his every bidding and that he exercised mind control over his followers. To the outside world, Koresh was a transparent charlatan who had somehow hypnotised a group of naive people into pandering to his lust for power, sex and glory. Privately, the FBI negotiators shared the public's view. One of them later wrote that Koresh was 'as close to pure evil as any human being I had ever heard of – devious, calculating, self-absorbed, charming, and completely sadistic'.

The FBI's goals were clear: get everyone out of the compound, and avoid further violence. The Branch Davidians – well, nobody was quite sure what they wanted. Some speculated that they were preparing for the End of Days, and that they had been planning to invade the local town and kill everyone in sight, or that they were about to blow themselves up.

At first, a quick resolution had seemed possible. Davidian leaders agreed to the handover of nineteen young children from Mount Carmel. But after this initial breakthrough the negotiation entered a tortured stalemate. Ninety-eight people remained in the building, twenty-three of them children (including Koresh's own). One stumbling block was that the FBI treated this as a hostage situation, while Koresh and the other Davidians insisted that everyone inside was staying of their own free will.

FBI: What I'm saying is that if you could make an agreement with
     your people that they're walking out of there and you could –
Koresh: I am not going to tell them what to do. I never have and
     never will. I show them out of a book what God teaches. Then
     it's for them to decide.

At one point, the FBI asked the Davidians to make videotapes of people inside the building so that they could see everyone was OK. The Davidians happily complied. The videos included Davidian women explaining, with apparent authenticity, that they lived at Mount Carmel because they liked it there. Koresh himself appeared, asking why the ATF couldn't have just arrested him 'at the side of the road' one day, instead of pointing guns at the women and children of Mount Carmel. The FBI did not release the tapes to the public.

The FBI continued to believe they were dealing with dupes being controlled by a psychopath. The Davidians thought of themselves as intelligent, spiritual people who had freely chosen to live in a community that did not conform to society's norms. The two sides also had radically different ideas about what kind of conversation they were having. The FBI negotiators approached it as an exercise in pragmatism. Their aim was to drain the conversation of emotion in order to engage in a bargaining process: *You give me this, I'll give you that.* The Davidians were not interested in bargaining. Like Schneider in that opening exchange, they wanted to talk about what was happening in the context of God, scripture and the meaning of existence. But whenever Koresh or the other Davidians offered a religious interpretation of events, they were dismissed or ignored. The FBI kept trying to bring the conversation back to what they took to be the real issues; to the Davidians, God *was* the real issue.

Early on, the FBI and Koresh came to an agreement that the Davidians would leave the compound if a message, recorded by Koresh, was broadcast on national radio. The broadcast was made, but the agreement dissolved when Koresh told negotiators that God had ordered him to wait. The negotiators began pressing him on what they perceived as a personal commitment:

FBI: Okay. I need to know, are you going to live up to your promise? What are you planning to do?

Koresh: Let me explain. See, in verse two –

FBI: Yes, I know. Please tell me what you're going to do.

Koresh: I am trying. Please look at verse two of Nahum.

FBI: Let's not talk in those terms, please.

Koresh: No. Then you don't understand my doctrine.

The conversations often had the flavour of a parent–teenager row. The negotiators took a paternalistic tone, only pretending to take the Davidian talk of God seriously. The Davidians sensed their condescension and became more resistant. A common reason that negotiations and disagreements of any kind go bad is that one side, or both, has not made an effort to see things from the other's perspective. That can require not just the effort to consider another opinion, but to consider a whole other cultural worldview, which, however bizarre it seems to you, is just as rich and real as your own.

• • •

In 1934, Victor Houteff, a Bulgarian immigrant, and a disillusioned Seventh Day Adventist, formed a commune outside Waco to await the Second Coming of Christ. The group, which later became known as the Branch Davidians, built themselves a compound called Mount Carmel. The Davidians were part of American Christianity's millennialist tradition, which also spawned Mormonism and the Jehovah's Witnesses. Millennialists believe that a close reading of the Bible offers specific clues to when and how the Second Coming, and the end of the world, will arrive, and often rely on certain individuals, privileged to be God's messengers, to interpret those clues. The Davidians paid particular attention to passages from the Book of Revelation which suggest that a mysterious figure known as the Lamb of God will one day open the Seven Seals, a book held in the right hand of God, heralding the return of the Messiah and the end of time.

In 1981, a long-haired 23-year-old high-school dropout and rock guitarist named Vernon Howell pulled up to Mount Carmel in a yellow Buick and asked to join the community. Howell was charismatic in an unconventional way, softly spoken but intense, with a sharp sense of humour, and an extraordinarily detailed knowledge of scripture, which he could recite by heart for hours. When Howell opened a Bible, people gathered expectantly. Scruffily dressed in T-shirt and sneakers and streaked with grease from the garage where he loved to tinker with cars, he embarked on marathon storytelling sessions that could last for twelve hours at a stretch. He would start off chatty and low-key, gradually building towards peaks of intensity. As an observer put it, 'When he read scripture it was as if he were actually there taking part in the events.'

Howell soon assumed spiritual leadership of the group, and changed his name to David Koresh – David after the biblical king,

Koresh for Cyrus, the ancient Persian king. Koresh convinced the Mount Carmel community that *he* was the Lamb of God – the one chosen by God to open the way for the Messiah. He told the group that God's chosen would soon fight a terrible battle against the forces of Satan, represented by the United Nations and led by the United States government. Despite this, the Davidians were not hostile to the outside world. They were often seen in Waco, where they were regarded as eccentric but harmless. One of them ran a legal practice there. Koresh himself sometimes ventured into town and even made trips to other countries, including the UK, where he successfully recruited new members from black churches. One Davidian who joined around this time remembered Mount Carmel as an 'open and friendly' place.

The community's hundred or so members included people from Mexico, Australia, New Zealand, the Philippines and Canada. Some were poor, some rich, and some highly educated – the lawyer, an African American called Wayne Martin, was a Harvard graduate.

The Davidians were at once more 'normal' than the FBI imagined, and stranger. The point of the commune was to live by different rules to the rest of society. Koresh, who was married to a fellow Davidian, took numerous 'spiritual wives' from among the Mount Carmel community, and fathered over a dozen children, purportedly in order to create a dynasty that would rule the world after the return of Christ. These 'wives' included the partners of his male followers, and at least one underage girl (the younger sister of his legal wife). Most of us would find all of this morally repellent. Within the community Koresh's sexual conduct was understood as ordained by biblical teachings (although it was the group's main source of friction). The Davidians didn't worship Koresh or believe him to be a deity. He was simply the one through whom God had chosen to speak. When Koresh and the Davidians said they were waiting to discover what they should do next, they meant it.

The FBI understood that the Davidians had their own very particular belief system. What they could not quite bring themselves to accept was that the Davidians really believed in it. That failure of imagination was linked to another one, even more fundamental: the FBI couldn't see its *own* culture.

At Mount Carmel, the two sides spoke across a cultural divide. One regarded itself as rational and analytical, while the other believed it was living a biblically ordained narrative. But the Davidians showed more understanding of the FBI than the FBI did of the Davidians. You get a sense of that in this brief exchange between an FBI negotiator and Koresh's lieutenant, Steve Schneider:

FBI: But that [waiting for God's word] was not our agreement, Steve.

Schneider: I understand. I know in this world you don't believe that there is a supernatural power that speaks audibly to a person.

FBI: No.

The FBI's transactional tone is typical of professional bureaucracies and would have been normal to them, but it was very different to how the Davidians thought or spoke. The result was an endlessly frustrating back-and-forth in which neither side could even agree on what the conversation was about or how to conduct it. In the following exchange, Koresh notes that the FBI have their own gods, and that unless both sides can acknowledge that they have a particular worldview, neither will really hear the other:

FBI: The bottom line is you're the one that's going to hear God, right?

Koresh: Yes, I'm the one listening to God and you're the one listening to the law, your system.

FBI: And I'm listening to you.

Koresh: That's not true. You're listening *at* me and I'm listening *at* you.

When negotiation guides cover cultural differences, they usually advise learning something about the other side's culture. That's a good start, but you should make yourself aware that you have a culture too, which is hard to do if you believe your worldview is somehow not a worldview at all, but just the natural way to see things. Seeing your own culture isn't just a challenge for professional negotiators, but for everyone who interacts with people with different worldviews to our own. We all have our own gods, which seem entirely normal where we come from.

• • •

When he was a graduate student in anthropology at UCLA, Joe Henrich travelled to the jungles of Peru to carry out fieldwork among the Machiguenga, a people indigenous to the Amazon basin. Henrich ran a behavioural experiment used by Western economists to test people's instinct for fairness. He expected to find that, even in an isolated culture like this one, people would play the game in roughly the same way as Westerners, since the prevailing assumption among social scientists was that humans share the same psychological hardwiring. The experiment was a bargaining game, in which two participants had to agree to split a given amount of money in a way satisfactory to both. When the game was played with American students, people's instinct for fairness meant they would reject a low offer of cash from the other individual even if it meant both walking away with nothing. But, as it turned out, the Machiguenga found this absurd. Why would anyone turn down free money?

Henrich wondered if the assumption of universalism made by economists and psychologists was deeply misleading. He led a study of fourteen other isolated, small societies, from Tanzania to Indonesia, and found that all of them played the game differently to North Americans and Europeans. Together with collaborators, Henrich went on to reveal that a whole range of established findings in psychology, from spatial awareness to moral reasoning, did not apply to people who were from cultures other than Western industrialised countries. This work culminated in a 2010 paper entitled 'The Weirdest People in the World?' By *WEIRD*, Henrich and his fellow authors meant the 15 per cent of humans who are *W*estern, *E*ducated, *I*ndustrialised, *R*ich and *D*emocratic. Henrich wanted to convey that the Western mindset was not just different to the rest of the world, it was deeply, interestingly odd – that if anything, it is we in the West, not people like the Machiguenga, who are the truly exotic tribe. Until scientists understand that, they cannot claim to understand humans at all.

People with a *WEIRD* mindset are more likely to 'punish' people who seem to be cheating them with a lowball offer, because they live in societies in which strangers often do business with one another. People from close-knit societies like the Machiguenga perceive the offer as a gift that comes with obligations – the Machiguenga in Joe Henrich's test, for example, had been more likely to reject the generous offers than the modest ones. The larger the gift, the more burdensome the obligation. *WEIRD* people tend to be more analytical, breaking up situations into parts and assigning them to abstract categories. Those with a more holistic mindset, like East Asians, focus on the *relationships* between things and between people, relying more on intuition to figure out what's going on. For instance, when study respondents are presented with a diagram showing a scarf, a glove and a hand, and are asked to pick the two most closely related objects, Westerners tend to pick the scarf and glove, because both are pieces of winter clothing, while East Asians are more likely to pick the hand and glove, because of their close relationship to one another.

Inspired by Henrich's work, cultural psychologist Thomas Talhelm ran tests like this with groups of American conservatives and liberals. He found that liberals and conservatives think as though they are from completely different cultures – 'almost as different as East and West'. Liberals are more *WEIRD* than conservatives: more analytical, readier to think in abstractions. No wonder that American liberals and conservatives have so many dysfunctional disagreements: they perceive reality in fundamentally different ways.

While both sides think their worldview is normal, their mutual misunderstanding is not symmetrical. Jonathan Haidt, a political psychologist, also ran a study in the USA, one that asked liberals and conservatives the same set of questions about moral and political issues. Then he asked the liberals to answer like conservatives and the conservatives to answer like liberals. The conservatives were significantly better at predicting how liberals would respond than vice versa.

'Conservatives understand liberals better than liberals understand conservatives,' Haidt concluded.

• • •

After the first group of children were sent out of Mount Carmel, Koresh and the community were under the impression that the FBI had agreed to send in milk for the remaining children. But the milk did not arrive, because the FBI had decided to use it as a bargaining chip. Their position was that they would only deliver milk if more children were released. A Davidian, Kathryn Schroeder, raised the issue with one of the negotiators:

FBI: I can only provide it to you, I can only provide it to you –

Schroeder: If we send out four more kids, that doesn't make sense.

FBI: Listen, I'll, I'll get the milk to you for two kids.

Schroeder: You get the milk to me for the two kids that went out Friday.

FBI: Kathy, perhaps we're wasting one another's time. All right? Put somebody else on.

Schroeder: I mean all you want, all you want to do is bargain?

FBI: Kathy!

Schroeder: Are you going to bargain with human lives?

If any one conversation between the FBI and the Davidians exemplified the problem of cultural mismatch, it was the argument over milk. The FBI talked about the children as if they were tradeable objects, when, to the Davidians, they were sacred entities. This discrepancy wasn't because the FBI negotiators were inhumane – the whole point of focusing on children was because they felt the children should be put out of harm's way. It was because they were locked into the technocratic mindset of negotiators. The FBI saw themselves as the rational ones; they never imagined that there might be a different kind of rationality to the behaviour of the Davidians. The children left at Mount

Carmel included Koresh's own, who were considered particularly special, with a significant role to play in the End of Time. They, of all children, couldn't just be handed over for milk.

When the FBI negotiator stresses that his prime concern is for the welfare of the children, Schroeder is sceptical: 'It doesn't *sound* like you're concerned.' 'I'll be happy to talk with you,' he replies, 'if you want to use reason.' According to Jayne Docherty, author of a perceptive book on the Waco negotiations, this was typical of how the male FBI negotiators behaved with female Davidians: they implied that they were too emotional to think straight. In many types of disagreement, there is often a party who seeks to play the game by their rules of engagement, and a party who questions those rules. One side sees themselves as reasonable; the other as if they are being ever so politely stamped upon. Pain and rage can build up under the surface of an apparently polite conversation, unacknowledged – until there is an eruption.

Indicating his growing impatience with the conversation, the FBI negotiator repeats his proposed bargain to Schroeder: 'Send the children out, the milk will be there . . .' He simply cannot understand why she does not grasp his logic. But it's not that Schroeder doesn't grasp it, it's that she resists it, because she feels like she is being pushed around:

Schroeder: If, if I don't . . . what I'm saying is you're saying that we don't have anything to say to each other because I don't agree with your stipulations. That's – it's like who's controlling whose mind here? Dave is not controlling my mind. You're trying to control my mind.

The negotiator persists, until Schroeder boils over:

FBI: . . . I'm willing to bring the milk out . . . What are you willing
to do to get the milk? That's the question. What are you willing
to do?

Schroeder: I'm willing to, myself, walk out that gate and be shot
by your Bradleys if I have to and I'll go get that milk.

There were two moments during the long stand-off at Mount
Carmel that suggested a more fruitful conversation was possible.
One of them came right at the beginning, another towards
the end.

Three minutes into the ATF raid that sparked the siege, Wayne
Martin, the Davidian lawyer, made a panicked 911 call. The
operator patched him through to Lieutenant Larry Lynch, from
the local sheriff's department:

Lynch: Yeah, this is Lieutenant Lynch, may I help you?

Martin: Yeah, there're seventy-five men around our building and
they're shooting at us at Mount Carmel . . . Tell them there's
women and children in here and to call it off.

Lynch had not expected any drama that day. He knew the raid
was going to happen; he did not know the ATF were going to
be so heavy-handed. He was on duty that Sunday because he
expected that Mount Carmel's neighbours would be calling to
express annoyance at the blockaded roads around the property.
('Because I'm old and fat, that's why I'm here,' he later confided to
Martin.)

As soon as the FBI arrived, Lynch took a backseat, which was
a pity, because he may just have been the best negotiator of all.
He displayed a kind of intuitive sensitivity that was rare among
the FBI negotiators. Lynch immediately recognised the urgency

of Martin's call, and made a human connection with Martin by explicitly accepting his priorities:

Lynch: Okay, Wayne . . . Talk to me Wayne, let's, let's take care of the children and the women.

With the word 'let's', Lynch indicated that he and the caller shared a desire to protect the women and children, and that they could work together to solve the crisis. Later, after the ATF withdrew, leaving the bodies of dead colleagues behind, Lynch gently tried to draw out a dazed Martin, acknowledging his emotion, starting where he was at:

Lynch: Are you okay? You sound – is there a problem?
Martin: No, there's no problem.
Lynch: You sound upset.
Martin: Well, everything is, huh . . .
Lynch: Everything is what, huh?

Lynch stayed on the line to Martin for the next fourteen hours, calming the situation, and negotiating a ceasefire before the FBI took over.

• • •

Later on, as March turned into April, came a different and more deliberate attempt to communicate with the Davidians on their own terms. A biblical scholar, James Tabor, got in touch with the FBI after watching events unfold on TV. He had immediately realised that the FBI had no idea about the Old Testament world inhabited by the Davidians and knew that any chance of a peaceful resolution would depend on the negotiators speaking the language of scripture. After approaching the FBI, Tabor and a fellow theologian Philip Arnold were permitted to begin direct discussions with Livingstone Fagan, a senior Davidian, considered by the Davidians to be a scholarly authority. Tabor and Arnold gained a greater understanding from Fagan of why the Davidians didn't want to move – they believed the Bible was instructing them to wait.

The FBI's display of military hardware was intended to intimidate the Davidians into surrender. What the FBI didn't understand is that the Davidians were much more worried about another kind of threat, as Steve Schneider had tried to explain:

Schneider: ... the only reason why we're staying here together as a unit still is because of that one word, wait. It's not because we fear man. There's a higher power we have learned to fear more so that – I mean when that God says he can destroy your soul and you know what he's talking about, we actually believe that is a reality more so than this world which will pass away.

Tabor and Arnold realised that Koresh needed another way to make sense of the prophecies in the Book of Revelation. They taped a long, technical discussion of the Seven Seals, offering an alternative reading, and sent it to Koresh, who was intrigued. At last, someone on the other side was at least taking his beliefs seriously, instead of insulting him or offering bargains. On 14 April, Koresh announced that God had directed him to write out the messages of the Seven Seals. After he had completed this, he said, 'I will be freed of my waiting period ... As soon as I can see that people like Jim Tabor and Phil Arnold have a copy, I will come out.' Inside Mount Carmel, there was rejoicing, as the ordeal seemed on the verge of ending. But the FBI was unimpressed by Koresh's declaration. To them, it seemed like another delaying tactic. On 16 April, a negotiator questioned Koresh's sincerity:

FBI: Now listen. Let's get back to the point in hand. This ah – you know – the writing of the seals. OK. You've got to do that in there, and its gonna take you *x* amount of time. But – just tell me this, David – are you saying that when you finish that manuscript –

Koresh: Then I'm not bound any longer.

FBI: No. But see, that doesn't answer the question.

Koresh: Then I'll be out – yes – definitely.

FBI: I know you'll be out. But that could mean a lot of things, David.

Koresh: I'll be in custody in the jailhouse.

One danger of an overly technocratic approach to a deep-rooted disagreement is that it can drive the other side mad; another is that, caught up in the disagreement's dynamic, the technocrats rationally persuade themselves to do something crazy. On 19 April, just five days after Koresh had changed position and said the Davidians would surrender once he had finished his translation of the Seven Seals, the FBI's leaders lost patience and, after receiving approval from Attorney General Janet Reno, ordered an assault on Mount Carmel. The Davidians may have had guns but they had shown no appetite for aggression or violence, except in self-defence. Now, a force capable of military combat was unleashed upon a small group of American civilians. The FBI shot about 400 canisters of tear gas – flammable under certain conditions – into a building lit by candlelight. Through a loudspeaker, an agent told everyone inside to come out. 'THIS IS NOT AN ASSAULT,' he said, even as the mechanical arms of Bradley armoured vehicles were smashing through the building's walls. The residents of Mount Carmel huddled in fear, as chunks of concrete crashed down around them. Somehow, the compound caught fire, and was soon engulfed in flames. Koresh and seventy-three other Davidians were killed, including twenty-one children. Over the loudspeaker, an FBI agent intoned, 'DAVID, YOU HAVE HAD YOUR FIFTEEN MINUTES OF FAME . . . HE IS NO LONGER THE MESSIAH.'

• • •

It is one thing, at our vast and comfortable distance from the awful tragedy of Waco, to identify what the FBI negotiators got wrong, entirely another to assume that any of us would have had more success. The truth is, it's incredibly hard to step outside your own cultural bubble and see how odd it might seem to others, or to enter another's and get a sense of how it might feel normal to them.

Culture to human beings is like water to fish: we can't see it because we live in it. It rarely shows itself in our conversations with others like us, precisely because it constitutes all the things we don't have to say. It doesn't feel like a particular way of seeing the world; it feels like reality. *Of course the world is this way. That's just the way it is.* But the truth is, we are all partially sighted. This might be even more true of those of us who pride ourselves in being objective and analytical, since we have a pronounced tendency to assume ours is the only valid way to perceive the world.

Cultural difference isn't just a matter of East *versus* West or Britain *versus* France. A country has a unique culture, but so do towns, workplaces, families and long-standing relationships, which is why the adage about never judging another's marriage is so wise – we don't know the culture. In fact, even among people who have grown up in the same places, attended similar schools and watched the same shows, each individual will still have acquired their very own quirks, habits and rituals. An individual is a micro-culture; we are all, each of us, a little odd. One way to think about any disagreement, then, is as a culture clash.

It's usually only when we bump up against someone with a different way of seeing the world that we get a glimpse of the medium in which we swim. An encounter like this can trigger a threat state, leading us to dismiss or demonise the other. But that stops us hearing what they are saying. To make yourself less prone to this reaction during a disagreement, try thinking about yourself as a visitor from a distant land with a very distinctive culture. You'll need to work hard at understanding the culture of your host, but you'll also need to reflect on your own. What experiences shaped your point of view? What are your blind spots likely to be? Which beliefs and habits of thought have you inherited from your forebears? Be an anthropologist to yourself.

9. Get Curious

*The rush to judgement stops us listening and learning.
Instead of trying to win the argument, try to be interested –
and interesting.*

Daniel Kahan, a professor of law at Yale University, studies the way
that our political opinions dumb us down. More specifically, he
investigates how people unconsciously distort new information to
make it fit what they already believe, on controversial topics from
vaccination to climate change. A commonly heard complaint about
political culture is that voters aren't presented with enough facts.
Kahan's work suggests that giving people facts won't necessarily
help.

In one of his studies, people were given a maths problem to solve.
Using data from a (fictional) clinical trial, the respondents had to
make a series of calculations to work out whether a new skin cream
had been shown to increase or decrease a rash. Most respondents
got the answer right. Next, they were invited to interpret exactly
the same set of statistics, this time in the guise of a question about
gun laws, a highly polarising topic in the United States. Some
respondents were given data suggesting that gun crime was on the
rise after a change in the law, others that it was falling. This time,
how accurately people answered the statistical question depended
on their political persuasion. Faced with a result they didn't like,
pro-gun respondents suddenly got worse at maths; the same went
for anti-gun respondents.

Kahan points out that this shouldn't be so surprising. If a person
reads about a potentially dangerous skin cream, or a change in how
much tax they pay, it makes sense to absorb the new information

rather than sticking to what they already believe. To do otherwise would clearly be self-defeating. But most people get little tangible benefit from being correct about, say climate change. They do, however, get an immediate benefit from expressing beliefs that others like them share: the feeling of belonging. We care more about people than being right, and the risk of changing a shared belief is that you no longer have people with whom to share it.

Say you're discussing the night sky with a friend and he mentions that Venus is Earth's nearest planetary neighbour. If you correct him (it's actually Mars), he'll probably accept he was wrong. Maybe he'll be mildly embarrassed, but the conversation will move on. Now imagine a similar conversation taking place in the seventeenth century. Your friend says something about the Sun going round the Earth, and you correct him, noting that according to the findings of this guy Galileo, it's the other way around. Your friend is likely to get furious, to deny all the evidence you present, and to denounce you as a wicked heretic. That's because, at the time, astronomy was not just about astronomy. It was bound up with people's deeply held beliefs about the social and spiritual order. By telling your friend that the Earth goes round the Sun, you were not just correcting an error in his conception of the physical universe, you were threatening his place in the social universe and thus his very sense of self. That's why, faced with information on a topic in which we have some personal investment, we perceive what supports our identity and ignore what does not.

Kahan's name for this phenomenon is 'Identity-Protective Cognition'. You might assume it only applies to people of low intelligence or education, but Kahan has found that highly intelligent and educated people are, if anything, *more* likely to distort and mould facts to fit their worldview. Clever people are better at finding reasons to support their beliefs, even when those beliefs are false. They make more convincing arguments, to others and to themselves, and they're better at reasoning away contradictory information. In the online forums on the flatness of the Earth or the lies of climate science, you can observe people using considerable scientific erudition to reach wholly erroneous conclusions.

For those hoping for more productive political disagreements, this suggests a bleak prognosis. More facts won't help, neither will better reasoning. So what might? Kahan discovered an answer to that question by accident, when he was approached by a group of documentary makers who wanted some guidelines on how to interest viewers in science-based topics. The group asked the professor to help them identify members of the public with high levels of scientific curiosity. Kahan and his team of researchers invented a survey tool, called the Science Curiosity Scale (SCS): a series of questions designed to predict how likely a person is to have their attention held by a science documentary. It includes questions about how likely the respondent is to read science books, and invites them to choose between a few articles with different levels of scientific content.

Kahan's team surveyed thousands of people and found that individuals with high levels of scientific curiosity were equally distributed across the population: men and women, lower class and upper class, right-leaning and left-leaning. They discovered something else, too – something totally unexpected. Out of his own curiosity, Kahan had inserted some questions on politically polarised issues into the survey. When the answers came back, he noticed that the higher a person's level of scientific curiosity, the less partisan bias she displayed.

For Kahan, this was counter-intuitive. Previously, he had established that more knowledgeable people were also more likely to be partisan thinkers. But what the survey had done was distinguish people high in *knowledge* from those high in *curiosity*. The curious people didn't necessarily know a lot about science, but they took a lot of pleasure in finding stuff out. It turned out that Republicans and Democrats who were highly curious were much closer in their views on, say, climate change, than Republicans and Democrats with significant levels of knowledge about it.

Kahan and his research colleagues designed another test. They gave participants a selection of articles about climate change and asked them to pick the one that they found most interesting. Some of the articles were supportive of climate change science, and some undermined it; some articles had headlines that framed the story as a surprise, others as confirmation of what was known.

Normally, partisan respondents would pick the article that supported their worldview. But science-curious Republicans picked articles that went against their prevailing political viewpoint when the headline framed the story as a surprise ('Scientists Report Surprising Evidence: Arctic Ice Melting Even Faster Than Expected'). The same was true of science-curious Democrats, in reverse. For the scientifically curious, Kahan concluded, the intrinsic pleasures of surprise and wonder trump their desire to have what they already know confirmed. Curiosity beats bias.

• • •

Powering up your desire to learn is often the only way to make the most out of a difficult encounter. If you're a climate change activist who meets someone who believes the whole thing is a hoax, the best you can do is be intrigued by how they arrived at that view. What experiences have they had, what have they read or heard, that got them there? Knowing that won't reconcile you to their view, but it gives you something to talk about.

You can get to a disagreement too soon. It's usually wise to defer the point at which you say, 'Well, actually . . .'; the longer you let the other person talk, unimpeded by interruption or the need to defend themselves, the more data you gather about their perspective. That inevitably puts you in a stronger position: either you will learn something that modifies your view or you'll have gained a better understanding of the other person's view, and of how to argue with them. And sometimes, the more a person talks, the more they talk themselves out of the position they started in.

Questions are good way of showing curiosity, but they can also be a way of avoiding it. If I ask, 'Are you *serious?*' I'm really saying that I don't take you seriously. Asking, 'Why do you believe that?' is better but not by much. It sounds like a demand to the other person to justify themselves. It positions you as the judge and puts them in the dock. Much better to ask, 'Can you tell me more?' or some variant. That kind of question shows that you're willing to listen and that you see this as a conversation of equals. 'Can you tell me more about why you believe that?' is different to, 'Why do you believe that?' in a subtle but significant way.

Some of this book was written during a stay in Paris. While there I was contacted by a businessman called Neil Janin who knew that I'd previously published a book on curiosity, the topic he wished to discuss. He didn't know I was writing a book on disagreement, but that turned out to be his speciality. Janin spent thirty years at the management consultancy McKinsey, many of them running its Paris office. Now semi-retired, he coaches senior executives in how to deal with difficult, conflict-ridden conversations. When we met, he was recovering from illness and had lost his voice. From across a café table, he fixed me with his penetrating gaze and delivered aphoristic wisdom in an intense, rasping whisper. 'The key to it all', he said, 'is connection. If you don't connect, you can't create. What stops me connecting to a colleague? Judgement. "*He's* stupid, *she* doesn't get it. *They* don't have the facts; once I give them the facts they will change their mind; if not, they're idiots."' When we are in a disagreement, he continued, we face a choice, with an easy option and a hard option. 'We love judgement. It helps us be "right", which is good for our ego, and requires no energy. Curiosity is energy-consuming, because you're trying to figure things out. But it's the only way through.'

Laurence Alison told me that in order to be effective, interrogators have to suspend moral judgement, no matter what terrible crime the suspect may have committed. 'There's a reason this person has ended up opposite you, and it's not just because they're evil. If you're not interested in why they're here, you're not going to be a good interrogator.' Janin echoes this sentiment in what he says is the most important piece of advice he gives his clients: 'SUSPEND JUDGEMENT. GET CURIOUS!'

Disagreement is hard work even for management consultants and their clients, who at least share a culture: analytical and logical, responsive to incentives and interests. What should you do if the person you're talking to seems emotionally led, irrational, possessed by bizarre beliefs? That's a question Jayne Docherty addresses in her book on the Waco negotiations. The key to it, she suggests, is to assume that they *are* being rational, and make it your job to figure out what kind of rationality they are using.

Max Weber, the great sociologist, argued that we use the term 'rational' too narrowly. It usually describes people acting in a logical way designed to achieve a material goal. Weber called that *instrumental* rationality and proposed three other types of rational behaviour. There is *affective* rationality, when I make my relationships central to whatever I say and do; that's the rationality used by the respondents in Daniel Kahan's study. There's *traditional* rationality, when we are happy to accept the steer that previous generations have given us, which is why we might put a tree in our house in December. Finally, there is *values* rationality, when everything we do is in the service of some higher value, almost regardless of outcome. That's what the Davidians were employing, to the befuddlement of the more instrumentally rational FBI.

Few people rely on just one mode of rationality; most of us switch between them or use more than one at once. Docherty points out that the Davidians could actually be quite practical and analytical and willing to problem-solve, as long as it didn't conflict with their ultimate values. This is one way that curiosity can help us. In a disagreement with someone who isn't using instrumental rationality – whether family member, colleague or political opponent – then, rather than assuming they're crazy, you can try and get curious about what mode of rationality they've moved into. When your daughter is being irrationally stubborn about going to bed later, she might be operating in affective rationality; she is looking for a way to spend more time with you. What's the deeper logic of the other person's behaviour? Come to think of it, what's the deeper logic of your own?

• • •

You're not only trying to get curious yourself, you're trying to stimulate the other person's curiosity. So how do you do that?

Gregory Trevors, a psychologist from the University of South Carolina, has studied 'the backfire effect': the paradoxical tendency for people to strengthen a belief in false information after the falsity of that information is pointed out to them (the term was coined by political scientists who found that, in 2009, people who believed that Iraq was behind 9/11 were *more* likely to believe that proposition after being shown information which refuted it). It's a similar reaction to the one that addicts have on being told their habit is bad for them. The risk of correcting someone, as we've seen, is that you trigger an identity threat. That brings what Trevors calls 'moral emotions', like anger and anxiety, into play, which can quickly derail the conversation. Anger and anxiety lead people to focus narrowly on defending their position and attacking the source of any conflicting messages. An alternative strategy is to try and activate the other's 'epistemic emotions', like surprise and curiosity, which, according to Trevors, act as an antidote to anxiety and anger. Carli Leon, the former anti-vaccinator who spoke about how insults had made her dig her heels in, also said, 'What helped me was people asking me questions that got me to think.'

Earlier on we discussed how to avoid triggering a threat reaction: convey your regard for the other person before getting into the disagreement (being curious about what they have to say is one way to do that). Other than affirmation, you can also frame new information or new arguments in a way that intrigues them rather than putting them on the back foot. As Daniel Kahan found, surprise – *I didn't know that,* or, *I hadn't thought of it like that before* – loosens up rigid beliefs. Displaying your own curiosity about the topic indicates that you don't think you have all the answers and encourages them to feel curious too. Gregory Trevors suggested using stories, humour and metaphors to neutralise the other's defence system. In short, rather than trying to sound convincing, try to be interesting and interested.

It's always easier to be incurious than curious. As Neil Janin suggested, curiosity is hard because it requires the allocation of scarce resources: energy, time and attention. If you have a different opinion to me on, say, immigration, that might be because you have a different experience of it to me. But contemplating that gulf of difference demands an expenditure of brainpower on my part to which I'm often unwilling to commit. It's simply quicker and more efficient to dismiss you as bigoted than it is to be interested in what you're saying. In a world where we're bombarded with opinions, that can seem like a necessary reaction, but it's one we should resist. By shutting down our curiosity about different views we make ourselves less intelligent, less humane – and less interesting.

10. Make Wrong Strong

Mistakes can be positive if you apologise rapidly and authentically. They enable you to show humility, which can strengthen the relationship and ease the conversation.

'There is no wrong note, it has to do with how you resolve it.'
Thelonious Monk

You have just arrived at the scene of a potential suicide. A man is standing on the ledge of a tall building, threatening to jump. The police brief you on what they know about him, and you make your way up to the roof, where, from a distance at which he won't feel threatened, you attempt conversation. You begin by trying to make an emotional connection – by showing that you care about him as a person. 'Hello Ahmed,' you say. 'It looks as if you're having a hard time. I'd like to help if I can.'

At that moment, you realise – perhaps because he tells you, perhaps because you just know – that you've made an excruciating mistake. His name isn't Ahmed. It's Muhammed.

You have lost control of this situation before you even started. What now?

That was the question Paul Taylor, a professor at Lancaster University in the UK, and one of the world's foremost scholars of crisis negotiation, put to one of his graduate students, Miriam Oostinga, after realising that nobody had yet studied it. Oostinga was immediately gripped by it. In the tense, emotionally freighted situation of a suicide negotiation, one false note would seem to have the potential to destroy whatever fragile bond of trust the negotiator has established. But errors are inevitable – so how do negotiators cope with them? At Taylor's suggestion, Oostinga pursued the question for her PhD.

We all make errors of communication, the kind of error that has an instant and palpable effect on the participants, straining relationships. Think of the teacher who jokes about a pupil's hair-cut only to realise she has hurt his feelings; the politician who impulsively tweets an opinion he immediately regrets; a salesperson who unintentionally condescends to an upset customer. Even a minor error can have an emotional, even physiological effect, both for the person on the receiving end and on the person making it. Whether and how the maker of the error recovers from it can determine how well the rest of the conversation goes.

Oostinga recruited trained negotiators from the Dutch police and prison services to participate in her study of errors. Some were crisis negotiators, others were interrogators. I asked her what she made of them, as people – did they have similarities? 'I would say that they were all intrinsically interested in the person they're talking to,' she said. 'When they talked to me, they really gave me the feeling that they were interested in who I was and what I was doing.' Oostinga started by interviewing the participants, to get a feel for the problems that errors create for them. 'Nobody is capable of a 100 per cent perfect interaction,' one of them told her. 'There is always something that goes wrong.' The risk of making an error increases as the stakes get higher – when there are more lives at risk – and when negotiators are dealing with aggressive individuals who draw them into a struggle for dominance. Errors might be factual, like getting someone's name wrong, or mixing up the time and day of an event. Or they might be errors of judgement, like adopting an overly domineering tone, or saying 'I understand how you feel' when, as their interlocutor is immediately liable to point out, they patently do not.

What took Oostinga by surprise is that the negotiators were wary of the whole notion of errors. They regarded stray messages as an inevitable side-effect of thinking on their feet. Trying to avoid them would only ensure the conversation was superficial and impersonal. 'We should be cautious not to become small-talkers who do not say anything wrong,' one of them remarked. Another said, 'If we do not make errors, we are not human any more. We become like robots.' The negotiators felt that 'error' was too unambiguously negative a term to describe an event that can have positive consequences, if handled skilfully.

For the next stage of her study, Oostinga simulated crisis scenarios and found ways to trip the negotiators into errors. For instance, they might be told to speak to a person called Steven, who has barricaded himself into a room in a prison and is threatening to kill himself with a knife. The first time that the negotiator uses the name he has been given (negotiators are trained to use names) the perpetrator – played by an actor – would angrily respond, 'I'm not Steven.' Other scenarios simulated judgement errors. During a conversation, a suspect would react badly to the negotiator's tone – for instance, by accusing him of sounding formal and superior, or overly friendly. Oostinga was interested in how the negotiator reacted and in how the conversation developed afterwards.

The errors had some predictable effects: they raised the stress levels of the negotiator and made the conversation more stormy and volatile. But they also had unexpected benefits. The worst enemy of an interrogator or hostage negotiator is not deceit or anger but silence; their primary goal is to keep a conversation, any conversation, alive. Oostinga discovered that errors can be useful in that way. For instance, when describing a scene which the suspect had witnessed, an interviewer would get an important detail wrong (because she had been fed false information by

Oostinga). The suspect would respond indignantly: 'No, it wasn't like that.' Then he would go on to describe how things really were, in detail. The conversation would flow, and the interviewer would gain richer information.

Instead of dwelling on a mistake, the professionals would use it to build a closer relationship. They were practiced at making immediate and sincere apologies: 'You're right, my mistake'; 'Yep, that was a stupid thing to say. Can we start again?' Occasionally they would deflect, blaming the source of their information. But when they felt able, they would accept responsibility and expose a vulnerable side of themselves to the interviewee. Doing that can be productive, the negotiators told Oostinga, if it helps to rebalance an inherently lopsided power relationship. In other words, apologies can correct for the one-down effect – so long as they are believed in.

• • •

Saying sorry is an art few bother to master until it's too late. Benjamin Ho, an associate professor of economics at Vassar College, studies why some apologies work, while others are regarded as worthless and insincere. It might seem like an odd thing for an economist to focus on, but Ho is a behavioural economist, interested in the costs and benefits of social behaviour. After all, an economy doesn't run on money; it runs on human relationships (it has taken economists a long time to realise this). The mistakes we make in our social interactions can damage or break those relationships. Apologies are an important way of restoring them.

At the corporate level, apologies have real economic importance. When a company like Volkswagen or Facebook screws up, it needs to apologise effectively if it is to minimise the damage done to its relationships with consumers. A 2004 study, led by Fiona Lee of the University of Michigan, reviewed the corporate annual reports of fourteen companies over a twenty-one-year period, and analysed the way those companies talked about negative events, like poor earnings. Lee and her colleagues found that the companies that owned up to their mistakes in public had higher stock prices a year later than those that tried to bury them.

Inspired by Lee's work, Ben Ho looked for other ways to establish a link between apologies and economic outcomes. Together with his colleague Elaine Liu, he looked at the way that medical malpractice is handled in the United States. When doctors make mistakes that harm their patients, they can get caught in a bind. On the one hand, presuming they are honest, they want to apologise. On the other, by doing so they expose themselves to the threat of a ruinous legal action. Now, imagine what it is like to be a patient who does not get an apology from a doctor who has made your life, or the life of someone you love, unnecessarily painful. You would feel furious, wouldn't you? Even if you hadn't originally intended to sue, you'd probably want to do so now. And that was what was happening: patients were upset, yet doctors didn't feel able to apologise, which made patients angry enough to sue.

To break this vicious cycle, many American states – thirty-six at the time that Ho and Liu published their paper – have passed laws that make doctors' apologies inadmissible in court (a bill to that effect was introduced to the Senate in 2005, by Senators Barack Obama and Hillary Clinton). The idea is to create a safe haven for doctors to say sorry, thereby improving their relationship with the patient and making legal action less likely. Since some but not all states passed the law, Ho and Liu found that in states which had passed 'apology laws', there was a reduction in claims filed of 16–18 per cent and malpractice cases were settled almost 20 per cent faster. That's a huge reduction in the number of costly, draining legal disputes, and all because people were able to hear a figure in authority say 'sorry'. This finding helped Ho put a concrete value on apologies, and it confirmed a theory he was already developing: that for an apology to be effective, it must appear hard to make.

Whether it's a doctor, builder or politician, we have to place deep trust in an expert for our relationship with them to work. When the expert makes a mistake, the relationship is jeopardised. Whether or not the expert can repair that damage with an apology depends, says Ho, on whether or not the apology is seen to cost them something. Ho draws on game theory, a branch of mathematics influential in economics and biology. In game theory, a 'costly signal' is one where an agent communicates in a way that is difficult to fake. The classic example from biology is the male peacock's tail, the existence of which made Charles Darwin despair because he couldn't discern the evolutionary logic behind such an elaborate, heavy adornment. The game theorists' explanation is that the tail's excessiveness is the point: the male peacock is signalling its extraordinary fitness, like a king who builds an absurdly elaborate palace to display his wealth and power. To signal 'I'm fit' or 'I'm powerful' in a way that reliably convinces others, the signal must be hard to fake.

Ho thinks the same logic applies to apologies. When we feel that someone has wronged us, we want them to say 'I'm sorry', but often the words themselves are not enough for the apology to feel satisfying; we need to feel they've been tough to say. While relationship counsellors advise couples to apologise to their partner to help heal a rift, anyone who has been in a relationship will know that you can also apologise too quickly. If you say sorry without it seeming like you had to struggle to do so, the words come across as empty and glib. In fact, we sometimes punish the people we love for apologising to us, pressing them on their reasons for not saying it sooner. The reason we do this is that we want them to pay an emotional price for it. The same logic applies to corporate apologies. The jeering and humiliation that often follow a public apology from a company or politician aren't proof that the apology was a waste of time, says Ho; the jeering and humiliation are what makes the apology effective.

Ho enumerates a few different ways to make a costly apology. For instance, *I'm sorry – here are some flowers.* This is the most straightforward version of a costly apology. The cost here is obvious and tangible. The more expensive the flowers, the better. Then there is the 'commitment apology': *I'm sorry, I'll never do it again.* The cost here is that you are foreclosing or giving up some future option. Of course, if you then go on to do it again, it's less likely to work the next time. Then there is what I think of as the Englishman's apology: *I'm sorry, I'm an idiot.* This is a particularly interesting approach because what you're trading with is your right to be seen as competent and effective (Ho's term for it is a 'status apology'). Finally, there is what Miriam Oostinga refers to as the 'deflect' response: *I'm sorry, it wasn't my fault.* This is not a very effective way to restore a relationship, precisely because it is not costly to say. But in some circumstances it might still be the best thing to do, for example if your reputation for competence is paramount and you can show it wasn't your fault.

In 2018, Ho got an unexpected chance to test his theory of apologies against real-world data. He received a call from John List, a professor at the University of Chicago, renowned for running real-world experiments using large datasets. List was calling in his capacity as chief economist at Uber. He wanted Ho to help him quantify the value of an apology to the business. Like any service-based business, Uber sometimes annoys or upsets its customers – a car that doesn't arrive; the wrong choice of route.

List suspected that when a poorly served customer received an apology, they would be more likely to use Uber again in the future. But to convince Uber's management of that he needed to put a number on the value of apologising.

List and his team had already established that poor service was costly for Uber. Customers who were delivered to their destination 10–15 minutes late spent 5–10 per cent less on future trips. Ho and List wanted to find out if an apology would boost a customer's spending back up. Along with two fellow economists, Basil Halperin and Ian Muir, they devised an experiment to help Uber figure out what makes an effective apology, and how much one is worth.

The researchers had a big, real-time dataset to play with, garnering information from 1.6 million passengers across America's major cities. They were able to identify which passengers had recently had a bad trip and ensured that these people received an email containing an apology within the hour. The economists divided the passengers randomly into eight groups and sent different apologetic messages to all but a control group, which got no apology (the control group represented the status quo, since at that point it was not Uber policy to apologise for bad trips). Some received a basic apology with no elaboration. Some received a 'status apology', which included the phrase, 'We know our estimate was off.' Some received a 'commitment apology', which said that Uber would work hard to give the customer arrival times they can count on. All four groups (control, basic apology, status apology and commitment apology) were then split in two, and half of each group received a $5 coupon they could redeem against a future trip. The economists tracked the passengers' Uber purchases, the number of trips they took and how much they spent for the subsequent eighty-four days.

Ho and his co-authors discovered a few things from their results. First, apologies are not a panacea. They found almost no effect for the basic apology: just saying sorry had very little impact on the number and length of trips people went on to take. Second, the most effective apology was a costly one: giving people a coupon along with an apology actually led to a net *increase* in their spend with the company, by comparison to the period prior to the bad experience. Third, apologies can be overused. Some of the customers had more than one bad experience and so received multiple apologies. Those customers punished the company more than customers who never received an apology at all.

This echoed something the hostage negotiators interviewed by Miriam Oostinga mentioned. 'Saying sorry five times in five minutes won't make for a positive relationship,' one of them told her. The more apologies you get from someone, the less costly those apologies seem. At some point they start to feel cheap, even insulting.

• • •

Knowing how to apologise is far from simple, because the same apology can have different effects depending on who we are and what we do. Larissa Tiedens, a social psychologist at Stanford University, has studied how the emotions that politicians display in public influence the way that voters perceive them. In one experiment, Tiedens showed respondents one of two video clips of President Clinton, both extracted from the grand jury testimony he gave on the Monica Lewinsky scandal in 1998 (the fieldwork took place in 1999, when Clinton was still president, and his opponents had begun impeachment proceedings). In one clip, Clinton is visibly angry. He describes his treatment as inappropriate, wrong and unfair, and questions the motives of the investigators. He looks straight at the camera, slashing the air with his hands to emphasise his points. In the other clip, Clinton reflects on his relationship with Lewinsky, and his demeanour is very different. He says the affair was wrong. His head goes down, and he gazes off to the side.

At the time, there was a consensus among media commentators that Clinton needed to show remorse and guilt instead of anger if he wanted to repair his relationship with voters. Tiedens found the opposite: the respondents who viewed the angry clip were more positive about Clinton than those who viewed the remorseful clip. The reason, according to Tiedens, is that 'anger communicates competence'. Social psychologists have consistently found that people expressing anger are seen as more dominant and competent, even as they seem less friendly, warm and nice. Angry people are more likely to be perceived as high status than sad or remorseful people are. It wasn't that Clinton's apologetic style didn't have a positive effect on how the respondents saw him; they *liked* him better for it. But the people who saw the angry Clinton *respected* him more.

This trade-off between respect and warmth makes it hard to judge the right tone to strike when you're apologising. If you make a status apology ('I'm sorry, I'm an idiot') you're trading away some of your reputation for competence – that is, respect – in exchange for likeability. That can be risky. Whether or not you should do so depends on whether competence or likeability is more important to the relationship in question. Nobody wants to hear a doctor say, 'The thing is, I'm basically a bit crap at this,' but a husband or parent should prioritise warmth over authority.

For those who need a measure of both, like hostage negotiators, the question of when to admit error can be a fine judgement call.

Some of those Oostinga talked to told her they were reluctant to own up to a mistake unless they had to because of the need to be seen as competent by the person in crisis. For others, an error was an opportunity to equalise an inherently lopsided power relationship. By apologising, the negotiator can show themselves willing to be submissive, which lowers the suspect's guard and opens up a pathway to intimacy (one of the negotiators told Oostinga that she might even return to an error later in the conversation if she feels its effects lingering: 'I have a feeling that what I said is still upsetting you'). An error has the potential to bring negotiator and suspect together into a 'bubble', where the relationship has time to incubate and deepen. The stakes, the onlookers, the future – the weirdness of the whole situation – all can be forgotten for a while, as the participants pore over what the negotiator got wrong and why. 'They can bond inside that bubble,' Oostinga told me.

• • •

Disagreements should be full of mistakes. A disagreement in which the participants plot their every intervention like a chess move and take great care not to say the wrong thing is an arid and passionless affair. It is unlikely to be productive, either; as Oostinga's negotiators remind us, a conversation without errors is either trivial or robotic or both. Of course, that doesn't mean you should be happy when you realise you've been deaf to the emotions of the other person, when you find yourself talking down to them – or when you get their name wrong. But if this book helps with your disagreeable conversations it won't be because you have eliminated all the errors you can make; it will be because you are better at recognising those errors and at knowing how to respond to them.

Once you understand how and why disagreements go wrong, the prospect of disagreement's bumpy, uncomfortable ride seems less intimidating than it might do otherwise. First, because you realise that it's not just you – that people make similar mistakes all the time, except that usually they don't recognise them as mistakes. Second, you come to see your mistakes as opportunities in disguise. By correcting your own error – resolving your bum note – you can strengthen your relationship with the other person and make the conversation richer.

An error shakes things up. Or at least it should do. It's a mini cyclone blowing through the conversation, rearranging the landscape, creating fresh perspectives. It also gives you the opportunity to apologise well, which, as we've seen, is much more than a matter of courtesy. An apology should cost you something. I don't mean that every time you grossly misinterpret what the other person is saying you need to whip out a coupon promising her the next five opinions for free. I mean your acknowledgement of a mistake should be emotionally costly. When you say sorry, it has to mean something other than 'Let's move on'; otherwise it's hard to move on, at least it is for the person who feels offended or badly treated. When you back down from a position, it's OK to let the other person see how hard it is for you to do so – in fact, it's better that way.

One of the worst ways to apologise is to say, 'I'm sorry if . . .' The 'if' immediately renders your apology cheap and insincere, because you're not admitting to a mistake. If you're not sure that you've made a mistake, best not to apologise at all, until you're absolutely convinced you have.

If it feels bad, that's good.

11. Disrupt the Script

Hostile arguments get locked into simple and predictable patterns. To make the disagreement more productive, introduce novelty and variation. Be surprising.

In the autumn of 1990, a Norwegian sociologist named Terje Rød-Larsen and his wife Mona Juul, a diplomat, made a trip to Gaza, the battle-torn strip of land on Israel's border that at the time was home to a million Palestinians. Rød-Larsen was preparing a survey of the living conditions in what was the most densely populated spot on earth. As they were being escorted around a Palestinian refugee camp by a UN officer, the two Norwegians stumbled into a skirmish between Palestinian youths and Israeli soldiers.

Rød-Larsen and Juul froze, terrified, as Israeli bullets whistled past and Palestinian rocks crashed around them. While their escort attempted to calm the situation, Rød-Larsen and Juul found themselves transfixed by the faces of the young men fighting on both sides. They looked scared and defiant and unhappy. Most of all, they looked similar.

Over the next three years, with Juul's help, Rød-Larsen embarked on a series of visits to the region, meeting with Israelis and Palestinians. Although he met them in his capacity as a social scientist, he had decided to attempt something way beyond his remit as an academic. Rød-Larsen wanted to find a way to help the two sides recognise that the gap between them was not as great as they thought, that the hostile image they had of each other, forged over decades of fighting, was stopping them from seeing each other as they really were – as people with a common interest in peace.

It was moonshine, really, but Rød-Larsen was a stubborn optimist. Jane Corbin, a British reporter for the BBC, wrote of Rød-Larsen that he had 'complete conviction that anything that is worth doing can be done'. Self-confident without being arrogant, with a ready smile, Rød-Larsen was instantly likeable and had a way of inspiring trust in anyone he met. His maxim was that 'Sometimes the impossible is easier than the possible.'

Rød-Larsen believed that the road to peace led through the Palestinian Liberation Organisation (PLO). Officially, neither Israel nor the USA dealt with the PLO because they defined it as a terrorist organisation. When a Washington-led peace process opened in 1991, it involved other Palestinian leaders instead. After the fall of the Berlin Wall, there was optimism for a new world order, but by 1993 the talks were already foundering. The USA was not able to play the role of an even-handed mediator, because of both its alliance with Israel and its sheer military and economic might. The Palestinians mistrusted the Americans, while the Israelis railed against the pressure that the Americans put on them.

Rød-Larsen began to wonder if Norway could offer something the USA couldn't. Norway was a small country, incapable of pushing anyone around. It had good relations with both sides in the dispute. It had its own oil supply, and therefore minimal economic interest in the Middle East. With a population of just over four million, Norway's comparatively modest size gave it another advantage: small groups of influential people could introduce political innovations.

Mona Juul was friends with Jan Egeland, a former social scientist who was now Norway's deputy foreign minister. The co-author of Rød-Larsen's social study of Palestine was Marianne Heiberg, another sociologist, who was married to the new foreign minister, Johan Jorgen Holst. The fluid, informal nature of public life in Norway was in sharp contrast to the vast, bureaucratic and hierarchical structure of American government. In Norway, Rød-Larsen knew everyone and everyone knew him, and some of them were prepared to listen to his crazy idea.

Rød-Larsen proposed peace talks in Oslo, separate from the official negotiations in Washington. These talks would be hosted by the Norwegians, and they would be secret. There would be no grand diplomatic ceremonies, press conferences or fleets of limousines. Above all, there would be no playing to the gallery. Rød-Larsen had observed that the bright public spotlight on the Washington peace process had the effect of polarising the conversation. The Israelis and Palestinians were always aware of the audiences back home. There was intense pressure on them to maintain their 'face': the negotiators felt compelled to project strength above all, which made it very hard to exhibit flexibility. As a result, the two sides did not truly engage with each other. Instead, they staked out their positions and dug in, making the same predictable moves and counter-moves as in previous negotiations. The script might as well have been written in advance.

• • •

Peter Coleman, a professor of conflict resolution, runs the Difficult Conversations Laboratory at Columbia University. Coleman and his team have analysed hundreds of encounters between people with opposing views. They study the emotional dynamics of conversations; how they flow and how they get stuck. Then they graph them.

The lab employs a similar methodology to the one pioneered by relationship scientists. It matches strangers with strong and opposite views on a polarising issue and invites them to talk the issue through. Afterwards, each participant is played a recording of the conversation and asked to say how he or she felt at each moment. The results are coded for positive and negative emotions, and for particular thoughts and behaviours. The conversations can get heated; sometimes they have to be brought to an end early. Others go much better.

Coleman and his colleagues have identified a key difference between the more destructive conversations and the more constructive ones. The destructive conversations get locked into a tug-of-war dynamic early on and stay that way, becoming progressively more bad-tempered. Each person aligns themselves with a side, and each blames the other's side for the world's ills. Meanwhile, the constructive conversations are not necessarily serene or well mannered – they can involve verbal attacks and bad faith, and the participants can report feeling hurt and annoyed – but, at certain points, the participants are able to escape or subvert the dynamic. Positive emotions, like amusement, empathy, and insight make appearances, if only fleeting ones. The conversation is more expansive. It has *variety*.

'The more constructive dyads', Coleman reported, 'thought about the issues in more complex, nuanced and flexible ways. They felt many different types of emotions, both positive and negative, over the course of the discussions. And they behaved in more varied ways that demonstrated a greater degree of openness, flexibility, and curiosity in addition to a strong advocacy for their positions.'

When Coleman's team map the data on the emotions from each conversation on a grid, the shapes generated by constructive and productive conversations look very different. The constructive ones are, literally, all over the place, messy constellations of dots. The destructive ones are straight lines, like ruts. It's as if the participants

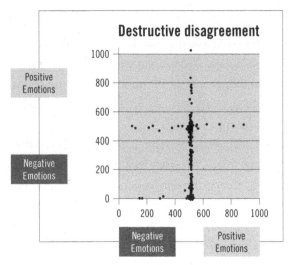

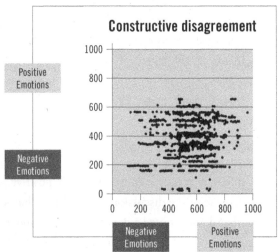

In session 1 (destructive), the dots are tightly organised along two lines, indicating a narrow emotional range of the discussion. In session 2 (constructive), the dots show that the emotions of the participants fluctuated back and forth as the discussion unfolded. Coleman measured thought and behaviour as well as emotion. On every dimension, the constructive conversations were more complex than the destructive ones.

in the destructive conversations have had their emotional range reduced to a narrow band. They have become wholly predictable.

Software engineers who design chatbots distinguish between 'stateful' and 'stateless' conversations. A stateful exchange is one in which the participants retain a memory of what is said during the conversation. Stateless dialogues are ones in which little or no conversational history is retained, and each new remark responds only to the last. They are so low context that they don't even have the context of the previous conversation.

For obvious reasons, it's easier to design bots for stateless conversations: picking an appropriate response to a single cue requires less processing power than attempting to engage with the flow of a conversation. The trade-off, for programmers, is that stateless bots sound 'robotic', dispensing pre-scripted replies without any indication that they really know what the conversation is *about*. But it's not as a big a trade-off as you might think, since a lot of human conversation is stateless.

Have you ever had an argument like this?

A: I really enjoyed that book.
B: Oh really? It's very poorly written.
A: Why do you have to make me feel bad about what I like?
B: Why do you have to play the victim all the time?
A: Oh, that's rich – you're always playing the victim.
B: Look, you're clearly just in a bad mood today.
A: I'm the one in a bad mood?

And so on. In an exchange like this, each remark is only about the last remark. The conversation has almost no memory of itself. Neither partner is learning anything from the other and both are becoming increasingly bad-tempered.

In 1989, an undergraduate computer programmer at the University of Dublin called Mark Humphrys wrote a chatbot program he called MGonz. Whenever MGonz lacked a clear cue for how to respond to a remark, it threw in an insult, like 'You are obviously an asshole,' or 'OK thats it im not talking to you anymore,' or 'Ah type something interesting or shut up.' When Humphrys left the program connected to his university's computer network overnight, he returned in the morning to discover that somebody had spent an hour and a half engaged in an argument with MGonz, obviously convinced that he was debating with a real person.

Humphrys had stumbled across a truth about human arguments: they tend towards statelessness. Arguments that start off as being 'about' something quickly become about nothing but themselves, locking the participants into a pattern of negative reciprocation. The conversation becomes as simple and simplistic as a straight line.

Stateless arguments can run on indefinitely and fruitlessly since there is nothing to solve or conclude. As they do so they usually become more unpleasant. Like water, argument becomes diffuse as it heats, but in this case, the resulting gas is toxic. You might forget what your argument with your partner was about, but you will probably remember how it made you feel.

The science writer Brian Christian observes that, 'Verbal abuse is simply *less complex* than other forms of communication.' MGonz's anonymous correspondent replied to the bot's insults with insults of his own. However witty or stinging his retorts may have been, he was making things easy for the bot by retorting at all. If he'd just asked a few questions, he would have quickly discovered the limited range of his interlocutor. Chatbots find it near impossible to respond convincingly to enquiries such as, 'What do you mean by that?' and, 'How so?' because requests for elaboration rely on context; they prompt the participants to widen the conversation rather than just taking a cue from the last remark.

Similarly, to make a conversation between people more human and less robotic, we need to ask questions that can't be answered with a pre-prepared script. Hence the crucial roles for empathy, curiosity and surprise in conflict-ridden conversations. In Memphis, Don Gulla played the Memphis cops a video of an attempted arrest (there are many such clips online, taken on smartphones or bodycams). A man who has just committed an armed robbery stands in the forecourt of a store, facing off against an officer with a gun pointed at him. The criminal's gun is in his back pocket. He isn't reaching for it or attempting to flee, but he is refusing to obey the officer's request to get down on his knees.

The officer moves from requests to commands at a steadily increasing pitch of intensity: 'Get down on your knees,' he shouts. 'I am *not* going to tell you again!' The man refuses, the officer tells him again. The deadlock is only resolved when further officers arrive. After playing the video, Gulla said, 'The officer makes a dozen verbal commands. He should realise that what he's doing is not working. Don't continue a mistake just because you spent a lot of time making it.'

Gulla elucidated the psychology of a deadlock. 'The guy asks you to back off. Your ego says, "No, I'm the police." But who cares? Give the guy some space. Maybe ask his name. You could even lower your gun and offer him a cigarette. Ask yourself, why is he refusing to kneel? Maybe it would be humiliating for him. Say, "Will you at least sit down?"'

'Sometimes', he observed, 'you just need to switch gears.' Gulla told a story about an officer chasing a man on foot down a highway as cars screamed past. Then the officer, who was getting out of breath, had an idea: he stopped, and shouted, 'Hey, I'm too out of shape for this. Please stop!' The man stopped, turned around, and gave himself up. 'It was beautiful,' said Gulla, eyes twinkling.

• • •

On a snowy night in January 1993, two slightly dazed Israeli academics arrived at a Norwegian country house after a long drive from the airport. Ron Pundak and Yair Hirschfeld were acting as clandestine representatives of politicians back home. Their Palestinian counterparts Abu Ala, Maher El Kurd and Hassan Asfour arrived late, having been held up by immigration, much to their annoyance. A Norwegian businessman had given Rød-Larsen the use of the house, known as Borregaard, and its staff, without having to be told anything more than that it was for some international political activity.

The next day, the Palestinians and Israelis gathered in the sitting room. The atmosphere was, unsurprisingly, awkward: nobody was sure how this was going to go or whether they should even be there. Rød-Larsen gave a brief talk, explaining that the Norwegians, unlike the Americans, would be playing no role other than facilitation. 'If you two are going to manage to live together, you've got to solve this problem between you.' He advised them to spend their first hours together getting to know each other, to share stories about their homes and their children. After lunch, a fire was lit and the Israelis and Palestinians sank into red velvet sofas on either side of a low coffee table and began to talk.

At the heart of Rød-Larsen's vision was the stuff that conventional diplomacy overlooked or ignored: setting, mood, personality. He didn't see why Palestinians and Israeli negotiators should not be able to get along, even to like each other – just as he did not see why those boys in the streets of Gaza could not play together instead of fighting. Rød-Larsen believed that once the negotiators got to know their counterparts, the conversation would become less predictable and more creative. As he put it to me, 'Our goal was to get them off-script.' His job was to design the conditions which made that possible.

In Washington, the two sides sent delegations of more than a hundred people each. They stayed in different hotels, and met across vast tables, after holding separate press conferences, while American mediators brokered proposals and counter-proposals. At Borregaard, the Israelis and Palestinians lived together, ate together, and shared downtime. Rød-Larsen paid meticulous attention to details like the seating plan at dinner. Participants were served Norwegian specialities, like smoked fish, and potatoes baked in cream, while enjoying access to a ready flow of wine and whisky.

The negotiators, five in all, held sessions in different parts of the mansion, and sometimes ventured outside, arguing and discussing during long walks in the snowy woods under the stars. As Jane Corbin puts it, the atmosphere was one of 'a country house weekend: good food and good company and stimulating discussion late into the night'. For the negotiators, it felt a very long way from the corridors of power in capital cities. The novelty of the environment allowed a new, more emotionally expansive conversation to emerge. Relationships of trust were quickly forged.

Rød-Larsen's own role was a self-effacing one. He didn't participate in the discussions, but whenever a negotiator exited the meeting for a break, they would go to him and unburden themselves of whatever was on their mind, including their frustrations with the other side. Rød-Larsen would listen, reflect back what they were saying, and reassure them the conversations would bear fruit. One of the negotiators noticed that Rød-Larsen never asked him about the negotiation, only about what he felt. 'How did you feel about meeting your arch enemy?' Rød-Larsen would enquire casually. 'Did you ever think you would?'

• • •

There is a fundamental tension in the human psyche, says Peter Coleman, between *coherence* and *complexity*; he calls it the 'crude law' of our existence. We want resolution and closure at the same time as we want interest and novelty. We seek order, and we seek freedom. Problems arise when we feel pushed too far in one direction or the other. Societies that are too ordered become stifling and oppressive; those that have no coherence are unsettling and alienating. Mental health problems tend to result from an excessive drive for either order (obsessive compulsive syndrome), or chaos (schizophrenia).

When we're anxious or threatened or just tired, we have a strong drive to simplify – to take short-cuts to coherence. What happens when you're in an argument with someone? You feel stressed, attacked and weary. So you reach for ever simpler answers (she is an *idiot,* he is *evil*), while your opponent does the same. When a conflict of any kind escalates, says Coleman, there is a press for coherence, on both sides. Each party become increasingly rigid and inflexible. Nuance, irony and compromise collapse into binary oppositions: good versus evil, stupid versus smart. Curiosity about our opponents' point of view is rendered suspect, because it opens up questions we prefer to be closed down. So is empathy, which might smudge the clarity of our moral vision. The only allowable question becomes, whose side are you on?

Disrupting this dynamic requires a lateral approach. Rather than going directly after a conflict, Coleman's advice is to 'stop making sense'. The main task is to find a way, any way, of fostering positive feelings between the parties: 'This may seem simplistic, but it's everything. In fact, the more distant these attempts are from rational persuasion, and from obvious attempts at swaying emotions, the better.' Negotiators are trained to analyse and rationalise; they think in straight lines. But when straight lines are the problem, what's required is imagination.

It sometimes takes a third party to introduce creative dissonance to an us-and-them dynamic. In the Oslo process, that role was played by the Norwegians. In Liberia in the early 2000s, a group of ordinary, albeit exceptionally brave women – mums, aunts, grand-mothers – formed an organisation known as the Women's International Peace Network (WIPN), which helped end a decades-long civil war. When UN peacekeepers were stuck in an armed stand-off with a group of rebel forces in the jungle, they called the WIPN. The women arrived on the scene in their white T-shirts and headdresses. They entered the jungle with hands raised, dancing and singing. The WIPN intervention introduced surprise, tonal variation, and good feeling to the stalemate. After two days, the women brought the rebels out of the jungle.

• • •

The first Oslo meeting ended after three days. In February, the participants reconvened at Borregaard, with the tacit blessing of their respective leaders. The Oslo channel, which remained a secret from the outside world, was now considered by both sides to be a serious counterpart to the official talks. Over the next few months, over a series of meetings in different Norwegian country houses, the participants argued their way towards a revolutionary agreement.

Being a social scientist, Rød-Larsen paid close attention to group dynamics. A micro-culture had formed at Borregaard, and he looked for ways to preserve its fluidity and prevent it hardening into protocol, even as new, more senior negotiators were introduced. When a very senior Israeli official joined a meeting for the first time, Rød-Larsen seized Ala, the Palestinian negotiator, by the hand and, pulling the men together, said, 'Meet your public enemy number one!' The remark sounded spontaneous, but Rød-Larsen had planned his words carefully. In conventional diplomatic terms, it made no sense. But the joke provoked a smile from both Israeli and Palestinian. Later, the same men would go on walks in the woods together, interspersing intense discussions with dirty jokes.

For eight months, day and night, Rød-Larsen acted as a go-between for the negotiating teams and their respective leaders in Tunis and Tel Aviv. He worked hard at maintaining the group's camaraderie – its sense of 'us against the world'. He knew that only within the context of this strange solidarity between antagonists would new ways of seeing the world emerge. It was an emotionally and physically punishing endeavour, but Rød-Larsen succeeded in creating the conditions in which arch enemies were able to recognise each other as human beings – as individuals who understood the pain of exile and bereavement; as parents with hopes for their children; as men who shared a taste for bad jokes.

The Oslo process culminated in a meeting that took place one morning in September 1993. Under a blue sky, two men faced each other on the White House lawn before an invited audience of world leaders; millions more watched on TV. One of the men was Yitzhak Rabin, the Prime Minister of Israel, a former general in the Israeli Army, and veteran of bloody battles with Israel's neighbours, including the Palestinians. The other was Yasser Arafat, leader of the PLO, which had fought an insurgent war against the Israeli state for forty years.

Less than nine months after Rød-Larsen hosted that first clandestine meeting at Borregaard, the two leaders had come together to sign a joint declaration of principles, known as the Oslo Accords. This was the first time the PLO and Israel had even recognised each other as legitimate antagonists – something that most people thought was impossible, until it happened. Standing between the two men was the President of the United States, Bill Clinton, who invited the two enemies to shake hands. Arafat reached out first. Rabin hesitated, as if to convey how hard this was for him. Then they shook.

Shortly after this handshake, negotiations on the fine details of the agreement ran into the ground. Rabin, perhaps the only Israeli leader held in sufficient esteem at home to make the deal work, was assassinated in 1995. Five years later, the process set in train by the Oslo Accords ended definitively with the outbreak of the Second Intifada, a period of intensified violence between Palestinians and Israelis.

Oslo was a failure, but a valuable one. The spirit of the agreement endures in the very notion of a peaceful, two-state solution. So does the story of the Oslo channel, whose embers glow faintly in the darkness. If the impossible suddenly seemed possible once, it might seem so again.

• • •

Peter Coleman cites a study which estimates that about one in twenty conflicts are classified as 'intractable' – that is, extremely hard to solve. The figure is said to apply not just to diplomatic and political clashes, but to the conflicts of everyday life between family members, friends or colleagues. Intractable disputes may be rare, but they exert a powerful influence over the lives of the participants and those around them, draining energy and generating hostility. We are used to referring to them as 'complex', but in a sense, as we've seen, the problem is the opposite, which implies something about how to approach them. As Coleman put it to me, 'In conflict you are pulled to simplify, and so you need to offset it with more complexity of feeling, thought and action.'

Arguments with our friends and relatives often follow regular patterns. Once the argument begins, you can predict how things will unfold, like an expert chess player can predict the next eight moves in a game from a glance at the board. As the familiar script plays out, we find ourselves almost irresistibly swept along with it, playing our parts in a stale drama. To stop this happening, mix things up – say what the other person isn't expecting you to say, agree on something unexpectedly, or switch topic for a while. You can vary how you say things as well as what you say: the language you use and the tone you deploy. It might be a note of humour or a touch of warmth, or even just something that doesn't quite make sense. If you always have the argument in the kitchen or in an office, find somewhere else to have it out.

What you're trying to do is create space, literal and figurative, for a new way of communicating with each other. In fact, you might want to think about it as opening a secret back channel to your antagonist.

12. Share Constraints

Disagreement benefits from a set of agreed norms and boundaries that support self-expression. Rules create freedom.

In 2013, when Kal Turnbull was seventeen and in his final year of secondary school in Nairn, Scotland, he became aware that he and his group of friends all tended towards similar views, whether on politics or music or TV. Turnbull started to wonder, where do you go if you want to hear from people who see things differently?

It is not as simple a question as it seems. Anyone who has lived in the same place for long tends to spend their time with people who see the world in roughly the same way they do. It's not always easy to find conversation partners who have strongly different views to your own. Even when you do, there's a social pressure to agree on things, since, as we've seen, disagreement can feel awkward and unpleasant. You can go online, of course. But when Turnbull looked at debates on social media he saw a lot of posturing and pile-ons and little real engagement. There didn't seem to be a place you could go to have your views probed and challenged without feeling as though you were under fire. So Turnbull decided to create one. He started a forum on reddit.com called Change My View. Within five years it had over half a million subscribers.

Change My View (CMV) is a place you can go to explore the limits of your own opinions. Perhaps you have formed a point of view on something – on how to run the country, on whether God exists, on the most overrated movie of the year – but you have a feeling you're not seeing all sides of the question, that you might be missing something important? Then take your opinion to

CMV, and its community of users will help you think it through by politely disagreeing with you. Whether or not you end up changing your view, you will see things differently.

• • •

When people celebrate the value of disagreement, they often emphasise free expression. But, as social media platforms have revealed, when people are allowed to express themselves however they want, disagreements tend to degenerate into acrimony and abuse. CMV is not a place where anything goes. Turnbull worked with a team of more than twenty moderators, enlisted from the group's regular contributors, to maintain a tightly drawn code of conduct. Rule-breakers are warned, then thrown off the platform if they ignore those warnings. 'We have restrictive rules, but what they provide is freedom for certain conversations,' he told me. The rules were not designed by Turnbull at the outset: they evolved organically over time, as he and the user community gradually figured out what makes for a good disagreement and what does not.

CMV works like this. First, you submit a view that you would like challenging: 'Zoos are immoral'; 'Heroin should be legalised'; 'Radiohead is the best band of all time'. The site does not set any rules about the content of the belief – it can be anything. But it does have to be *your* belief: you can't say, 'I've got this friend who says . . .' You should also be genuinely willing to accept your belief is wrong. This last condition is hard to enforce, since it's impossible to know for sure what's in someone's mind, but Turnbull and his team have identified some reliable proxies for bad faith. Submitters who offer the same justification for their view over and over, or who engage in repetitive rants without seeming to absorb or reflect on any of the questions from commenters, violate what is informally known as the 'no soapboxing' rule.

CMV asks users to 'enter with a mindset for conversation, not debate' since the latter implies a competition between people who will never change their mind, where the object is winning, not learning. The very act of submitting a view to CMV signals that the submitter, like someone volunteering for therapy, is *ambivalent*; some part of their mind is open to change. Indeed, Turnbull told me that he wants CMV to feel like a clinic people can visit to learn why they're wrong.

When you're submitting a question, CMV asks you not just to state your view baldly but to give a summary of why you believe it. That might include your reasoning, although the most valuable information, says Turnbull, usually has to do with *how* you came to believe it. Does your view have something to do with your personal life, the home you grew up in, a specific experience? A philosopher might argue that how someone came to a view is irrelevant information – that whether or not a belief is wrong or right can be established purely on logical or factual grounds. But Turnbull and CMV's users have found that embedding the opinion in someone's life has a way of improving the conversation.

Knowing something about where the submitter is coming from helps commenters shape their questions and arguments. The users who are most successful at changing views tend not to post off-the-peg arguments that could be used on anyone, but tailor their comments to the person behind the view. The more that commenters feel they're talking to a real person, the less likely they are to denigrate the view and the more likely they are to show that they are truly listening – and people who feel they've been listened to are more open to having their mind changed. 'What does listening look like in a text-based forum?' asks Turnbull. 'I think it's about referring to someone's reasons for their view and the path they took to get there.'

In most social media forums, he told me, people usually jump straight to the point of disagreement without taking time to understand each other first. The result is that they scrabble around on the surface of an issue without digging beneath. *I think this! Well, I think this!* 'Sometimes it's better to take your time getting to the point where you disagree,' Turnbull said. 'Start at the beginning, take a walk around the question, then see where you get to.' Another benefit of asking submitters to spend time articulating their view is that it begins the process of opening their mind to flaws in their own position. As people discuss things in more detail, they often discover that they are less certain than they thought they were.

Commenters are required to disagree with the submitted view. Turnbull didn't want this to be a place where people can come simply to have their views affirmed – after all, there are plenty of places for that. Crucially, however, the disagreement must be expressed courteously and respectfully. The first rule to be agreed on was the simplest: *don't be rude or hostile*. Turnbull's team of moderators are vigilant for any signs of rudeness or aggression. The prohibition of hostility, he says, is fundamental: 'It's very important people don't break this rule because if they do it just throws off the conversation and makes it hard for anyone else to get through to the author of the post after that point. It changes the tone.'

This is worth dwelling on. Tone is sometimes discussed as if it's a secondary characteristic of human interaction. ('Why are you worrying about tone? Focus on the substance.') But tone is *more important* than content. It goes deeper than words. It is the medium through which we express the relationship we expect to have with who we're talking to. Your tone efficiently communicates how you see yourself in relation to me: as more intelligent or less; as dominant or deferential; as somebody with whom I can be serious or playful. And as we've seen throughout, until people establish a mutually agreeable relationship, a disagreement is bound to go badly.

Turnbull notes that when people break the rule against hostility on CMV, they often do so without realising and immediately apologise. 'They want to change the view of the other person. So by being rude, it's going against their own interests, because they're less likely to get through to them.' This should be obvious, but people often forget it in the heat of the moment. CMV's most ingenious rule is one that keeps people focused on why they are there in the first place: submitters give awards to commenters who have shown them they are wrong. If and when a submitter decides that their view has been modified by a CMV conversation, they bestow, on the commenter who made the difference, a delta: Δ (in maths and physics, the delta sign signifies change).

A person with a high delta score gains status within the community, since they have a proven ability to change other people's views. 'The first time I got a delta,' one participant told a researcher who has studied CMV, 'it felt like a big deal.' Commenters have a strong incentive to maintain good relations with submitters, because otherwise they won't be able to persuade them of anything.

• • •

In the early days of the site, Turnbull and his fellow moderators noticed a problem: people who had their views swayed by a discussion had a tendency not to admit it. Despite adopting a different position to the one they started with, they would pretend, perhaps as much to themselves as anyone else, that they had pretty much held the same opinion all along. Turnbull wanted people to admit that they had been wrong. Not because he wanted them to feel humiliated – quite the opposite. He wanted to de-stigmatise wrongness. 'Nobody likes to be wrong. It's not a great feeling. But if you approach it positively, it's a chance to learn, gain insight and lose some of your ignorance. It doesn't have to feel like an attack.' Over 2,000 years after Socrates tried to reassure Athenians, the message still needed sending.

When we talk about 'changing my mind' we tend to think in terms of a 180-degree reversal – a Damascene conversion. The trouble with this is that it puts a high price on the act of changing your mind. At CMV, participants are encouraged to award deltas merely when they feel that the discussion has led to a deeper understanding of the topic, or when they have learnt something from their challengers. 'It helps to literally think in terms of *view*,' says Turnbull. 'If you've moved even slightly around, then you've got a new perspective.'

Turnbull has noticed that the people who are really good at changing minds – users with high delta scores – are skilled at asking productive questions. They don't use questions as a way to flay the other person ('What on earth makes you think . . . ?') but to understand their view more fully. Sometimes their questions expose a contradiction at the heart of the submitter's position, prompting them to rethink (personally, I know that the moment I hear someone summarising my point of view fairly is when I get the fear). But this only works when the questions spring from genuine curiosity – those who ask questions in a forensic, prosecutorial style are less effective at changing minds. As Turnbull puts it, 'It might seem to contradict the whole idea of CMV, but starting with the intention of changing someone's view can actually ruin the process a little.'

We've seen how the righting reflex can backfire. A better approach to changing minds is to become someone's partner in an exploration. Successful delta-accumulators often exhibit a little uncertainty about their own position. The act of having your mind changed and the act of seeking to change someone else's mind start in the same place, with questions that point simultaneously at the questioned and the questioner – don't you think?

• • •

CMV is a fertile source of data for academic researchers interested in how and why people change their minds. A team of computer scientists at Cornell University analysed over two years of postings on the platform. They found that about a third of submitters to the site had their mind changed. That may not sound high, but in context of previous research on persuasion and attitude-change, it's exceptional. The Cornell researchers ran numbers on which kinds of conversation resulted in deltas and which did not. Their findings echo and augment Turnbull's observations.

For instance, the factor most associated with successful persuasion was using different words to those used in the original post. That's intriguing, because it implies that to change a view, you need somehow to reframe the argument in different terms, putting it in a fresh context. It links to another finding the researchers made: the use of specific examples really helps to change minds, as does the use of facts and statistics; the best recipe is a combination of storytelling and hard evidence.

Longer replies tended to perform better than shorter ones (although not if the commenter is seen to be soapboxing).

A person's view was more likely to be changed over the course of a conversation with a commenter, rather than by one devastating point. But if it wasn't changed after five rounds of back-and-forth exchanges, it was unlikely to be changed at all (this has been useful to me in knowing when to bail out of Twitter arguments).

The researchers also found that 'hedging' helps. Arguments that included phrases like 'it could be the case' tended to be more persuasive than those that projected certainty. When a commenter signals with his tone that he's not entirely sure of himself, the submitter lets their guard down. Weakness is power.

• • •

Experts on traffic know it only takes two or three drivers on a crowded highway to do something that disturbs the traffic flow for hundreds of cars to coalesce into a jam. The same principle applies to online debate. A small number of deliberately disruptive or bad-tempered participants can force their way to the forefront of everyone's attention and before you know it, a new normal has been set, resulting in bad-tempered gridlock.

Most people don't make a decision to be rude, any more than they are implacably determined to remain polite. Whatever environment we're communicating in, we instinctively take cues from how others are behaving. That's true at the basic level of a dyad: when two people are talking and one injects even a hint of hostility into the discussion, the other notices immediately and feels an urge to follow suit. Online, that dynamic plays out at scale. Without thinking about it, participants look around and ask, is this the kind of place where I'm expected to let fly with sick burns, or to engage in respectful debate?

This places a certain responsibility on each individual. These days we're used to the idea that what we buy or how we travel has environmental effects. How we communicate has environmental effects, too. With each remark we make, we can choose either to improve or to pollute the discourse. In fact, what you say may be less important than how you say it. After all, you cannot know for sure that you are right. What you can be sure of – what you can control – is the example you set.

Improving the quality of online disagreement isn't just down to individuals, though: well-designed rules make a difference too, as Change My View has shown us. Even the simplest of rules can help, providing people are made aware of them. Some worry that strict rules can have a chilling effect on participation and free expression. In 2016, Nathan Matias, a professor of communication at Cornell University, looked into this. He conducted a study with Reddit's science discussion community, which had 13.5 million subscribers at the time. Matias arranged things so that users in some threads saw an announcement of the community's rules, which include a prohibition on hostile language. Compared with discussions in which users were not shown the announcement, first-time commenters were significantly more likely to abide by the rules. Crucially, the participation rate of newcomers increased by an average of 70 per cent. They weren't being put off by the rules. Online, or in the workplace, simply making rules of interaction visible improves the conversation for everyone, most of all for those who haven't been around long enough to absorb the group's norms through osmosis. Shared constraints create space for livelier disagreements.

Rules are important not so much because people need telling what to do or not do, but because they feel better about expressing themselves within a structure to which everyone is expected to adhere. Arguments can always get out of hand, either because people knowingly break rules or because they didn't know the rules in the first place. But when people do get into a messy argument, they usually want to find a way out, and a clearly articulated set of rules can lead them there.

This is a principle that hostage negotiators understand. They often have to de-escalate situations that are on the verge of chaos. In order to do that, Professor William Donohue told me, they try and provide a structure through which the hostage-taker can express himself. 'The negotiator enters this highly contentious, identity driven, emotionally fraught moshpit of confusion, and they have to impose order on it. They feed back what they're hearing in a structured manner: "The first thing you're concerned about is this, the second thing is this . . ."' Experts in tough conversations are trained to do this, but as Donohue pointed out to me, it's something skilled communicators do instinctively: 'A good friend listens to your emotional diatribe and helps you find a shape for it. They turn your mess into something you can get a handle on – so that you can do something about it.'

Donohue likened this process to a political system. 'It's where democracy starts. The idea of Magna Carta was to take back rights from a capricious king who was making decisions on the spur of the moment. A democratic society needs due process, so that every demand or grievance isn't settled by the whim of the king. In my research, I see the same forces at work. Negotiators and mediators create a map of the issues and propose a process for working them through. When that structure falls apart, it opens up the need for people to grab power and impose their will.'

13. Only Get Mad on Purpose

No amount of theorising can fully prepare us for the emotional experience of a disagreement. Sometimes your worst adversary is yourself.

Back to where we started: an anonymous hotel meeting room, somewhere deep in the English countryside, on a winter's night. This is what I know: a young woman was raped in an underpass last Sunday. A video of the incident had been uploaded to a website from a phone that belonged to a local delivery firm with seventeen male drivers. The last text message sent from the phone pinged off a mast close to the home of this Frank Barnet, a man with a history of domestic violence.

The man I was looking at wasn't really Frank Barnet, and he wasn't really a rape suspect. He was an actor. Laurence Alison had offered me the chance to take part in the kind of role play that forms the backbone of his training for police interviewers. It was Laurence who briefed me on the case, addressing me as 'Detective Inspector Leslie'.

So why was my stomach turning over? Because even the simulation of a high-pressure conversation has the power to trigger your nervous system, regardless of how much your rational brain might tell you it's not real. Alison had warned me that role-play interviews often feel all too authentic. Hardened police interviewers can be driven to the edge in training simulations. In the real world, professional interrogators sometimes need therapy in the aftermath of an intensive period of interviewing.

What I took away from this brief but intense simulation is that in order to make a disagreement productive, you need to influence the other person, but the first person you need to influence is you. Mastering your own emotions, your own reactions, is the hardest skill of all.

• • •

FB: I don't give a fuck about *people*, why are you talking to *me*? Frank Barnet. Why me?

The man playing Barnet was Lloyd Smith, a regular participant in Alison's courses. Lloyd has been interviewed by more police officers than almost anyone else alive. He has been a Rwandan warlord, an Islamist terrorist and a Brazilian gangster. He has been a murderer, a paedophile, a rapist. He is sometimes aggressive and borderline violent, sometimes charming and evasive, sometimes determinedly silent. For each case, he absorbs a character profile written by Alison, together with information about the crime or crimes the character has committed. It is his job to give the interviewer as hard a time as possible, and he does so with tremendous skill and guile. Lloyd has not studied interrogation tactics in an academic context, but he has taken part in so many interviews, with so many different interviewers, that he has a profound understanding of their dynamics.

He is also just an extremely good actor. To me, in that room, he wasn't Lloyd. He was Frank Barnet. I explained to him, in a voice that I tried and failed to make self-assured, that we were interviewing several drivers who worked for the delivery company.

FB: So you believe I might be a rapist?

I didn't know how to answer. How do you answer that? I just repeated myself, telling him, in a more convoluted way than last time, that he was one of a number of people we were talking to. I sounded like a politician evading a straightforward question.

FB: It's a yes or no question. Do you believe I could be a rapist?

Finally, I said yes.

FB: You should know I don't have no love for you people.
IL: Which people?
FB: The police. You've been pestering me and beating me since I was a kid.

I tried to return to the question of what he was doing that Sunday afternoon, but Barnet had other ideas.

FB: Do you think I'm a cunt?
IL: No, I don't.
FB: Don't you think a rapist is a cunt?

I ignored the question. In an officious-sounding voice, I asked again about that Sunday. Barnet peered at the ring on my left hand.

FB: You're married, ain't you?
IL: Yes.
FB: If I raped your wife, would you consider me a cunt?
IL: [stunned silence] Yes, probably.

I already felt hot, nervous and itchy with discomfort. Now, I felt furious. Why the hell did this guy think it was OK to talk about raping my wife? Why was he asking *me* questions? I wasn't the one suspected of a crime. Laurence, who had been observing, paused the interview, and asked me how I felt. I told him. He nodded. The challenge, he said, was to avoid getting sucked into Barnet's force field – into the conversation he wanted to have. 'You're thinking, God this guy is being a real jerk to me. But a really good interviewer is able to step back and think, "Ah, that's interesting – this guy is behaving like a jerk. What is that about?"'

Lloyd, out of character now, explained that I needed to get better at knowing when to give way. 'I don't think you should be afraid to use the words I use – my language. These are little hurdles I'm setting for you. If I know you're battling to hold those words in, I will keep pushing. If you say, "Yes, I would think he was a cunt," there's nowhere for me to go with that. Or when I asked you if you thought I could be a rapist – just say yes! Then I've got nothing to push back on.' Sometimes he puts his feet on the table, he said, to lure the interviewer into a futile argument. Less experienced interviewers see this as a threat to their authority and get diverted by it; smart interviewers ignore it. 'After a while, it gets uncomfortable for me and I take my feet down anyway.'

When Frank Barnet tried to rattle me by personalising the conversation, said Laurence, I should have gently returned to the question I wanted to pursue. 'You could have said, "Yes, of course I'd think – in your words – he was a cunt, but my feelings are neither here nor there. I'm here to interview you about the rape of a young girl. That's the job I have to do."'

But my biggest error, said Lawrence, was not exploring *why* Barnet was behaving so unpleasantly. He thought I had missed an opening when Barnet said he didn't like the police. 'You could have reflected that back,' said Lawrence. 'You could have said, "Did the police have it in for you?"' Lloyd agreed. 'It's a human experience, a truth of his life. You don't have to take personal responsibility for it, but you could have acknowledged it. You could have said, "That sounds like a bad experience."' Asking him about it might have helped me understand who I was talking to, and it would have had another subtle benefit: 'It has a subconscious impact,' said Lloyd. 'I get into the mode of actually *talking*, rather than just giving short answers and blunt questions.'

By showing interest in his life, I might have lowered his defences. But it's hard to be curious when you feel angry. In fact, it's hard to think straight at all.

• • •

A team of psychologists at University College London invited subjects into the lab in pairs. The first person was hooked up to a little squeezing machine, which applied a very small force on her finger. She was then instructed to press down on the other person's finger *using exactly the same amount of force*. Crucially, the other person had no idea about this part of the instruction.

The second person was then instructed to push back on the first person's finger, using exactly the same amount of force as they felt. The two individuals traded finger pushes, while the scientists measured the precise force they used. In every pair of pushers tested, the use of force escalated quickly, until the two people were pushing down on each other's finger with about twenty times the original force.

It's an experiment that offers an ominous glimpse into the dynamics of human escalation. Each participant thought they were behaving proportionately to the other, and while nobody was deliberately raising the stakes, somehow the pressure rose anyway. This raises a question: why don't all of our conflicts escalate in the same way?

One answer is that some people react slowly to the emotional signals they receive from others. Researchers who study marital communication find that couples who reciprocate each other's negativity are more likely to be unhappy (for although, as we've seen, negativity can be helpful to a relationship, too much bad feeling is obviously unhealthy; what matters is the *ratio* of positive to negative feelings over time). More surprisingly, this is also true of couples who reciprocate each other's positivity. Unhappy marriages and families are just more febrile; feelings fly around at a faster rate than in happier ones. In his lab, the relationship scientist John Gottman has measured the effect of argument on the *physiology* of married partners – on heart rate and sweat glands – and correlated it with the longevity of the marriage. If one partner's behaviour affects the other's physical functioning this way, the marriage is likely to end in divorce.

Individuals who have 'emotional inertia' – who tend to stay close to the same emotional state, whatever is going on – also act as stabilising influences. If you are frustrated by the way that your partner or a colleague doesn't seem to respond immediately to your mood, good or bad, there may be reason to be grateful for it. A measure of emotional inertia is healthy in a relationship, or a group. When you're putting together a team or choosing a partner, it might be wise to think about the mix of personalities through this lens. A good team should have passionate, creative people in it, but unless it has sceptical or just plain unexcitable individuals too, disagreements are liable to race out of control in unpredictable ways. The Beatles really needed Ringo.

Getting the right mix of personalities is one thing, but just as important to preventing escalations is to try and be your inner Ringo – to calm your more volatile responses when you need to. The participants in the finger-pushing experiment were acting in a manner that the relationship scientist Alan Sillars calls, in the context of marital rows, 'mindless reciprocation'. Each was instinctively responding to the other's last move and neither was asking themselves how to respond to it (to be clear, nobody had asked them to). Since they had no goal to achieve, they exerted little self-control.

Huthwaite International, a UK-based company that provides training in sales and negotiation skills, has been collecting data on the behaviour of negotiators for over fifty years. It has carried out a series of long-term studies using a consistent methodology based on direct observation of real negotiations. One of the aims of this research has been to establish differences in behaviour between highly skilled negotiators and average ones (negotiators deemed as highly effective have to be rated as such by both sides, and to have a track record of success).

One of the major differences identified by Huthwaite's researchers is the way that negotiators handle conflict. Like anyone else, negotiators sometimes get mad with their counterparts when they come up against a disagreement. Huthwaite uses the term 'defending/attacking' for emotionally heated behaviour, in which the negotiator either displays aggression towards the other party or makes an emotional defence of themselves. The company's researchers have observed that the behaviour has a tendency to form 'a spiral of increasing intensity'. As one party attacks, the other defends, in a way that the other perceives as an attack. As a result, defensive and offensive moves become hard to tell apart.

Average negotiators are most likely to react defensively to dis-agreement or implied criticism, using phrases like 'You can't blame us for that' or 'It's not our fault.' But all this does is provoke a sharp reaction from the other side, setting off a spiral. In fact, average negotiators engage in defend–attack spirals *three times* as often as skilled ones. They also follow a pattern of escalation that relationship scientists have identified as common in marital rows, starting their attacking behaviour slowly, with low-level sniping, and gradually increasing its intensity, as the other side does the same, until a full-on confrontation ensues.

More skilled negotiators handle things differently. It's not that they never employ hostility, but they do so rarely, and when they attack, they hit hard and without warning. What this suggests is that skilled negotiators exert more conscious control over their aggression than less skilled ones. When they get hot, it's because they are using heat as a means to an end. Perhaps they want to send a signal about what they care about, or to move the discussion out of a rut. Whatever it is, what they never do is let the conversation control them.

In the negotiations leading up the Good Friday Agreement of 1998, the UK government's chief negotiator, Jonathan Powell, spent endless hours with politicians and officials from all sides of the Northern Ireland conflict, patiently mediating arguments, soaking up anger and blame. Powell has a typically diplomatic temperament, level-headed and calm, but the strain of his role took a toll on him. In his book about the negotiations, *Great Hatred, Little Room*, he describes a moment in which he lost his self-control altogether. At a meeting attended by his boss, the British prime minister Tony Blair, Powell exploded in fury at a Unionist official, who he thought was going to great lengths to needle the British. He grabbed the man by the lapels and had to be pulled away by Blair. Powell knew he had made a mistake. Afterwards, Blair took him aside and told him, 'You should never lose your temper by accident.'

Skilful communicators, says Alan Sillars, refuse to submit to the logic of reciprocity without considering, first, if that's the wise thing to do. They deliberately slow the conversation down and consider their options. They're not just thinking about what they want to do, but how what they do affects the other, and about the best way to reach their goal for the conversation. That's not easy when you are feeling a surge of rage or fear, which raises your heart rate, priming you to take quick, impulsive decisions, often bad ones. But just being aware of what is causing your reaction can help you bring it under control.

• • •

Don Gulla, of Polis, suggested I talk to Ellis Amdur. Amdur is a specialist in anger – his own and others. He works with police officers and other professionals who have anger-filled encounters in the course of their job. Raised in a middle-class household in Pittsburgh, Pennsylvania, Amdur grew up with an acute sense of vulnerability to existential harm. 'I'm Jewish, this was the 1950s. My parents taught me to never trust a Christian. When the holocaust comes, they said, the Christians will either participate or turn their back.' He went to a school where kids were free with their fists and, after losing one fight badly, he decided to learn the art of combat.

After studying psychology at Yale, Amdur spent nearly fourteen years in Japan at a number of martial arts schools. He returned to the USA to study a form of psychotherapy influenced by phenomenology, which explores how we perceive the world as shaped by what we believe. 'I was drawn to a way of thinking that says you have to be able to bracket your preconceptions to see what's in front of your eyes. A good police officer, or anyone who is skilled in crisis, can identify the salient data in an encounter and screen out what isn't important. To do that, you need to study your own reactions and be aware of them.'

To Amdur, anger is never just anger. He teaches officers how to assess, to a finely calibrated degree, the kind of anger a person is displaying, and how to handle it. 'Chaotic rage – delirium. Terrified rage – a cornered wolf who doesn't want to fight but will. Cool rage – a predator maintaining control. Hot rage – like a bear that wants to tear you up. Manipulative rage – like a rat that needs to get through a maze to a goal. Deceptive rage – like a snake in tall grass. You need a different approach for each type.'

Amdur talks about the brain as having three levels: human, mammal and reptile ('It's not neurologically accurate but it's a useful metaphor for aggression'). In human-brain, he says, 'We can have some heat in the encounter but we're interested in what the other person is trying to say. We're trying to achieve a win–win outcome. Another word for it is dialogue.' When a disagreement raises the heart rate, we can move into mammal-brain. The encounter becomes a struggle over dominance, with the dominant emotion being anger. *Who do you think you are?* 'My focus becomes on what *I* have to say and I have little interest in what others are saying. That's why you hear people saying, *You're not listening. Give me a chance to talk. You don't get it.*' The reptile-brain is different again: 'This is when anger takes over. An angry person cares only about winning the argument. That goal may overlap with truth – they may be right – but truth is not the goal. You cannot problem solve with an angry person.' You can't even ask questions of them, since, to the angry person, your questions confirm that you haven't been listening to them. 'If you say, "Are you mad?" they'll reply, "What the fuck do you think?" Better to say, "I see you're mad."' In reptile brain, rage takes over.

Amdur asks his students to reflect on their own psychological hot buttons – what kinds of things are liable to send them into a rage? He tells cops that it's crucial to prepare for the possibility that someone might push one of their buttons that day. 'Let's say you have a certain insecurity. You don't think about it most of the time, until someone activates it. By reminding myself of what my buttons are, I'm more likely to roll with it when it happens. I won't have that intense threat reaction. I'm prepared.'

In Memphis, the Polis trainers often returned to the importance of self-mastery under pressure, while noting that sometimes they needed a little help from colleagues. 'Everybody has triggers,' Mike O'Neill told the room. 'Mine was any domestic violence [DV] incident. My parents fought. If I was dealing with a DV, I could explode in a New York second. My partner knew that about me. He'd say, "I got this, Mike."'

One of the Memphis officers, a man, spoke up. 'My trigger is when children are involved. I visited an apartment, and it was in a horrible mess. I could see the guy spent all his money on beer. There were cockroaches everywhere – and this little kid was on the sofa. I started losing it. My partner had to take me outside.'

• • •

My brief encounter with Frank Barnet brought home to me how insanely hard it is to do what expert interrogators do. Your mind has to operate at full capacity on at least three levels at once. First, you are playing a cognitive chess game, focusing on what you know about this suspect, what they know about what you know, and what you need to get from them. Second, you are trying to establish an emotional relationship of rapport or trust with an individual who is doing their best to push you away. Third, you're in a struggle with yourself.

I knew it was a bad idea to lose my temper with Frank or to react to his provocations. But that did not mean I found it easy to stop myself from doing so, and if I couldn't control my own behaviour, I had little hope of influencing his. Of course, this isn't true only of encounters in police cells and military camps. In any heated conversation, the conflict we're having with another person is entwined in a conflict we're having within ourselves.

I find it helpful to think about this internal argument as a struggle between competing goals. Whatever we're doing, there's always a goal or goals we're trying to achieve, whether we're fully aware of them or not. Behavioural scientist William T. Powers envisioned the mind as a series of goal-driven systems, stacked in a hierarchy. The lowest systems control our body – the central nervous system, our muscles – while the highest levels involve conscious awareness and purpose. At the lowest levels, actions can be performed automatically and unthinkingly, because they have instructions from above; when you're driving a car you don't have to think about every movement you make, because you've set yourself the goal of driving. That goal is itself in the service of a higher, more strategic goal – visiting the furniture store. Our problems arise, said Powers, when systems get into conflict with each other. Maybe your body has set you the goal of staying on the sofa, but your higher system is demanding you visit the store, because the sofa needs replacing. So you feel anxious and unhappy until one side or the other wins out.

In a confrontation of any kind – with your partner, with a colleague, with a stranger – we often get stuck in one of these inner struggles. Our lower, more instinctual system has set us the goal of winning the argument in front of us, while a higher system has set goal of maintaining a good relationship with this person. The competition is not necessarily an even match. Those lower systems are powerful; they can bully us. We get so focused on the goal in front of us – to win the argument, to best this person, to display our superior intelligence and wit – that we lose awareness of any higher goal altogether. Even when the error signals are loud and clear – when the argument feels stressful and painful – we charge ahead, blinkers on.

When someone is being rude or hostile to you, it's almost like an invitation to you to do the same. A part of you naturally wants to accept the invitation and rip right into them. When that happens, we're allowing them to control our reactions, instead of remembering that we have a choice of goals. Maybe your goal *is* to make that person feel bad about themselves, or to humiliate them – maybe you don't care about burning the relationship. In which case, go ahead. Pursue that goal mindfully.

But often, it's better to refuse their invitation and choose your own tone. If you're talking to someone with whom you want or need to have a good ongoing relationship, following them down to the low ground will be a bad move for both of you. In which case, the best thing to do is to back up, slow down, and consciously choose your own path, instead of the one you have been invited to follow.

William Powers provided a useful way of thinking about this: whenever we get stuck in an internal conflict we should kick the problem up to the next level, like an employee passing the buck to his line manager. In other words, we should try and get more perspective on our behaviour and more clarity on our goals. Specifically, we can ask *why* and *how*. The *how* question shines the spotlight down to our lower-level behaviours. So, in an unpleasant argument with someone, we might take a mental step back and ask, how am I conducting myself in this argument? Am I being bad-tempered, sarcastic, aggressive? The *why* question shines the spotlight up to our higher goals. Why am I engaging in this row – what am I after, what's the *point*? When you know the answer to *why*, you can decide on what to do about *how*. You might change your tone and become warmer or more playful – or, if the moment calls for it, more aggressive, like those expert negotiators did at moments of their choosing.

Moving up a level like this does not guarantee your interlocutor will respond in the manner you're inviting them to. For instance, they might respond to your warmer tone with more aggression. But at the very least, it lifts *you* up and out of the moment you're in. Winning the argument right now suddenly feels less important. Even if you can't reach a reconciliation with the other person, you'll be reconciled with yourself.

14. Golden Rule: Be Real

All rules are subordinate to the golden rule: make an honest human connection.

Back in the room, and it's time for round two. Same case, same suspect. Only this time, Frank Barnet would be a different kind of character. I'd asked Laurence and Lloyd to give me a taste of the range of challenges a police interviewer can face.

When Barnet sat down opposite me this time, he didn't stare suspiciously, and he didn't put his feet on the table. He looked at the floor, as if he didn't want to make eye contact. When he spoke, it was in a soft, hesitant voice. I asked him what he had been doing on the day in question. He started to answer before tailing off. He asked, 'Is the girl all right?'

I gave a cursory answer before returning to my questions on the events of his day. After a long pause, he said, in a small voice, 'I want to help, but I'm just confused. I wouldn't do something like this. They arrested me in front of the school, when I was with my kids.' I said that must have difficult for him, then continued my enquiry.

Laurence paused the interview and asked me how it was going. I said I felt more confident this time, more in control. Laurence frowned. 'I thought you were strangely un-empathetic. Your tone was almost exactly the same as the first interview, albeit a bit less nervous. There was no modulation.'

I realised he was right. I was so concerned with sounding like Detective Inspector Leslie – authoritative, in charge – that I had forgotten the need to adapt my tone to the person in front of me.

Lloyd joined in. 'If you're going to say, "That must be very difficult for you," and it hasn't got the right emotion behind it, it's not worth saying,' he told me.

This was a crucial lesson: sympathy without feeling is worse than no sympathy at all. 'Unless you sound like you actually care about what happened to me, I just feel like I'm part of a process, and you're just moving me along.'

It was important, continued Lloyd, to appear persuadable. 'If a police officer seems open-minded and non-judgemental there's more chance I'm going to talk. Maybe it's just because I think I can con you. Either way, if you give the impression you've already made up your mind, there's no reason for me to talk.'

So the best interviewers have an ability to come across as if they have an open mind? 'It's not so much an ability,' said Laurence, 'as being genuinely interested in finding out the truth.'

• • •

British police officer Jake Rollnick (whose father Stephen was the co-founder of Motivational Interviewing whom we met earlier) told me about how he patiently builds rapport with people in crisis, before getting down to the action that needs taking – whether that's an arrest or, just as often, getting them to a safe place. But as we wrapped up our conversation, Jake had one more point to make:

Rapport is important, but there are different ways to get there. My sergeant is a big bloke, rugby player, real Cardiff man. He always goes in confrontational, and it always works. I remember this suicidal lad who had slit his wrists and taken an overdose. I sat with him for ages, gently persuading him to let me take him to the hospital. Then Sarge walks in and starts shouting:

'WHAT DO YOU WANT ME TO DO? DO YOU WANT ME
TO TAKE YOU TO THE HOSPITAL OR WHAT? I CAN'T SOLVE
YOUR PROBLEMS FOR YOU. I'VE GOT WORK TO DO. IF
YOU WANT TO GO TO THE HOSPITAL, I'LL TAKE YOU – OR
YOU CAN SIT HERE AND DIE.'

'It was all wrong,' said Jake. 'I sat there thinking to myself,
he's messed up all my good work. But the lad went with us to
the hospital. And I've seen the sergeant do that again and again.
Somehow he always ends up making a connection. There are no
rules.'

It might seem odd, in a book of rules, to say this, but Jake is
right: there are no hard and fast rules. Well, almost none. There is
a golden thread running through all the conversations I had with
people in the course of researching and writing this book, and it's
this: you can't handle disagreement and conflict successfully if you
don't make a truthful human connection. If you have one, then
all rules are moot. If you don't have one, then the techniques and
tactics you use are likely to do more harm than good.

• • •

During the stand-off with the Davidians, the FBI tried a series
of persuasion tactics that were clumsy and counter-productive,
as persuasion tactics tend to be when divorced from genuine
empathy and curiosity. One of the techniques taught in
negotiation textbooks is to identify common ground in order to
develop rapport. It's a fine principle – one that I have advanced
here – but done clumsily it can sound insincere and cynical. For
instance, one of the negotiators, proposing a plan to Koresh, told
him that it had been sanctioned by his superior only after his boss,

'a very devout Christian' had prayed to God, 'as we all do'. Koresh was unimpressed. Another of the FBI's persuasion tactics was to send photos and videos of the released children, and messages written by the children, into the compound, so that the children's parents would be motivated to come out and be reunited with them. Unsurprisingly, the Davidians were angered by this blatant attempt at manipulation.

Even the people you believe to be less intelligent than you (always a risky bet) may have a finely honed sense of the relationship signals you're sending. Polis trainer Don Gulla emphasised that officers should never feign compassion and should always assume others are smart enough to see through any tricks, no matter who they are. 'Mentally ill people are intelligent. They're just ill. They know when you're lying to them. Don't try and be someone you're not. Be real.'

One of Laurence Alison's refrains is, 'You've got to mean it.' An interrogator's curiosity should never be faked; it must be authentic. Laurence warned repeatedly against relying on 'tricks': techniques of manipulation that make the interrogator feel clever but are often seen through by interviewees. Tricks are attractive because they make us feel smart and in control, but they're rarely as effective as promised, and can backfire. Niël Barnard, a former head of South African intelligence and one of the figures involved in brokering Mandela's release from prison, had a rule of thumb for negotiation: 'cleverness is stupidity'.

When Alfred Wilson decided to ask the truck driver about his life, he wasn't deploying a trick; he really was interested. Charlan Nemeth found that the devil's advocate game only works if the advocate really believes in her view. The hostage negotiators who spoke to Miriam Oostinga emphasised that an apology only works if it's genuine. Viljoen knew that Mandela was for real when Mandela told him how much Afrikaners had hurt him.

• • •

Polis founder Jonathan Wender told me that when he was a cop, the thing he found hardest about the job was what he calls 'the bureaucratic paradox'. It is only as a police officer, a wearer of the uniform, that he had licence to intrude upon people's lives. But at the same time, it was only when he transcended his official role that he was able to influence them. 'If my job as an officer is to build a sense of trust, I can't do that by acting as a rigid bureaucrat. As long as I saw things through the technical lens of the law I could not influence people in a lasting way. I must be humanly authentic myself.'

Wender grew up in New Jersey, in a household full of books and ideas. 'I was an intellectually inclined child.' His parents owned an independent bookstore, his grandfather was a history professor. He studied philosophy and Middle Eastern languages at university, before joining a police department near Seattle. Six years into his police career, Wender began studying for a PhD that applied the work of the German philosopher Martin Heidegger to law enforcement. His thesis later became a book, entitled *Policing and the Poetics of Everyday Life*.

Talking to Wender is like listening to a continental philosopher who happens to know the most efficient way to execute an arm-lock. I asked him what it was about police work that he found so stimulating. 'The world thinks about policing in terms of aggression, but for me, police work is intimate. You are interacting with people, over and again, at their moments of greatest vulnerability. You see people being born and you see them die. You talk to them about why their marriage is broken or why they tried to kill themselves. It is human nature in the raw.'

He returned, as he often does, to philosophy. 'A human is not like a tree or a rock. We make meaning. A jet moving across a sky leaves a contrail of smoke, a boat moving through water leaves a wake; there's no other way they can move. The same is true of a person moving through the world. When you walk into a room, you radiate meaning like a star gives off light.' He paused. 'So if that's true, then good interaction with others means having a good purpose. Never objectify someone. Understand that they have a soul, and you have a soul.'

PART THREE

Staying in the Room

PART THREE

15. The Infinite Game

Productive disagreement is not the same as good manners,
but some minimal form of civility is required to keep our
disagreements going.

'Where there is much desire to learn, there of necessity will be
much arguing.' John Milton

In 1962, the philosopher and advocate for liberal causes Bertrand
Russell received a series of letters from Oswald Mosley, former
leader of the British Union of Fascists. Mosley wanted Russell to
engage in a debate about the morality of fascism. Finally, Russell,
then almost ninety, replied. In a short letter, he explained why he
would not engage with Mosley:

It is always difficult to respond to people whose ethos is so alien,
and in fact, repellent, to one's own. It is not that I take exception
to the general points made by you but that every ounce of my
energy has been devoted to an active opposition to cruel bigotry,
compulsive violence, and the sadistic persecution which has
characterised the philosophy and practice of fascism.
   I feel obliged to say that the emotional universes we inhabit are
so distinct, and in deepest ways opposed, that nothing fruitful or
sincere could ever emerge from association between us.

If I was to disagree with myself about the premise of this book,
here's where I'd start: productive disagreement is all very well, but
the truth is that some people don't deserve it. Yes, we can learn
from our opponents, but not all of them have something to teach

us. Of course we should try to engage our antagonists, but not those who hold views that make them unworthy of our attention. Some opponents must either be ignored or defeated. Fight or flight are sometimes the only good options, and it's dangerously naive to think otherwise.

Maybe. But it's difficult to identify who those people are in advance. Very few people are separated from each other by an impassable gulf of belief. Liberals and white supremacists? What, so Mandela shouldn't have negotiated with Viljoen – or, come to that, the South African government? You might argue he only did so because he had to – because he needed something from them. But that's the point. We often need something from people whose views we find repugnant, even if it's only fair treatment or peaceful cohabitation. Diplomats have successfully negotiated or mediated disputes with some of the most terrible people on earth. Interrogators, too, talk to people who have committed awful crimes and hold vile beliefs, and still manage to develop productive conversations. Russell didn't need to engage with Mosley, because Mosley was a spent force by then, an irrelevance, and Russell's own time was pressingly short.

I don't think we can say that some people are impossible to engage with on the basis of the views they hold. What I do believe, though, is that some people are impossible to engage with because of *the way they disagree*. There are those who are relentlessly closed-minded, aggressive and mean-spirited, who always assume bad faith, who always grandstand and never listen. This is a sensibility or attitude, not an ideology, and it can be found anywhere, not just in politics. Within relationships, families and workplaces, you will always find people who fundamentally do not want to play anybody's game but their own: people who might pretend to disagree productively, only to suck you into futile battles. Note that Russell refers to Mosley's 'emotional universe' being very different to his own.

Having said that, we have a persistent, habitual tendency to over-estimate the size of this group. Especially when we haven't had much sleep. By which I mean, our brains are always looking for ways to conserve energy, and one way to do that is to shrink the number of people and views that we deem worthy of our attention. So we reach for labels – racists, deplorables, idiots – that give us an out. That surge of certainty you feel when you dismiss someone isn't a signal that you're right, it's the satisfaction of getting out of some work. Many of those we quickly judge to be a waste of our time are worth engaging with, either because they might teach us something or because they are more ambivalent than they appear at first. Alfred Wilson could have dismissed the guy with a Confederate flag as not worthy of his effort. He's glad he didn't.

• • •

Still, this is all very *reasonable*, isn't it? This is an eminently reasonable book, with its emphasis on hearing each other out, on listening attentively, on seeing each other's perspective. It's so . . . polite.

I value politeness. But then, I live a comfortable life, relatively free from fear. People who are desperate, who are afraid, who feel they've been screwed over, might wish for something other than polite discourse. The very notion of productive disagreement can seem, from where they're standing, like an item of luxury furniture. What use is it when the roof is falling in? Besides, some things are worth getting angry over – even unreasonably angry. Politeness can get in the way of honesty. Even I don't want to live in a world where everyone has to be respectful of everyone's feelings all the time. Some people's views – and some people – are just irredeemably awful. There can be a bracing truthfulness to *fuck you.*

Injunctions to be polite can be a way of preserving the status quo. What did genteel Southern whites say about civil rights protesters in the 1960s? That they were uncouth, and not worth listening to, let alone disagreeing with. In his 'Letter from Birmingham Jail', Martin Luther King expressed impatience with white Americans who said they supported his cause but could not support direct action. The white moderate, said King, 'is more devoted to "order" than to justice'.

Change is uncomfortable and even painful for those who stand to lose from it, and placing a high importance on good manners can be a way of putting it off. In corporate boardrooms, people are only taken seriously if they conform to certain rules of self-presentation, especially in formal, high-context organisational cultures. It becomes practically impossible to stand up and shout: UNLESS WE CHANGE AND CHANGE FAST WE ARE TOTALLY SCREWED – even though many bankruptcies and disastrous decisions might have been averted had somebody felt able to do so.

Politeness can also be a means of controlling the conversation – a power move. It can ramify into a complex code that, like any code, hands an advantage to those who know it. The British class system is still full of fine distinctions about allowable ways to speak, which has helped to keep the whole dusty edifice in place. In its extreme form, political correctness gets used like this – as a linguistic technology used to distinguish insiders from outsiders, enabling educated elites to hoard authority. People who have something discomforting to tell us are kept out of the conversation: 'He's just offensive. She's too emotional.'

Disagreement shouldn't be a blood sport, but it shouldn't be a bloodless one either. If all public discourse was conducted like a dinner party, we wouldn't hear cries of pain and shouts of rage. Sometimes we must throw ourselves into argument without thinking too hard about which rules we're breaking or whose sensibilities we might offend. But this raises a hard question. What's the difference between being righteous and being rude, between speaking truth in someone's face and humiliating them?

• • •

Anyone who thinks that online political disagreements are uniquely vituperative should take a look at religious arguments from 500 years ago. Here is Martin Luther giving his opinion on popes:

You are desperate, thorough arch-rascals, the very scum of all the most evil people on earth. You are full of all the worst devils in hell – full, full, and so full that you can do nothing but vomit, throw and blow out devils!

Luther's rudeness (he also once wrote about the 'dear little ass-pope' who licks the devil's anus) was strategic. He didn't think it was possible to call out the pervasive and grotesque corruption of the Roman Catholic Church politely – to do so would be to neuter the potency of his anger. To protest effectively, he and his followers would have to disrupt *how* the establishment spoke as well as *what* it said. They had a moral duty to offend delicate sensibilities.

Teresa Bejan, a political philosopher at Oxford University, has studied how the modern idea of 'civility' was formed in the religious and political controversies that raged in the long wake of Luther's Reformation, as people in Europe and the New World struggled with the new problem of 'tolerance' – whether and how it was possible for people to live alongside those whose beliefs they despised. Bejan noticed something that the debates of colonial America had in common with those of the present: handwringing about a decline in civility. Anglicans would lecture atheists on how offensive their views were, without addressing their arguments. Quakers were shunned for not doffing hats and for their disgusting habit of shaking hands – if they couldn't even be civil, didn't they deserve to be persecuted?

Bejan set out to write a book arguing that 'civility' is a tool fashioned by the powerful with the aim of suppressing dissent and disagreement. But in the course of her research, she changed her mind. Someone persuaded her that the true purpose of civility is to create space for uncomfortable and even angry disagreements. That person was an Englishman, born in 1603.

• • •

In January 1636, Roger Williams put on a heavy coat, stuffed his pockets with as much dried corn paste as would fit, and stepped out of his house into a freezing New England night. Williams didn't know where he was going, but he knew he had to go. Soldiers from Boston were on their way to arrest him. Their orders were to put him on a ship back to England, where he would be thrown in jail.

Carrying corn paste for sustenance was a trick Williams had learnt from the American Indian tribes he had got to know over the years. He would need every ounce of it. It was a violently cold winter – some thirty-five years later, Williams recalled 'the snow wch I feel yet' – and he had no place to go. For fourteen weeks, he did not know 'what Bread or Bed did meane'. He would not have survived had local tribes not taken him in.

Williams was a man of exceptional energy, confidence and charm. He also had a ferocious appetite for argument. Born in London, the son of a tailor, Williams somehow came to the attention of Sir Edward Coke, an English barrister and judge famous for his defences of civil rights against the crown. Coke saw something in the young man and scooped him up, appointing him to his household as a secretary. Williams was vaulted into England's elite, attending first Charterhouse School and then Cambridge University, where he became friends with the poet John Milton.

Like Milton, Williams was intensely curious about the world, and bursting with religious zeal. Both men were drawn to the rebellious, anti-establishment Protestant movement known as Puritanism. On graduation, Williams took holy orders and became a private chaplain to a Puritan aristocrat. But the English government under Charles I was cracking down on these troublesome non-conformists so, in 1631, Williams set sail for New England to join the Massachusetts Bay Colony.

Even by the standards of Puritans, Williams was uncompromising. Almost as soon as he got off the boat in America, aged twenty-eight, he was invited to be theologian to the Boston church, a prestigious position that would afford him a leading role in the creation of this new society. It was the opportunity of a lifetime, yet Williams spurned it. He declared the local Puritans to be insufficiently pious, since they allowed their congregations to mix with worshippers from the Church of England. He also disagreed with the Bay's leaders about the extent of their authority: Williams believed government should have nothing to do with religion. Scandalised, Boston's leaders made it clear to Williams he was no longer welcome. Williams moved to Salem, where he hoped to find a purer Christian society. Unfortunately, he found faults everywhere in Salem as well and loudly declared them, much to the annoyance of his neighbours.

Around this time, Williams began visiting the Wampanoag and Narragansett tribes, making trading partners and friendships. He learnt their languages, partly so that he could debate religion with them and also because he was curious about how they lived. He wanted to know about how they hunted, how they raised children, how they governed themselves, how they worshipped. Remarkably for his time, Williams didn't regard Indian civilisation to be inferior to that of Europeans. He thought the Indians were heathens who would burn in hell, but he treated them as equals, stating that, 'Nature knows no difference between Europe and Americans in blood, birth, bodies, &c.' Williams went so far as to publicly accuse the colonists of stealing the natives' land, declaring the entire American project to be a fraud.

His fellow Puritans, who regarded the tribes as barbarians, were outraged. Fed up with this troublemaker who refused to hold his tongue, the Massachusetts authorities voted to banish Williams from the colony. He was ordered to leave within six weeks or face imprisonment, or worse. They sent soldiers: hence his escape in the middle of the night.

After wandering in the unforgiving wilderness, Williams was offered shelter and food by first the Wampanoag and then the Narragansett. He never forgot their hospitality. His friendships with them opened the door to his next and greatest act.

• • •

In exile from societies he didn't want to live in, Williams reflected on the kind of society in which he did. He knew that everyone would be free to worship how they wanted. This was not, to be clear, because he was open-minded in the way we would recognise today. Williams was a religious fundamentalist. As far as he was concerned, anyone who didn't meet his exacting standards of worship – which was pretty much everyone – was damned. Teresa Bejan writes, 'By the end of his life, he worshipped in a congregation of only two, him and his wife – and he may not have been entirely sure about her.' But he had a fierce commitment to the integrity of everyone's personal conscience, and believed people should be allowed to go to hell in their own way. His ideal society was one in which everyone was trying to convert each other but nobody could force anyone to do so.

The chief of the Narragansett effectively gifted Williams some land on a cove, where Williams started a settlement. He later wrote, 'Having, of a sense of God's merciful providence unto me in my distress, called the place PROVIDENCE, I desired it might be for a shelter for persons distressed for conscience.' His family and those of a dozen or so followers from Salem joined him. Williams relinquished his rights to the land to the common ownership of the town. He drafted a constitution which, unlike the founding documents of Massachusetts, or of every other European settlement in the Americas, made no mention of religion. Williams, the most devout of men, believed that it was shamefully arrogant of humans to enlist God into the mundane business of government.

So it was that Providence, Rhode Island, became a magnet for all the radicals, heretics, troublemakers and contrarians in New England. Anyone who was 'distressed for conscience' – who wished to escape the enforced orthodoxy of neighbouring colonies – made their way there. They included Quakers, Jews and Catholics. Almost in spite of himself, Roger Williams, Puritan firebrand, founded the most tolerant society the world had ever seen.

• • •

In 1643 Williams sailed back to England on a perilous mission to secure a patent for his fledgling colony. During his stay, he wrote a document that became his most important written legacy. In London, he reconnected with Milton, who put him in touch with a publisher. *The Bloudy Tenent of Persecution for Cause of Conscience* was published in 1644, when England was at war with itself, and the state was clamping down on pamphlets and books spreading unorthodox opinions.

The Bloudy Tenent made a powerful case for extending toleration not only to all Protestant sects but to American Indians, Jews, Muslims and even to those he called 'Antichristians' – Catholics. This went well beyond what anyone had argued for before, and it made *The Bloudy Tenent* incendiary. On publication, the English parliament ordered it to be burned, and might have had Williams arrested were he not already on a boat back to America, patent in hand.

Williams's version of toleration meant more than a grudging consent to let others live as they saw fit. While he was very clear that the only true religion was his brand of Christianity, he believed that unbelievers must be actively engaged in an effort of 'civill converse and conversation' in order to save their souls. He really did mean conversation – a back and forth. After he told the Indians the story of Adam and Eve, Williams would listen as they told him their creation story, if only to equip himself better for argument with them.

At the same time that Williams founded his colony, William Penn led another group of dissenters in Pennsylvania. The early Quakers were uncompromising social radicals who deliberately engaged in offensive behaviour, such as going naked in the streets, or walking into church services and shouting down the minister while banging pots. Williams hated this behaviour. It implied, he said, that 'There are no Men to be respected in the World but themselves.' A functioning, tolerant society, he said, depended on 'the Bond of *Civility*'. By this he didn't mean what we usually associate with that word: decorum, manners, tact – Williams, as you may have gathered, was not a very decorous man. He meant whatever it was that enabled everyone to speak their minds. Williams expected people to disagree with each other about the things they cared about, passionately and unapologetically. To do otherwise, he thought, would be a betrayal of conscience. Toleration required freedom of speech so that people could compete for converts and try to persuade one another. The 'war of words' was evidence of an honest society.

For Williams, living with people who disagree with us about the most important things in life may be tense, unpleasant and infuriating, but it's still better than living with people with whom we only pretend to agree. It was everyone's duty, not to seek harmony or to stay silent, but to keep on disagreeing about the things that matter. In his sense, civility is not a code so much as a principle: the minimum standard of behaviour necessary to encourage your opponent to talk back.

Roger Williams helped Teresa Bejan to conceive of civility, not as etiquette or manners, but as whatever the participants in a tough conversation need to do to keep each other in the room, whether that room has four walls or constitutes a whole society. After all, even the fiercest critics of civility expect some minimal civility from those with whom they argue. The alternative is not arguing at all.

During the eighteenth century, religious divisions receded as commercial society brought more people into frequent contact with others from different backgrounds. English aristocrats bought supplies from Jewish merchants; Anglicans did business with Catholics. Politeness oiled the wheels of this complex cross-cultural dance. The Enlightenment philosopher Anthony Ashley-Cooper was the first to use the word 'politeness' in the modern sense. He took a term associated with jewellery – with polished stones – and elevated it to a social virtue: 'We polish one another, and rub off our Corners and rough Sides, by a sort of amicable collision.' Unlike decorum, which was a sign of your class, politeness was democratic: the French novelist Mademoiselle de Scudéry described it as 'wanting not to be the *tyrant* of conversation'.

Politeness is not merely superficial or decorative. Adhering to a shared set of rules is a way of liberating conversation among people who don't know each other well, as Kal Turnbull's experiment showed us. The linguist Robin Lakoff (once married to George Lakoff, quoted in the first chapter) boiled down polite behaviour to three guidelines: *Don't impose. Give options. Make your interlocutor feel good.* I love the simplicity of this and, as you'll note, Lakoff's rules are echoed and elaborated on in this book. But ultimately all rules are a crutch, or a guiderail, that we can dispense with if the relationship is strong enough. We should be civil with those we don't know, and aim to know them well enough that we can be uncivil.

• • •

In recent years there has been a spate of books and articles on *persuasion* – on how to overcome people's stubborn resistance to reasoned argument. The question these tracts really seem to be answering is, 'How can *we* – the enlightened, the reasonable, the informed – win *them* – the bigoted, the backward, the tribal – over?' It's as if the authors and their implied readers somehow stand outside or above the messiness of human discourse, coolly assessing its flaws.

Online, people love to *smash*, *destroy* and *cancel*. The unspoken aim is an end to disagreement itself. The same impulse is buried in those treatises on persuasion. No wonder the people on the other end of this persuasion often turn out to be stubborn and resistant to the point of bloody-mindedness. I have been that person too, digging in unreasonably because I don't want to be pushed over. You dig in because you sense that this is a power game, in which the persuader demands that you be open-minded while remaining resolutely closed-minded himself.

Disagreement should be a way of helping each other overcome the blindspots and refusals of reality that we all have. But if you're focused only on persuasion, you won't really hear the other person, because you've closed off the possibility that you might change your own mind. When listening becomes a mere tactic, it's no longer listening. A better question than 'How can I persuade?' might be: 'How can I make this disagreement fruitful?'

In his book, *Finite and Infinite Games*, James Carse made a profound distinction: 'A finite game is played for the purpose of winning, an infinite game for the purpose of continuing the play.' A *finite* game – for example, a game of chess or football – has a precisely defined beginning and end. The game is over when someone has won and the other has lost, or when an agreed period of time runs out. An *infinite* game has no defined end and cannot be definitively won or lost. The players win or lose in the course of play but their wins and losses are just moments in an endless unfolding. A game of football is a finite game; the game of football is an infinite game.

In a finite game, the rules exist so that a winner can be agreed and the game can come to an end. In an infinite game, the rules are there to prevent anyone from winning definitively. The players in an infinite game are always looking for ways to extend it. When the game is threatened by the definitive victory of one party, the rules are changed to prevent that happening. The whole point is to keep the game going, and to bring as many people as possible into play. In ancient Athens, Socrates turned debate from a finite game into an infinite one.

Athens was the birthplace of democracy, which is itself an infinite game. Its rules are designed to maintain equilibrium; to balance competing interests and powers, containing but not abolishing conflict. That includes elections, which are finite games, with victors and losers. Elections are fiercely fought, but there is – or should be – a recognition by all the players that no party, no person, is bigger than the infinite game. The rules of a democracy change when the need arises, because they are designed so that no one party can dominate for ever. As more people feel free to take part in the game, more talents are unlocked, more new ideas are generated, more progress can be made. The aim of democracy is more democracy.

The same is true at every level of human collaboration. Meetings and marriages go better when the participants see their disagreements as part of an infinite game. The aim of a marital argument should be to reset the relationship in a way that makes it stronger; the aim of a workplace dispute should be a better future for the organisation. Sometimes we want to win so badly we forget that. Unscrupulous politicians bend or break the rules that make a democracy work; business executives put their self-interest before that of their team; couples say wounding things to each other that imperil the relationship. In an infinite game, even when you disagree fiercely with someone, you want to connect to and learn from them because you want the conversation to continue. The aim is to find new ways to disagree. It's not like a game of tennis, when you're trying to smash an unreturnable volley over the net. It's more like a group of friends keeping a beach ball in the air.

Earlier on I referred to the custom of not discussing religion or politics at the dinner table. Like all customs, this one is not universal. When I mentioned it to the French writer Clementine Goldszal she was bemused. Why would you want to miss out on the best part of dinner? 'It's a French tradition to argue at the dinner table. We argue about politics. We argue about everything. It's a tradition: the family dinner turns into a political fight.' In the first few minutes of a meal, as Clementine described it to me, there is a sense of anticipation: who will be first to raise the controversy of the day? Finally, somebody tosses in a hand grenade, and boom. 'Everyone goes, "OK! Let's get into it!" It's exciting.'

You and I might not live in an argumentative culture. But we can still aspire to this vision of good argument as something nourishing and mind-expanding rather than threatening and stressful. If you treat disagreement as one move in an infinite game, rather than as a finite game in which victors walk away triumphant and losers are humiliated, it's much more fun.

What do the French do that we don't? Clementine told me, 'You have to be able to separate the person from the position they are taking.' This stops you from getting too personal and ending up in a defence–attack spiral. 'In the course of a conversation, your thought is moving. So you say things you don't necessarily agree with, for the sake of taking the argument further. I do it often.' Sometimes the argument we're making is intensely personal to us, rooted in our experience or deepest beliefs. But when there is a little distance between you and the position you're taking, you can tease out better arguments from around the table.

It helps if everyone recognises that's what you are doing; if there's an unspoken acceptance around the table that sometimes people will offer opinions they aren't fully sure of themselves yet, in order to further the discussion. But that means people need to trust each other not to say things only to upset or annoy. They need to see themselves as bound together in a shared adventure, even if it's one that only lasts until coffee. In that context, being a disagreeable person is good. It means you're taking part.

• • •

'As long as we think of difference as that which divides us, we shall dislike it; when we think of it as that which unites us we shall cherish it.' Mary Parker Follett

In the first section, we looked at how disagreement is an engine of innovation and new ideas. But it's also an act of creativity *in itself*, at least it is if it's done right. A purposeful disagreement takes two and two and makes five. What defines a pointless disagreement? I think it's a disagreement that isn't interested in creating something new.

The thinker who made me see this most clearly is Mary Parker Follett, who, though admired by scholars of management, is relatively little known today. Follett made for an unlikely management guru. Born to a prominent Boston family at the end of the nineteenth century, she studied philosophy and psychology at Harvard and Cambridge, before throwing herself into social activism. For decades, Follett worked among the poorest communities in Boston, teaching social skills to young men and helping the unemployed find jobs.

While serving on the Minimum Wage Board of Massachusetts, Follett started thinking about the nature of conflict. This was an era of frequent clashes between bosses and workers. Some bosses believed the only option was to fight the unions and crush dissent. The more thoughtful ones were open to some kind of co-operation. In 1924 Follett set out her ideas on how to deal with conflicts in a series of lectures at a club for industrialists, which put her much in demand as a consultant.

Follett told businessmen that people usually respond to conflict, of any kind, in two ways, both of which are erroneous. One is that they seek victory – they try to dominate the other. That might be OK in a competition, but it doesn't work in any situation where you need to work together. The other mistake is to *compromise*. Follett didn't believe in bargaining, in meeting halfway. She believed that when two opposing ideas clash, the optimal solution is to create a third. 'When two people arrive at a common decision, that decision is only really satisfactory if it represents an integration.' Follett was writing at a time when Darwinism was heavily in the air. To her, the clash of views was a means of generation and variation.

Follett cherished human differences of any kind. Long before it became the buzzword it is today, it was the unprecedented *diversity* of the United States that excited her. Millions of immigrants were arriving on American shores every year, and there was a fierce debate over national identity. Follett disapproved of words like 'fuse', 'melt', or 'assimilate' because they implied that people had to give up their identities; mere tolerance was intolerable to her.

She wanted any clash of different cultures to lead to 'something new which neither side possesses'.

To Follett, differences of opinion should give birth to new thinking – to progress. That meant everyone being proud to hold their own opinions even as they listened to those of everyone else. She remarked:

A friend of mine said to me, 'Open-mindedness is the whole thing, isn't it?' No it isn't; it needs just as great a respect for your own view as for that of others, and a firm upholding of it until you are convinced. Mushy people are no more good at this than stubborn people.

Finding a new solution that meets the goals of both parties, she said, is an essentially creative task, requiring 'brilliant inventiveness'. The first step to doing so is self-examination. It's amazing how contemporary-sounding Follett is on this theme. To integrate differences of opinion truly, you must 'put your cards on the table, face the real issue, uncover the conflict, bring the whole thing into the open'. Your 'sub-articulate egoisms' – things you can barely admit to yourself and what we might now call triggers – must be unearthed. You also, said Follett, have to listen to the other party – *really* listen – to hear the unspoken as well as the spoken. All this requires a kind of emotional honesty that managers today, let alone in the 1920s, find hard.

When I read Follett's view of conflict it struck a resonant chord. The best disagreements, she showed me, neither reinforce nor eradicate a difference, but make something new out of it. Persuasion is a noble and necessary art, and I like it when I make someone think again, but my ultimate aim is not to get you to agree with me. I want your thinking to improve my thinking; your experience to modulate and enrich my own. I want us to disagree creatively: to make something new and better out of our diverse opinions than either of us could have conceived of alone. That way we both win.

As I write these words, the world is in the grip of a pandemic which has put most of our daily disagreements into humbling perspective, and served as a reminder of just how much energy we waste in futile argument. The best that can be said of it is that it represents a chance to reset entrenched habits of behaviour that have not been serving us as well as they might. I hope that can include the way we disagree.

It is often remarked that we humans must put our differences aside if we are to defeat our existential threats and face the future with justified optimism. I'm not sure that's quite right. Yes, it is vital we recognise that we sink or swim together. But we must also put our differences to work. Without robust, honest, creative disagreement, any progress we make will be too slow, any unity we achieve superficial. Maybe there is something of which I want to persuade you, after all.

16. Rules of Productive Argument Summarised

First, connect
Before getting to the content of the disagreement, establish a relationship of trust.

Let go of the rope
To disagree well you have to give up on trying to control what the other person thinks and feels.

Give face
Disagreements become toxic when they become status battles. The skilful disagreer makes every effort to make their adversary feel good about themselves.

Check your weirdness
Behind many disagreements is a clash of cultures that seem strange to each other. Don't assume that you are the normal one.

Get curious
The rush to judgement stops us listening and learning. Instead of trying to win the argument, try and be interested – and interesting.

Make wrong strong

Mistakes can be positive if you apologise rapidly and authentically. They enable you to show humility, which can strengthen the relationship and ease the conversation.

Disrupt the script

Hostile arguments get locked into simple and predictable patterns. To make the disagreement more productive, introduce novelty and variation. Be surprising.

Share constraints

Disagreement benefits from a set of agreed norms and boundaries that support self-expression. Rules create freedom.

Only get mad on purpose

No amount of theorising can fully prepare us for the emotional experience of a disagreement. Sometimes your worst adversary is yourself.

Golden rule: Be real

All rules are subordinate to the golden rule: make an honest human connection.

17. Toolkit of Productive Argument

Define the disagreement. A surprising amount of disagreements are not disagreements at all but misunderstandings or antipathies in disguise. When you're stuck in an unproductive argument, take a step back and ask, what precisely are we disagreeing about (if anything)?

Seek out good disagreers. We are often advised to open our minds and our social media feeds to people who have different views from us. That's fine in theory but in practice it can be counter-productive. What is crucial is to find people who say things you find objectionable in a way that makes you respect and like them.

Feel the burn. For those of us who are not naturally confrontational, it's always tempting to turn away from any conflict. But just as we learn to interpret the pain of exercise as a signal that we're getting stronger, so we can learn to welcome the discomfort of a disagreement.

Frame your opponents positively. You might have to fake it at first, but it always helps a conversation go well if you like and respect your interlocutor – and if they feel it. George Thompson, a former cop, used to say, 'The moment they sense you dislike them, they can ignore what you say.'

 # Feel the steel. It's sometimes said that we should argue with the strongest case for the opposing view, not the weakest. Instead of a straw man, build a 'steel man'. But this can't just be an intellectual exercise. Let yourself feel the emotional force of the other side's position – inhabit it somehow, if only partially and fleetingly.

 # Beware reactance. People are fiercely defensive of their own agency and autonomy, and in a tense conversation, any attempt at correction can trigger a reaction. Psychologists call this 'reactance'. It's why the righting reflex is counter-productive and it's behind the backfire effect. When primed for threats, people focus on the relationship signals and disregard the content. To be heard, you need to work harder at sending the right signals.

 # Preview the disagreement. To avoid triggering a threat state in the other person by taking them unawares, let them know you're about to disagree before getting into the disagreement. Acknowledge that you may be wrong and they may be right. This gives them a chance to adjust mentally before hearing you out (this can be particularly useful when disagreeing with a more powerful person).

 # Resist negative reciprocation. When a person is aggressive or hostile or sarcastic towards us, our instinct is to reciprocate. If the conversation is to stand a chance of being productive, someone needs to break the circuit.

 # Create a culture of positive argument. Whether it's at work, in a sports team or with your partner, make it normal for everyone to challenge decisions, speak up about doubts and address annoyances. When you're used to tackling the small issues this way, the big ones are less likely to tear you apart.

Reward dissenters. People who speak up in meetings to offer different views are often punished, albeit in subtle ways, for doing so. Leaders should make an effort to show they genuinely value challenges to a prevailing view, even when they disagree or overrule them.

Don't tell them what to do or how to feel. Never in the history of the world has anyone responded well to the imperative 'Grow up'. As with all injunctions ('Be reasonable'; 'Calm down') it simply annoys. Telling people how to behave, or worse, how to feel, nearly always backfires. Be alert to what's behind the other person's view: are you in an argument with their position or their emotion? If the latter, your clever arguments will not break the deadlock. Perhaps you need to acknowledge their underlying feelings.

Be wary of 'you'. In the midst of a disagreement, the word 'you' can trigger an identity threat in your interlocutor's mind ('*You* do this, *you* seem to think that . . .') Although it's not always possible to avoid it, use 'you' sparingly in tense conversations.

Cut the 'but'. As with 'you', it's unlikely you will be able to eradicate 'but'. But – hear me out – 'but' tends to snag on the other person's defences. Just replacing it with 'though' can soften a sentence's edge.

Go to the heat. At the workplace, conflicts are often avoided nobody wants to confront them. But that allows tensions to fester. Leaders should be unembarrassed about acknowledging conflicts

and they can organise meetings specifically to air them. Perhaps over beer.

Lead with weakness. Often the other person feels as if you're trying to dominate them or prove your superiority in some way (and, let's face it, often you are). To allay that suspicion, show vulnerability, admit anxiety, confess uncertainty, even – or especially – if you're in a position of authority. Unilaterally disarming is your best chance of getting others to lower their defences.

Check for understanding. *So if I'm hearing you right, what you're saying is . . .* The practice of checking in with your opposite number like this is good for both of you: you get clarity, and they are reassured that you're listening. Done honestly, it can open up the conversation.

Reverse the emotional polarity. It can be good to articulate your emotions directly in a disagreement, but to avoid escalation you can do so in a calm and even tone. Conversely, when discussing factual information, you can infuse some life and passion into it, so that you don't sound like you're holding forth from a chilly plateau of intellectual superiority.

Spot the truth in the other's mistake. Therapists dealing with delusional patients say that there is usually some kind of truth in the delusion, even if it's just an emotional one, and that part of their job is to identify what it is. In arguments, when you're encountering views with which you strongly disagree, make an effort to find a kernel of truth in what's being said. At the very least it will help you respect your interlocutor.

 # Stop trying to be right. Of course, we all love being right, but it's a cheap satisfaction compared to learning about something or someone, and it often gets in the way. Try not to let the urge to win the argument dominate your attitude to the conversation. Conversely, nobody wants to be told they're wrong, so if you first convey to the other person that they are *in some way right* they are more likely to be open to your point of view. After all, what matters is not that you are right, but that we are right.

 # Acknowledge expertise. You shouldn't always defer to experts, because sometimes experts are wrong. But when your interlocutor knows more than you about the topic at hand, either through experience or learning, it's wise to start in the one-down position and acknowledge their epistemic authority. That way, you're more likely to learn and they're more likely to listen.

 # Practise losing. I can't put this any better than Stephen Llano, an associate professor of rhetoric at St John's University in New York: 'Losing an argument is a very important democratic art that we never practise. It's vital that we learn how to live with our persuasive failures. There's no great secret to it, just practice. The more time we spend arguing with one another in low-stakes situations, the better we will be when the situation calls for serious consideration.'

 # Believe less. Outside of religious faith, believing is not an end in itself. People who *enjoy* believing tend to stop reflecting on *why* they believe what they believe. They also tend to lose the ability to listen to other views. The fewer beliefs you hold inviolate, the more cognitive freedom and empathy you have.

 # Be sceptical of your own tribe. Nearly all of us are aligned with groups, formal or informal, who share a similar set of opinions. There's nothing wrong with that, but when you follow the script of your group too closely, you surrender some of your own ability to think. That's not good for you and ultimately it's bad for the collective intelligence of your group, too. Use your disagreement skills to probe the beliefs of your own side, as well as those of the other.

 # Don't just correct – create. Following Mary Parker Follett, don't simply try to impose your view, and don't be satisfied with a compromise. Instead, seek out the integration: the alchemic reaction that occurs when opposing views collide and transform into something new. It's not always possible, but it's the prize.

Acknowledgements

This book is the product of many illuminating conversations and useful disagreements. My primary debt of thanks is to the practitioners and scholars who generously contributed their time, expertise and stories. They include Robert Agne, Ellis Amdur, Rob Bardsley, Emma Barrett, Teresa Bejan, Agnes Callard, Peter Coleman, Bill Donohue, Bertis Downs, Catarina Dutilh Novaes, Eleanor Fellowes, Clementine Goldszal, Ben Ho, Neil Janin, Steven Klein, Jeremy Lascelles, Terje Rød-Larsen, William Miller, Simon Napier-Bell, Mike O'Neill, Miriam Oostinga, Nickola Overall, Emmanuelle Peters, Gabrielle Rifkind, Jake Rollnick, Stephen Rollnick, Michelle Russell, Alan Sillars, Lloyd Smith, Nathan Smith, Elisa Sobo, Elizabeth Stokoe, Garry Tan, Paul Taylor, Kal Turnbull, Gregory Trevors, Bill Weger, Simon Wells, Jonathan Wender, Alfred Wilson, Warren Zanes. Thanks to Emily and Laurence Alison for sharing their work and their insights with me. Thanks to the Memphis police department, and to all the highly impressive officers who attended the Polis training and did not object to the presence of a weedy Englishman with a notebook. Thanks to Don Gulla and his team for their warmth and hospitality and for fascinating conversations over spare ribs and fried chicken. Special thanks to Susan Bro for talking to me, so eloquently, about the life and death of her remarkable daughter Heather Heyer.

Thank you to my agent Toby Mundy, who patiently helped me shape my inchoate thoughts into a viable book proposal. Thank you to everyone at Faber & Faber, especially Laura Hassan for her confidence in this book and her sustaining enthusiasm; Rowan Cope for the care and attentiveness she showed the manuscript, and for cracking the title; Marigold Atkey for her brilliant notes and moral support; Donald Sommerville for his assiduous copy edit. Thank you also to the highly professional team at HarperCollins, especially Hollis Heimbouch for positive energy and straight talk. I am lucky to have had an absurdly talented team of informal readers. Thank you, first of all, to the indispensable Stephen Brown, my emergency manuscript doctor: without you this book would not have made it out of its first draft alive, let alone become fit for publication. Thanks to Tom Stafford for science-checking a draft and for his helpful notes. Thank you to my brilliant friends Helen Lewis and Oliver Franklin-Wells and to Oli in particular for his notes on the opening chapter. Thank you to Jonathan Shainin and David Wolf of *The Guardian*, who commissioned and helped shape an article on interrogation which became the starting point for this book. Thanks to Teresa Bejan and Agnes Callard for reading and improving the chapters in which I cite their work. All errors are my own.

Profound thanks to Clydette de Groot, Audrey Chapuis, and the marvellous team at the American Library in Paris. I am so grateful for the opportunity to take up a fellowship there – working on this book in Paris is something I'll remember for the rest of my life. The library and its community proved vital sources of inspiration. Thanks to Pamela Druckerman and Simon Kuper; to Simon in particular for pointing me to John Carlin's book on Nelson Mandela. Thank you to the many friends, too many to mention here – also I'm scared of leaving someone out – who have talked through ideas, shared insights, or simply provided encouragement. Thank you to my mother Margaret and brother Stephen, who, along with my late father Bryan, grounded me in the arts of disagreement. Thank you to my children Io and Douglas, life; without you would contain fewer disagreements and yet be so much less agreeable. Thank you, finally, to my best editor and best friend, Alice Wignall, to whom I am lucky enough to be married. Alice, I love you and I look forward to many more arguments, productive and otherwise. Oh, and thanks for letting me take up that fellowship, it puts me for ever in your debt. You'll always have Paris.

Notes

For the most part I've mentioned my sources in the text and they can be found in the bibliography; here I'll note those I haven't explicitly cited, along with any additional observations.

PART ONE

1. Beyond Fight or Flight

The study of discussion threads in a BBC forum is by Chmiel et al. Edward Hall introduced the concept of high- and low-context cultures in his 1976 book *Beyond Culture*. The example of *bubuzuke* in Kyoto is cited in Nishimura et al. (its original source is literature from the Kyoto Tourist Board). The quote, 'the constant and sometimes never-ending use of words', is also from Nishimura. On this topic I also drew on papers by Croucher, and Kim. The study on the diversity of news diets is the Reuters Institute Digital News Report, reported on by Fletcher et al. in *NiemanLab*. The Columbia University study is by Sun and Slepian. The Harvard Business School study is by Noam Wasserman. For evidence on how anger affects the way we perceive people and make decisions, see DeSteno.

Since they are both classed as 'negative emotions' in psychology, sadness and anger are often studied together. It turns out that they have contrasting effects on our thinking. In a study by Litvak et al., undergraduates primed to feel either sad or angry were asked to imagine themselves in an emotionally charged scenario (for instance, you invite someone you've just met to your house party because you think there might be a chance of romance, and they turn up with a girlfriend, leaving you feeling embarrassed). People feeling sad were more likely to think reflectively and analytically about the ambiguities of the situation; those primed to be in an angry mood were quicker to assign blame and identify culprits.

The other studies I refer to on parent–child conflict are by Brett Laursen ('three or four conflicts with parents') and Ryan Adams, with Laursen ('a 2007 study').

2. How Disagreement Brings Us Closer

My account of William Ickes's experiments is drawn from his book, *Everyday Mind Reading*. The conversation between Penny and her husband is recorded in Sillars et al., 'Stepping into the stream of thought: Cognition during marital conflict'. My conversation with Alan Sillars was important to everything I say in this chapter, including the distinction between relationship and content. For the section on workplace conflict I drew on the meta-analysis by Carsten et al., as well as De Wit. 'Both male and female senior execs were expected to conform to dominant norms' is from Martin and Meyerson.

3. How Disagreement Makes Us Smarter

'Psychologists have now established beyond doubt that people are more likely to notice and consider evidence that confirms what they believe . . .' For a review of evidence for confirmation bias, see Nickerson. On evidence for 'intelligent and educated people are just better at persuading themselves they're right' – see for instance the paper by Richard West et al. The story of John Yudkin is based on my article for the *Guardian*, 'The Sugar Conspiracy'.

4. How Disagreement Inspires Us

For my account of the Wright Brothers' arguments I relied on Mark Eppler's marvellous book, *The Wright Way*. He called their approach to problem-solving in argument 'forging'. The stories and interviews about rock groups are largely drawn from my article for *1843* magazine, 'A Rocker's Guide To Management'. For anecdotes about the Beatles I relied on Mark Lewisohn's definitive history of the group's early years, *Tune In*. Bormann's theory is described in *Group Dynamics* by Donelson Forsyth. I found the story about Crick and Watson in Joshua Wolf Shenk's excellent book, *Powers of Two*.

PART TWO

5. First, Connect

The video and partial transcript of Susan Bro's eulogy for her daughter Heather Heyer can be found at https://www.buzzfeednews.com/article/coralewis/heres-heather-heyers-mothers-eulogy-they-wanted-to-shut-her. My account of Heather's murder is drawn from published accounts and from conversations with Susan Bro and Alfred Wilson. Susan told me that there is footage of Heather, shortly before she was killed, going over to one of the young neo-Nazis and attempting to engage her in conversation. 'Can you tell me why you came? Can you tell me why you believe what you believe?' The woman simply said, repeatedly, 'No comment.' Please visit the website of the Heather Heyer Foundation, which has established a scholarship programme providing financial assistance to young people passionate about social change.

The significance of a pause at the start of a phone conversation is observed in Elizabeth Stokoe's fascinating book *Talk: The Science of Conversation*. The observation by Eli Pariser was made in an interview with *Wired*, conducted by Jessi Hempel.

6. Let Go of the Rope

The interrogation video I witnessed, and my interviews with the Alisons, Stephen Rollnick, and Steven Klein, are based on an article for the *Guardian* I researched and wrote in 2017 (which was also informed by an interview with William Miller). Details have been changed including the name of the interviewee in the video. The quotes from the interrogation are verbatim. My permission to view the tape was negotiated with the UK counter-terrorist police when I was writing the piece.

Carli Leon is quoted in a 2018 *Voice of America News* article by Sadie Witkowski.

The reference to 'public health officials' and Emma Wagner is from a *New York Times* article by Jan Hoffman. The 2011 study on therapy is by Freda McManus et al., and the German study is by Ziem and Hoyer.

7. Give Face

For the Mandela story I relied on John Carlin's marvellous portrait of the man, *Knowing Mandela*, which I strongly recommend. The Twitter study is by Zhu and Lerman. The story of Laura Chasin is told in Peter Coleman's book, *The Five Percent*. A transcript and video of Ocasio-Cortez's discussion of disagreement can be found here https://theintercept.com/2019/03/09/alexandria-ocasio-cortez-aoc-sxsw.

8. Check Your Weirdness

I drew on multiple sources for my account of the Waco incident, including books by Thibodeau and Reavis. My biggest debt is to Jane Docherty's erudite and penetrating analysis of the negotiations, *Learning Lessons From Waco* (and a subsequent interview she gave, cited). I'm also indebted to Malcolm Gladwell's superb article for the *New Yorker*. The 'completely sadistic' quote is from Danny Coulson's memoir of working for the FBI's Hostage Rescue Team, *No Heroes*. For my account of Joe Henrich's work I drew on an interview with him conducted by Ethan Watters for *Pacific Standard*. For Richard Lewis's analysis of cultural differences in negotiation, see his book *When Cultures Collide*.

10. Make Wrong Strong

I owe thanks to Paul Taylor for my introduction to Miriam Oostinga's work on apologies in hostage negotiation. I made the connection to Ben Ho's work after hearing an episode of the excellent *Freakonomics* podcast, devoted to apology (the podcast is hosted by Stephen Dubner). Costly signals come in many forms. In the eighteenth century, pirates flew the skull and crossbones flag because nobody else would dare to. Piracy was illegal and punishable by death. The pirates' victims were therefore more likely to surrender without a struggle if they saw the flag, since they knew they were dealing with recklessly flamboyant criminals.

11. Disrupt the Script

For my account of the Oslo negotiations I relied on Jane Corbin's compelling and authoritative book, as well as an email conversation with Terje Rød-Larsen. I first came across the story after watching the brilliant play *Oslo* by J. T. Rogers. Peter Coleman also runs the Intractable Conflicts Lab, encountered earlier. For much more on the dynamics of conflict I recommend his excellent book, *The Five Percent*.

12. Share Constraints

Change My View continues at Reddit but Kal Turnbull has now established a new and independent website and app called Ceasefire (ceasefire.net).

I advise you to check it out and perhaps test some of your beliefs there. The Cornell study of CMV discussions is by Chenhao Tan et al. The finding that longer replies are more persuasive than shorter ones chimes with the findings of an investigation into a change that Twitter made to its platform in 2017, when it doubled the 140-character limit to 280. A statistical analysis published in the *Journal of Communication* (Jaidker et al.) revealed that the change made political discourse on the site more polite, analytical and constructive.

13. Only Get Mad on Purpose

The University College London study is by Shergill et al.

In Japan, Ellis Amdur studied a 400-year-old martial art called *araki-ryu*. For the first three months, the only technique that he was permitted to practise was serving sake to his teacher in a way that concealed his intention. He carried the sake on a *sanpo*: a traditional wooden tray that must be carried at eye level. At the very moment he served the tea he was to draw a concealed mock knife (made of oak) and attempt an assassination. If his teacher detected the merest hint of intent to attack, he would take out a wooden weapon and strike or stab his pupil, often leaving bruises.

The Huthwaite research findings have been summarised by the company's founder Neil Rackham in a paper called 'The Behaviour of Successful Negotiators'.

PART THREE

15. The Infinite Game

The Bertrand Russell letter is in Ronald Clark's biography of Russell.

My account of Roger Williams's life is drawn from Teresa Bejan's book and also from John Barry's excellent biography of him. In the same year as *The Bloudy Tenent* was published, his friend John Milton published *Areopagitica*, his polemic in praise of freedom of speech: 'Where there is much desire to learn, there of necessity will be much arguing, much writing, many opinions; for opinion in good men is but knowledge in the making.'

On democracy as an infinite game, I was also influenced by David Hume's argument that society should be built on a conflict that is always balanced and never resolved: 'In all governments, there is a perpetual intestine struggle, open or secret, between Authority and Liberty, *and neither of them can absolutely prevail in the contest.*'

On the French culture of argumentation: before the Normandy landings of 1944, the British Army issued a manual to its troops instructing them in native cultural habits. It included this warning: 'By and large, Frenchmen enjoy intellectual argument more than we do. You will often think that two Frenchmen are having a violent quarrel when they are simply arguing about some abstract point.'

Susan Bro puts great emphasis on being respectful, but civility, she told me, is not quite enough. 'Trying to talk civilly to everyone is not going to work because then they don't understand your anger. So you should be passionate, but you also have to try to hear what the other person is saying, even if you're not ever going to agree with them.'

I came across Mary Parker Follett in Peter Coleman's book *The Five Percent*, and then in Andrea Gabor's *Capitalist Philosophers*. I also drew on papers on Follett by Gary Nelson and Judy Whipps (the latter includes a marvellous quote from Follett: 'Truth emerges from difference . . . from all the countless differings of our daily lives.'

17. Toolkit of Productive Argument

George Thompson's quote can be found in his book *Verbal Judo*, which contains many other diamond-like aphorisms ('Insult strengthens resistance, civility weakens it'; 'When you stop thinking like the other, you lose your power over them') and much wisdom about how to handle conflict.

Bibliography

Adams, Ryan E., and Laursen, Brett, 'The Correlates of Conflict: Disagreement is Not Necessarily Detrimental', *Journal of Family Psychology*, 21 (3), September 2007

Agne, Robert R., 'Reframing Practices in Moral Conflict: Interaction Problems in the Negotiation Standoff at Waco', *Discourse and Society*, 18 (5), 2007

Arnold, K., and Vakhrusheva, J., 'Resist the negation reflex: minimising reactance in psychotherapy of delusions', *Psychosis*, 8 (2), 2015

Ayoko, O., Ashkanasy, N., Jehn, K., *Handbook of Conflict Management Research*, Edward Elgar Publishing, 2014

Azoulay, P., et al., 'Does Science Advance One Funeral at a Time?', *American Economic Review*, 109 (8), August 2019

Barry, John, *Roger Williams and the Creation of the American Soul: Church, State and the Birth of Liberty*, Duckworth Overlook, 2012

Bejan, Teresa, *Mere Civility: Disagreement and the Limits of Toleration*, Harvard University Press, 2017

Bradbury, T. N., and Cohan, C. L., 'Negative Life Events, Marital Interaction, and the Longitudinal Course of Newlywed Marriage', *Journal of Personal and Social Psychology*, 73 (1), August 1997

Brady, William, et al., 'Emotion shapes the diffusion of moralised content in social networks', *Proceedings of the National Academy of Sciences*, 114 (28), 2017

Budiansky, Stephen, 'Truth Extraction', *The Atlantic*, June 2005

Buffett, Warren, 'Letter to Shareholders', *Berkshire Hathaway Annual Report*, 2009

Canary, Daniel J., Lakey, Sandra G., and Sillars, Alan L., 'Managing Conflict in a Competent Manner: A Mindful Look at Events that Matter', in *The SAGE Handbook of Conflict Communication*, ed. Oetzel and Ting-Toomey

Carlin, John, *Knowing Mandela*, Atlantic Books, 2014

Carnevale, P. J., https://www.researchgate.net/publication/228255884_Creativity_in_the_Outcomes_of_Conflict

Carse, James P., *Finite and Infinite Games: A Vision of Life as Play and Possibility*, Simon & Schuster, 1986

Chmiel, Anna, et al., 'Negative Emotions Boost Users' Activity at BBC Forum', *Physica A: Statistical Mechanics and its Applications*, 390 (16), 2011

Christian, Brian, *The Most Human Human: What Artificial Intelligence Teaches Us about Being Alive*, Penguin, 2012

Clark, Ronald, *The Life of Bertrand Russell*, Bloomsbury Reader, 2012

Coleman, Peter, *The Five Percent*, PublicAffairs, 2011

Corbin, Jane, *Gaza First: The Secret Norway Channel to Peace between Israel and the PLO*, Bloomsbury, 1994

Coulson, Danny, and Shannon, Elaine, *No Heroes: Inside the FBI's Secret Counter-Terror Force*, Pocket Books, 1999

Crockett, M. J., 'Moral outrage in the digital age', *Nature Human Behaviour*, 1, 2017

Crouch, Tom, *The Bishop's Boys: A Life of Wilbur and Orville Wright*, W. W. Norton & Co., 1991

Croucher, Stephen M., et al., 'Conflict Styles and High–Low Context Cultures, A Cross-Cultural Extension', *Communication Research Reports*, 29 (1), 2012

Cusk, Rachel, *Coventry: Essays*, Faber & Faber, 2019

De Dreu, K. W., and Weingart, L. R., 'Task Versus Relationship Conflict, Team Performance, and Team Member Satisfaction: A Meta-Analysis', *Journal of Applied Psychology*, 88 (4), 2003

DeSteno, David, et al., 'Prejudice from thin air: the effect of emotion on automatic intergroup attitudes', *Psychological Science*, 15 (5), June 2004

De Wit, Frank R. C., et al., 'The paradox of intragroup conflict: a meta-analysis', *Journal of Applied Psychology*, 97 (2), 2012

Docherty, Jayne, *Learning Lessons from Waco: When the Parties Bring Their Gods to the Negotiation Table*, Syracuse University Press, 2001

——, interview retrieved from https://www.beyondintractability.org/audiodisplay/docherty-j

Donohue, W. A., and Taylor, P. J., 'Role Effects in Negotiation: The one-down phenomenon', *Negotiation Journal*, 23 (3), 2007

Druckman, Daniel, 'Stages, Turning Points, and Crises: Negotiating Military Base Rights, Spain and the United States', *Dans Négociations*, 2 (28), 2017

Dutilh Novaes, C., 'What is logic?', *Aeon* magazine, 2017, retrieved from https://aeon.co/essays/the-rise-and-fall-and-rise-of-logic

Eppler, Mark, *The Wright Way: Seven Problem-Solving Principles from the Wright Brothers That Can Make Your Business Soar*, Amacom, 2003

Faber, Adele, and Mazlish, Elaine, *How to Talk so Kids Will Listen and Listen so Kids Will Talk*, 3rd edn, Piccadilly Press, 2013

Fletcher, Richard, and Nielsen, Rasmus Kleis, 'Using Social Media Appears to Diversify Your News Diet, Not Narrow It', *NiemanLab* report on 2017 Reuters Institute Digital News Report

Forsyth, Donelson, *Group Dynamics*, Wadsworth Publishing, 1980

Gabor, Andrea, *Capitalist Philosophers: The Geniuses of Modern Business – Their Lives, Times, and Ideas*, John Wiley & Sons, 2020

Galef, Julia, Rationally Speaking podcast, episode 206, April 2018, interview with Kal Turnbull of ChangeMyView

Gallagher, Brian, interview with James Evans and Misha Teplitskiy, 'Wikipedia and the Wisdom of Polarised Crowds', *Nautilus*, 14 March 2019

Gallo, Amy, 'How to Disagree with Someone More Powerful Than You', *Harvard Business Review*, 17 March 2016

Gawande, Atul, commencement speech to UCLA Medical School, published in the *New Yorker*, 2 June 2018

Gelfand, M., Harrington J., Leslie, L., 'Conflict cultures: a new frontier for conflict management and practice', in Ayoko et al.

Gittell, Jody Hoffer, *The Southwest Airlines Way: Using the Power of Relationships to Achieve High Performance*, McGraw-Hill Education, 2005

Gladwell, Malcolm, 'Sacred and Profane: How Not to Negotiate with Believers', *New Yorker*, 31 March 2014

Goffman, Erving, *The Presentation of Self in Everyday Life*, Penguin, 1990

Goldberger, Ary L., 'Fractal Variability versus Pathologic Periodicity: Complexity Loss and Stereotypy in Disease', *Perspectives in Biology and Medicine*, 40 (4), 1997

Gottman, John, *The Relationship Cure*, Crown Publications, 2002

Gottman, John, Swanson, Catherine, and Swanson, Kristin, 'A General Systems Theory of Marriage: Nonlinear Difference Equation Modeling of Marital Interaction', *Personality and Social Psychology Review,* 6 (4), 2002

Graham, Paul, *How to Disagree*, March 2008, http://www.paulgraham.com/disagree.html

Greene, Joshua, *Moral Tribes*, Atlantic Books (UK), 2014

Grossman, Lev, 'Mark Zuckerberg, Person of the Year 2010', *Time*, 15 December 2010

Grubb, Amy Rose, 'Modern-day hostage [crisis] negotiation: the evolution of an art form within the policing arena', *Aggression and Violent Behaviour*, 15 (5), 2010

Haidt, J., et al., 'The Moral Stereotypes of Liberals and Conservatives: Exaggeration of Differences across the Political Spectrum', *PLoS ONE*, 7 (12), 2012, https://doi.org/10.1371/journal.pone.0050092

Hall, Edward T., *Beyond Culture*, Anchor, 1976

Halperin, Basil, Ho, Benjamin, List, John A., Muir, Ian, 'Towards an understanding of the economics of apologies: evidence from a large-scale natural field experiment', NBER Working Paper No. 25676, March 2019

Hempel, Jessi, 'Eli Pariser Predicted the Future. Now He Can't Escape It', *Wired*, 24 May 2017

Hendrick, Carl, 'The Growth Mindset Problem', *Aeon*, 11 March 2019

Henrich, J, Heine, S. J., Norenzayan, A., 'The Weirdest People in the World?', *Behavioral and Brain Science*, 33 (2–3), June 2010, https://doi.org/10.1017/S0140525X0999152X

Herman, Arthur, *The Scottish Enlightenment: The Scots' Invention of the Modern World*, Fourth Estate, 2003

Ho, Benjamin, and Liu, Elaine, 'Does Sorry Work? The Impact of Apology Laws on Medical Malpractice', *Journal of Risk and Uncertainty*, 43 (2), June 201

Hoffman, Jan, 'How Anti-Vaccine Sentiment Took Hold in the United States', *New York Times*, 23 September 2019

Horowitz, Ben, *The Hard Thing about Hard Things*, HarperCollins USA, 2014

Hughes, Bettany, *The Hemlock Cup: Socrates, Athens, and the Search for the Good Life*, Vintage 2011

Huthwaite International, *The Behaviour of Successful Negotiators*

Ickes, William, *Everyday Mind Reading: Understanding What Other People Think and Feel*, Prometheus Books, 2006

Jacobs, Alan, *How To Think: A Guide for the Perplexed*, Profile, 2017

Jaidker, K., Zhou, A., Lelkes, Y., 'Brevity is the soul of Twitter: The constraint affordance and political discussion', *Journal of Communication*, 69 (4), August 2019

Janis, Irving L., *Victims of Groupthink: A Psychological Study of Foreign-Policy Decisions and Fiascoes*, Houghton Mifflin, 1972

Jhaver, S., Vora, P., Bruckman, A., 'Designing for Civil Conversations: Lessons Learned from ChangeMyView', GVU Technical Report, December 2017

Kahan, Dan, 'Ideology, motivated reasoning and cognitive reflection', *Judgement and Decision-Making*, 8 (4), July 2013

Kahan, Dan, et al., 'Science Curiosity and Political Information Processing', *Advances in Political Psychology*, 38 (S1), February 2017

Kahneman, Daniel, *Thinking, Fast and Slow*, Penguin 2012

Kaplan, Jonas T., Gimbel, Sarah I., Harris, Sam, 'Neural correlates of maintaining one's political beliefs in the face of counterevidence', *Scientific Reports* 6 (1), 2016, https://doi.org/10.1038.srep39589

Kim, D., Pan, Y., Park, H. S., 'High-context versus low-context culture: a comparison of Chinese, Korean and American cultures', *Psychology and Marketing*, 15 (6), 1998

Klar, Samara, and Krupnikov, Yanna, *Independent Politics: How American Disdain for Parties Leads to Political Inaction*, Cambridge University Press, 2016

Klein, Kristi, and Hodges, Sara D., 'Gender Differences, Motivation, and Empathic Accuracy: When It Pays to Understand', *Personality and Social Psychology Bulletin*, 27 (6), June 2001

Kolb, Deborah, et al., *When Talk Works: Profiles of Mediators*, Jossey Bass, 1994 (interview with Patrick Phear conducted by Austin Sarat)

Kramer, R., and Neale, M., *Power and Influence in Organizations*, SAGE, 1998

Lakoff, G., and Johnson, M., *Metaphors We Live By*, University of Chicago Press, 1980

Lakoff, R. T., *Language and Woman's Place*, Oxford University Press, 2004

Laursen B., and Collins, W. A., 'Interpersonal conflict during adolescence', *Psychological Bulletin*, 115 (2), 1994

Lee, Fiona, et al., 'Mea Culpa: Predicting Stock Prices from Organizational Attributions', *Personality and Social Psychology Bulletin*, 30 (12), 2004

Leslie, Ian, 'A Rocker's Guide to Management', *The Economist/1843*, 14 November 2018

——, 'The Scientists Persuading Terrorists to Spill Their Secrets', *The Guardian*, 13 October 2017

——, 'The Sugar Conspiracy', *The Guardian*, 7 April 2016

Lewis, Richard D., *When Cultures Collide*, 3rd edn, Nicholas Brealey Publishing, 2005

Lewisohn, Mark, *The Beatles – All These Years*, Volume One: *Tune In*, Little, Brown, 2013

Litvak, Paul M., et al., 'Fuel in the Fire: How Anger Impacts Judgment and Decision-Making', in M Potegal et al., *International Handbook of Anger*, Springer, 2010

Llano, Stephen, letter published in *The Atlantic*, 30 April 2019, retrieved from https://www.theatlantic.com/letters/archive/2019/04/how-argue-letters-erisology/588265/

Macduff, Ian, 'Here, There and Everywhere: Taking mediation online', *Kluwer Mediation Blog*, 28 March 2014; http://mediationblog.kluwerarbitration.com/2014/03/28/here-there-and-everywhere-taking-mediation-online/

Marken, Richard T., and Carey, Timothy A., *Controlling People: The Paradoxical Nature of Being Human*, Australian Academic Press, 2015

Martin, J. and Meyerson, D., 'Women in Power: Conformity, Resistance, and Disorganized Coaction', in Kramer and Neale, *Power and Influence in Organizations*

Matias, J. N., 'Preventing harrassment and increasing group participation through social norms in 2,190 online science discussions', *Proceedings of the National Academy of Sciences of the United States of America*, 116 (20), April 2019, https://doi.org/10.1073/pnas.1813486116

McManus, Freda, et al., 'An investigation of the accuracy of therapists' self-assessment of cognitive-behaviour therapy skills', *British Journal of Clinical Psychology*, 51 (3), September 2012

McNulty, James K., 'When Positive Processes Hurt Relationships', *Current Directions in Psychological Science*, 19 (3), 2010

McNulty, James K., and Russell, V. Michelle, 'When "Negative" Behaviors Are Positive: A Contextual Analysis of the Long Term Effects of Problem-Solving Behaviours on Changes in Relationship Satisfaction', *Journal of Personality and Social Psychology*, 98 (4), 2010

Mercier, Hugo, and Sperber, Dan, *The Enigma of Reason: A New Theory of Human Understanding*, Penguin 2018

Miller, William, and Rollnick, Stephen, *Motivational Interviewing: Helping People Change*, 3rd edn, Guilford Press, 2012

Montaigne, Michel de, *Essays*, trans. Charles Cotton, via Project Gutenberg

Morrill, Calvin, *The Executive Way*, University of Chicago Press, 1995

Moshman, David, and Gell, Molly, 'Collaborative Reasoning: Evidence for Collective Rationality', *Thinking and Reasoning*, 4 (3), July 1998

Nelson, Gary M., 'Mary Parker Follett – Creativity and Democracy', *Human Service Organizations: Management, Leadership and Governance*, 41 (2), 2017

Nemeth, Charlan, *No! The Power of Disagreement in a World that Wants to Get Along*, Atlantic Books (UK), 2019

Nemeth, Charlan, Brown, K., Rogers, J., 'Devil's Advocate versus Authentic Dissent: Stimulating Quantity and Quality', *European Journal of Social Psychology*, 31 (6), 2001

Nemeth, Charlan, et al., 'The liberating role of conflict in group creativity: a study in two countries', *European Journal of Social Psychology*, 34 (4), 2004

Nickerson, Raymond S., 'Confirmation Bias: A Ubiquitous Phenomenon in Many Guises', *Review of General Psychology*, 2 (2), June 1998

Nishimura, Shoji, Nevgi, Anne, Tello, Seppa, 'Communication Style and Cultural Features in High/Low Context Communication Cultures: A Case Study of Finland, Japan, and India', University of Helsinki Department of Applied Sciences of Education, Research Report 299, 2008

Nissen-Lie, Helene A., 'Humility and self-doubt are hallmarks of a good therapist', *Aeon*, 5 February 2020

Nyhan, B., and Reifler, J., 'When corrections fail: The persistence of political misperceptions', *Political Behavior*, 32 (2), 2010

Oostinga, M., 'Breaking [the] ice: communication error management in law enforcement interactions', PhD thesis, University of Twente, 2018

Overall, Nickola, 'Does Partners' Negative-Direct Communication During Conflict Help Sustain Perceived Commitment and Relationship Quality Across Time?' *Social Psychological and Personality Science*, 9 (4), 2018

Overall, Nickola C., et al., 'Regulating Partners in Intimate Relationships: the costs and benefits of different communication strategies', *Journal of Personal Social Psychology*, 96 (3), 2009

Overall, N. C., and McNulty, J. K., 'What type of communication during conflict is beneficial for intimate relationships?', *Current Opinion in Psychology*, 13, 2017

Perlow, Leslie, *When You Say Yes but You Mean No*, Crown Business, 2003

Plato, *Complete Works*, ed. Cooper, John M., Hackett, 1997

Powell, Jonathan, *Great Hatred, Little Room: Making Peace in Northern Ireland*, Vintage, 2009

——, *Talking To Terrorists: How to End Armed Conflicts*, Vintage, 2015

Rackham, Neil, 'The Behaviour of Successful Negotiators', in *Negotiation: Readings, Exercises and Classes*, ed. Lewicki, Litterer, Saunders, and Minton, McGraw Hill, 2014

Rackham, Neil, and Morgan, Terry, *Behaviour Analysis in Training*, McGraw-Hill UK, 1977

Reavis, Dick J., *The Ashes of Waco: An Investigation*, Simon & Schuster, 1995

Resnick, Brian, 'There may be an antidote to politically motivated reasoning. And it's wonderfully simple', *Vox*, 7 February 2017

273

Richards, Keith, *Life: Keith Richards*, Weidenfeld & Nicolson, 2011

Rozenblit, L., and Keil, F., 'The misunderstood limits of folk science: an illusion of explanatory depth', *Cognitive Science*, 26 (5), 2002

Shergill, S. S., Bays, P. M., et al., 'Two eyes for an eye: the neuroscience of force escalation', *Science* 301 (5630), 2003

Shi, F., et al., 'The Wisdom of Polarised Crowds', *Nature Human Behaviour* 3 (4), 2019

Sillars, Alan, et al., 'Cognition and Communication during Marital Conflict: How Alcohol Affects Subjective Coding of Interaction in Aggressive and Nonaggressive Couples', in P. Noller and J. A. Feeney (eds), *Understanding marriage: Developments in the study of couple interaction*, Cambridge University Press, 2002

Sillars, Alan, et al., 'Stepping into the stream of thought: Cognition during marital conflict', in V. Manusov and J. H. Harvey (eds), *Attribution, Communication Behavior, and Close Relationships*, Cambridge University Press, 2001

Sloman, Steven, and Fernbach, Philip, *The Knowledge Illusion: the myth of individual thought and the power of collective wisdom*, Pan, 2018

Smith, Dana, interview with James Evans: 'The Wisdom of Crowds Requires the Political Left and Right to Work Together', *Scientific American*, 8 March 2019

Sobo, Elisa, 'Theorising (Vaccine) Refusal: Through the Looking Glass', *Cultural Anthropology*, 31 (3), 2016

Stokoe, Elizabeth, *Talk: The Science of Conversation*, Little Brown, 2018

Sun, Katherine Q., and Slepian, Michael L., 'The conversations we seek to avoid', *Organizational Behaviour and Human Decision Processes*, 60, September 2020

Talhelm, Thomas, et al., 'Liberals Think More Analytically (More "WEIRD") Than Conservatives', *Personality and Social Psychology Bulletin*, 41 (2), 24 December 2014

Tan, Chenhao, et al., 'Winning Arguments: Interaction Dynamics and Persuasion Strategies in Good-faith Online Discussions', *Proceedings of the 25th International World Wide Web Conference*, 2016)

Tesser, Abraham, et al., 'Conflict: the role of calm and angry parent–child discussion in adolescent adjustment', *Journal of Social and Clinical Psychology*, 8 (3), 1989

Thibodeau, David, and Whiteson, Leon, *A Place Called Waco*, PublicAffairs, 1999

Thompson, George, *Verbal Judo: The Gentle Art of Persuasion*, HarperCollins USA, 2014

Tiedens, Larissa Z., 'Anger and Advancement versus Sadness and Subjugation: The Effect of Negative Emotion Expressions on Social Status Conferral', *Journal of Personality and Social Psychology,* 80 (1), 2001

Trevors, Gregory, et al., 'Identity and Epistemic Emotions During Knowledge Revision: A Potential Account for the Backfire Effect', *Discourse Processes,* 53 (5), January 2016

Wallace, David Foster, 'Tense Present: Democracy, English, and the Wars over Usage', in *Consider the Lobster and Other Essays,* Little Brown 2006

Wasserman, Noam, *The Founder's Dilemmas,* Princeton University Press, 2013

Watters, Ethan, 'We Aren't the World', *Pacific Standard,* 25 February 2013

Wender, Jonathan, *Policing and the Poetics of Everyday Life,* University of Illinois Press, 2009

West, Richard F., et al., 'Cognitive Sophistication Does Not Attenuate the Bias Blind Spot', *Journal of Personality and Social Psychology,* 103 (3), 2012

Whipps, Judy D., 'A Pragmatist Reading of Mary Parker Follett's Integrative Process', *Faculty Peer Reviewed Articles,* 8, 2014, https://scholarworks.gvso.edu/lib-articles/8

Witkowski, Sadie, 'Psychology Researchers Explore How Vaccine Beliefs Are Formed', *Voice of America News,* 16 August 2018

Wolf Shenk, Joshua, *Powers of Two: Finding the Essence of Innovation in Creative Pairs,* John Murray, 2014

Zanes, Warren, *Petty: The Biography,* Macmillan USA, 2015

Zartman, I. W., and Aurik, J., 'Power Strategies in De-escalation', in L. Kriesberg and J. Thomson (eds), *Timing the De-escalation of International Conflicts,* Syracuse University Press, 1991

Zhu, Linhong, and Lerman, Kristina, 'Attention Inequality in Social Media', *ArXiv,* 2016, abs/1601.07200

Ziem, M., and Hoyer, J., 'Modest, yet progressive: Effective therapists tend to rate therapeutic change less positively than their patients', *Psychotherapy Research,* 30 (4), 2020

Index

Page numbers for figures are shown in *italics*. Endnotes are denoted by n, e.g. 264n11.

Index

Index

Oostinga, Miriam, 172–5, 178, 226
organisations *see* workplace
Oslo Accord negotiations, 184–6, 192–4, 195–7, 264n11
Overall, Nickola, 24, 31, 44

Palestinian–Israeli conflict *see* Arab–Israeli conflict
parents: modelling reasoning, 60; power struggles with adolescents, 113, 130; 'righting' reflex and behaviour, 114–15
Pariser, Eli, 99, 263n5
passive aggression: in marriage and romantic relationships, 25; as never helpful, 45; in the workplace, 37, 39–40
peacocks' tails (as 'costly signals'), 177
Penn, William, 241
Perlow, Leslie, 39
personality mix in teams, 214
personality traits, 20
persuasive argument: vs constructive conflict, 243, 248–9; as 'righting' behaviour, 243; strategies for, 204–6
Peters, Emmanuelle, 118–19
Phear, Patrick, 93
phone conversations, pause before initial 'hello', 90, 263n5
physiological responses: and emotional reciprocity/inertia, 214; fight or flight response, 15; research studies, 41, 214; threat vs challenge states, 40–2
pirates, skull and crossbones (as 'costly signals'), 264n10
Planck, Max, 68
Plato, 49; *Gorgias*, 49; *Hippias Minor*, 48; *Republic*, 48–9
police: communication (de-escalation) skills, 95–9, 137, 191–2; humiliation of suspects, 137–8; importance of authenticity, 227–8; Jonathan Wender's philosophy, 227–8; listening skills, 98; training simulations, 209;

understanding own reactions and emotions, 217–19
politeness and civility *see* civility and politeness
political discourse: cultural differences, 154, 245; and Identity-Protective Cognition, 163; and increased tweet length, 265n12; 'one-down' status of electorate, 131; in person, 17–18, 245; research studies, 154, 165–6, 265n12; in social media, 16, 265n12; Susan Bro's work, 104
political polarisation, and group decision-making (Wikipedia edits), 56–8
politicians' apologies, 178, 180–1
Posterous (microblogging platform), 18, 19
Powell, Jonathan, *Great Hatred, Little Room*, 216
power imbalances and struggles: with adolescents, 113, 130; in general, 106–7; during interrogation, 105–7, 108, 130, 210–12; 'one-down' parties (status imbalance), 128–32, 137, 175, 182; in online communication, 243
Powers, William T., 220, 221
privacy during negotiation, benefits, 135–6, 186, 193
productive disagreement *see* constructive conflict
protecting face, 134–6, 138–9, 186, 256; *see also* 'facework' (first impressions); giving face; 'wrongness', stigma of
Providence, USA, 239–40
Pundak, Ron, 192

questioning *see* curiosity and questioning

Rabin, Yitzhak, 196–7
racial/ethnic tensions and conflict: South Africa, 124–5, 139–40; USA,